VIRTUE IN BEING

SUNY series in Contemporary Continental Philosophy
Dennis J. Schmidt, editor

VIRTUE IN BEING

Towards an Ethics of the Unconditioned

ANDREW BENJAMIN

Published by State University of New York Press, Albany

© 2016 State University of New York

All rights reserved

Printed in the United States of America

No part of this book may be used or reproduced in any manner whatsoever without written permission. No part of this book may be stored in a retrieval system or transmitted in any form or by any means including electronic, electrostatic, magnetic tape, mechanical, photocopying, recording, or otherwise without the prior permission in writing of the publisher.

For information, contact State University of New York Press, Albany, NY
www.sunypress.edu

Production, Diane Ganeles
Marketing, Michael Campochiaro

Library of Congress Cataloging-in-Publication Data

Names: Benjamin, Andrew E.
Title: Virtue in being : towards an ethics of the unconditioned / Andrew Benjamin.
Description: Albany : State University of New York Press, 2016. | Series: SUNY series in contemporary Continental philosophy | Includes bibliographical references and index.
Identifiers: LCCN 2015036642 | ISBN 9781438461618 (hardcover : alk. paper) | ISBN 9781438461625 (paperback : alk. paper) | ISBN 9781438461632 (e-book)
Subjects: LCSH: Ethics. | Philosophical anthropology.
Classification: LCC BJ41 .B46 2016 | DDC 170--dc23 LC record available at http://lccn.loc.gov/2015036642

10 9 8 7 6 5 4 3 2 1

CONTENTS

Acknowledgments vii

Introduction 1

Chapter 1. Toward the Unconditioned:
Kant, Epicurus and *Glückseligkeit* 15

Chapter 2. Arendt and the Time of the Pardon 51

Chapter 3. Kant, Evil, and the Unconditioned 87

Chapter 4. Judgment after Derrida 125

Notes 169

Bibliography 199

Index 207

ACKNOWLEDGMENTS

The chapters of this book were first delivered as lectures at the Collegium Phenomenologicun held at Citta di Castello, Italy, in July 2014. I wish to thank María del Rosario Acosta López for the kind invitation to give a weeklong course. I have allowed the book as it now stands to retain the overall structure of the lectures. During the writings of the lectures and during the preparatory study conversations and critical exchanges with friends and colleagues were fundamental. Let me thank Kristie Sweet, Ted George, Peg Birmingham, Claire Katz, Rick Lee, Simon Morgan Wortham, Howard Caygill, Elina Steikou, Dimitris Vardoulakis, Dennis Schmidt, and Miguel de Beistegui. I also want to thank James Kent for his help in the preparation of the manuscript.

INTRODUCTION

The address of this book is straightforward. It involves the argument that a philosophical thinking of life, and thus the development of a philosophical anthropology in which human being is present as an entity within a generalized relational ontology, should be premised on the identification of an already present and thus original relationship between the ontological and the ethical. The uncovering of the relationship, a relationship that has an existent reality, would be the identification of its effective presence. In other words, the identification of a relationship that has an already present structuring force within philosophy. There are therefore two opening claims. The first affirms the presence of this formulation of the relationship between the ethical and the ontological. The second is that the possibility of the relationship's recovery indicates that it has always been at work within the history of philosophy, even if it awaited recognition rather than its exercise being an automatic and, as a consequence, its results already determined. Allowing for its presence gives rise to a different approach to the ethical. Rather than uncovering ways of connecting the ontological and the ethical, what their already existent relation identifies is the presence of what will henceforth be described as *virtue in being*.

Staged by this formulation is the *anoriginal* inscription of the ethical within the ontological. While this is a position that will continue to be made, the argument is that the ethical is not a contingent addition to the ontological. Rather the ontological is already the site of the ethical. That already present status is identified by the claim of an already present, hence *anoriginal*, inscription.

The term *anoriginal* is fundamental to this project. It has two interrelated determinations that are at work here. First, it bears an important connection to Derrida's term *différance*.[1] An affinity arises as both terms—*anoriginal* and *différance*—bring into play a conception of original irreducibility that is thought in terms of space and time. However, in contradistinction to Derrida the term *anoriginal* allows for a reworking of the ontological. The *anoriginal* stages that reworking in terms of the development of a relational ontology. Hence, the *anoriginal* as a term within the philosophical, is intended to be part of what can best be described as a reappropriation and therefore a repositioning of the ontological itself. The *anoriginal* is difference at the origin. It pertains to what is. As such, it locates and names a sense of irreducibility that is ontological in nature. When Kant argues, in a passage that will be central to the project of this book that the "I" belongs both to the sensible and the intelligible worlds, not only is there the undoing of the opposition between the sensible and the intelligible, were that opposition to be equated with an either/or, what is also occurring is a repositioning of the subject such that it becomes the site of this founding irreducibility. Irreducibility inscribes spacing within the subject such that the subject is the locus of anoriginal irreducibility. This is the subject's constitution. It is also the case that what holds the irreducible elements both "apart" and as "a part" of the subject is a form of temporal simultaneity. These elements pertain at the same time. It is this conception of time that will be developed here in terms of *at-the-same-timeness*. Equally, if more abstractly, the self/other relation once take as primary, and thus as an original setup, identifies the presence of *anoriginal* relationality as another instance of a founding irreducibility. The claim is straightforward. There is not self or other prior to the relation. Any singularity therefore would be an after effect of the relation. Irreducibility is original. *Anoriginal* difference names this irreducibility. The occurrence of any one instance is the event of plurality. The plural event names therefore a setup in which any one singularity is marked by its being the aftereffect of an original relation. (Hence anoriginal relationality.)

The second determination of the term *anoriginal* concerns origins. It signals a way of denoting the presence, and thus the being, of that which is always already at work (where work involves the distinction between potentiality and actuality). Again, the affinity with Derrida is clear. To argue for the anoriginality of a relation is therefore to assume both irreducibility and the already present status of that relation. Equally, it is possible to deploy the term *anoriginal* to identify the already present. Again this underscores that what is at stake in every instance is an account of existence, of what exists and thus the ontological. Accepting anoriginality as a point of departure—and therefore as its own an-origin—means that the philosophical task entails accounting for the work of the anoriginal rather than offering an account of its origin. Centrality is to be attributed therefore to the effect of anoriginal presence: a presence that defines the origin in terms of an already present effecting relation.

Relationality is an already present force; a force that continues to take on different forms. Note the following two moments both of which need to be understood as an affirmation of the being of being human as *being-in-relation*.[2] The first is Hegel's dramatic opening to the section titled, "Independence and the Dependence of Self-Consciousness" (§178) in the *Phenomenology of Spirit*. The second occurs in chapter XII—the chapter concerned with education—in Mary Wollstonecraft's *Vindication of the Rights of Women*. As is well known, Hegel writes that: "Self-consciousness exists in and for itself when, and by the fact that, it exists for another: that is, it exists only in being acknowledged."[3] Mary Wollstonecraft's evocation of relationality, while just as insistent, takes on a different form. She argues that it is, ". . . only by the jostlings of equality can we form a just opinion of ourselves."[4] Both passages have elicited sustained critical commentary. Here all that will be noted are three elements. The first is that what the "dialectic of recognition" identifies is, inter alia, that were self-consciousness to be posited as a singularity then such a position would be an aftereffect of an original relation. Consistent with the position noted above, implicit in the formulation of this position is that relationality precedes singularity. The second is that "being acknowledged" and the "jostlings of equality" are activities. Relationality therefore *is*—that is, is what it is—in its being acted out. In being acted out, an acting out that is marked by an inevitable contingency as to content, the relationship between potentiality and actuality is brought into play. Third, what are described as "just" opinions, understood as both accurate opinions and an opinion of human being as bound up with both a sense of propriety and thus a sense of justice, occur as a result of activity and are given within reflection. Life and the just life delimited by an original sense of propriety have a possible and thus potential coincidence. A coincidence the setting of which has to be this life and which underscores the presence of what has already been identified as *virtue in being*. The coincidence is not a fait accompli. It actualization continues to meet sites of resistance. Resistance in this context is that which inhibits or restricts the actualization of a potentiality. They can be identified as the disequilibria of power that play a structuring role within relationality.

———◁○▷———

The substantive point is that the presence of the *anoriginal* understood as irreducibility is a claim that defines the being of being human. There will always be differing modalities of anoriginality. In general however, once it can be argued that the relationship between the ethical and the ontological is *anoriginal*, what this then entails is that there is an already present relation. There is no need to account for how the ontological could come to attain or acquire an ethical dimension. The position would be that they are always already related. There is the original inscription of one within the other. An inscription in which their "apartness" is equally their "a partness."

Virtue in being is therefore a formulation identifying a world in which finitude has an insistent quality while also comprising the formulation in terms of which this anoriginal relation will be thought and that grounds of judgment have force. Leaving aside any immediate attempt to justify this overall point of departure, given that a great deal of the justification emerges within the argumentation to come, the initial problem to be addressed is how would such a position be shown? In part the answer to this question resides in the already stated presupposition that the relationship between ontology and ethics is at work within the history of philosophy. The refusal to recognize that formulations of the being of being human have ethical concerns inscribed within them creates the problem—even though it is ultimately a false problem—of having then to establish the relationship between human being and the ethical. Though the converse of this position can also be undone as it is premised on the failure to understand the nature of contingency. A failure signaled by the retention of the assumption that acts can be both contingent and value free. Here one of the central claims of this project is that contingency needs to be attributed a different location. The claim is contingency is held within the interplay of the conditioned and the unconditioned. It is this positioning that makes it possible to judge contingent individual actions. The presence of contestability as a result of contingency does not entail the impossibility of judgment. In fact the opposite is the case. The presence of contingency underscores the necessity for judgment. Indeed, it would be the sign of philosophical vacuity to posit the presence of the contingent as though it were independent of the conditions of judgment. While contingency (or singularity) need not be determined by universality—hence there is a way out of a certain Hegelianism—it remains the case that contingency acts allow for judgment precisely because such acts occur within the setting that is itself, what can be described as the enacted presence of virtue in being.

Part of what has to be undertaken in order to realize this project involves indicating the ways certain philosophical texts, which in this setting are texts by Aristotle, Epicurus, Kant, Arendt, and Derrida, engage, *albeit* in importantly different ways, with the *anoriginal* relationship between the ethical and the ontological. Working through these sites means that all these texts are reworked such that their concerns take on an-other life; they come to have an afterlife. They are therefore marshaled to a different project. And yet, it should be noted that philosophical texts cannot be taken as providing ends in themselves. Arguing for the relationship between ontology and ethics, an argument that cannot be separated from that relation's own recovery, will be approached here *via* three different topics or locals of investigation. The topics that organize what is at stake in the project of thinking life philosophically are: *violence, evil,* and *the pardon*. Each exerts a structuring force on the explicit concerns of the chapters to come. Names, texts, and topics come to be interrelated, constructing settings in which to progress the threefold argument that is at work continually throughout this book. (Indeed the choice of topics is linked to the effective staging of the argumentative positions to be made.) While these positions are sustained and developed in the proceeding, their component parts can be stated in advance. Their already present interrelation means that these parts are not presented in a sequential order.

The first element of the overall argument resides in the already suggested claim that the only adequate way to address the question of life philosophically, which is the development of a philosophical anthropology, is in terms of the distinction between the conditioned and the unconditioned. Moreover, that distinction finds its most exacting and productive formulation in the writings of Immanuel Kant. The project here starts from the premises that this distinction can be recovered from those writings and put to work. This distinction between the conditioned and the unconditioned, which is also deployed by Derrida, though with a different inflection, needs to be interpreted, first, as stemming from an affirmation of the originality of the relationship between the ontological and the ethical and then, second, as providing the concepts through which the originality of that relationship can itself then be developed. While the detail will have to wait, part of the argument is going to be that integral to the presence of this distinction is the space that it constructs. Any distinction involves a form of separation. However, the distinction between the conditioned and the unconditioned establishes the possibility for judgment precisely because of the presence of that distinction within life (where life has the quality of activity; life as *vita activa*[5]). The separation takes on the quality of an inscribed, anoriginal spacing; a spacing with its own temporal determinations. Activity rather than either pragmatically determined and delimited by forms of calculation or naturalization is positioned and thus lived out in relation to the unconditionality of the unconditioned. Human being is the site in which the irreducibility of the unconditioned and the conditioned is at work. They are present at the same time. Their *at-the-same-timeness* has a profound effect, as will continue to be argued, on how human being is thought insofar as it necessitates a recasting of human being in terms of the *anoriginal*. Hence, *anoriginality* becomes a term integral to the development of a philosophical anthropology.

The second element concerns what can be described most straightforwardly as the relationship between commonality and place. This is a position that continues to be noted within the history of philosophy. When, for example, Kant argues, first, that the results of Enlightenment are best achieved through "our cooperation" (*unsere Mitwirkung*) and then, second, in the *Critique of the Power of Judgment* that the *senus communis* even though it is "the idea of a communal sense" presupposes, nonetheless, an open public realm in which judgments of taste can be both communicated and disputed, he needs to be interpreted as arguing for a version of the originality of *being-in-common* ("cooperation" as commonality) and *being-in-place* (the "open" as place). A further claim still has to be made, namely, that taken together *being-in-common* and *being-in-place* mark out and define that which is proper to the being of being human. The important consequence of this position is what is often taken to be the locus of the ethical—that is, the single moral agent—is repositioned such that the singular agent is only ever an after effect of an already existent, thus an original form of relationality. Commonality is relational. As a result *being-in-common* will be incorporated within *being-in-relation*. Relationality is placed. There will be the continual need therefore to note the interplay of commonality, relationality, and place. *Being-in-place* and *being-in-relation* need to be thought in terms of the network of diverse relations that they name. While there will be arguments advanced in greater detail in support of these positions the enduring presupposition is that "place" and "commonality" have an already affirmed status within the history of philosophy. They are not being adduced. While not given the prominence that is demanded "place" and "commonality" already inscribed within and thus firm part of the history of philosophy.

The final element is the most complex. Here the claim pertains to the concept of potentiality. This concept is integral to the argumentation of the book as a whole. Indeed, the overall conjecture is that were it not for the centrality of potentiality the relationship between the unconditioned and the conditioned could only be thought in deterministic and mechanical ways. Allowing for potentiality therefore circumvents that restriction on thought. There are two senses of potentiality at work in this project. Despite the difference between them what has to be emerge, and this forms a fundamental part of the argumentation in the ensuing chapters, is the continual demonstration of the differing ways that these senses of potentiality are related.

The first sense of potentiality is the potentiality for what is, that which is given, to be otherwise; this is a process that needs to be understood as *othering*. It is this sense of potentiality that resists the process of naturalization. Processes of naturalization demand that were there to be the possibility of being other then it could only occur within the continuity of transformation. Emphasis on continuity means that difference is variation within the developmental. Difference with this setting is thought in terms of modifications in which what "is," is maintained within its having been modified. This is the creation of a position that effaces the anoriginality of conflict and thus normalizes the presence of founding disequilibria of power. In other words, what such a formulation precludes, is the possibility that the present—the *now*—is, in addition to other determinations, also, and at the same time, a locus of conflict concerning the nature of that *now*. Throughout the development of the argumentation of this book the now will be written as *now*. The latter formulation means that while any one now has a specific determination insofar as it occurs at a point in time that can be both identified and described, and this will also be the case that decisions taken within it be adumbrated, harbored within this now is the possibility, thus the potentiality, for it to have been otherwise, and thus for it to be other. The now, even in having one determination, can never preclude the possibility of its having been other. *Othering* presupposes therefore that what continues to occur now has the potentiality to be other where that potentiality also pertains now; pertains as unactualized and thus is yet-to-be other. The term now becomes *now* in order to capture what can best be described as the anoriginal irreducibility of the *now*. As such the *now* cannot be reduced to a single determination. While the formulation "disequilibria of power" is accurate, it should nonetheless still be pointed out, and this will emerge with greater clarity when a turn is made to the work of Hannah Arendt, that this disequilibria is inextricably bound up with violence. Following Arendt, it will be argued that the *countermeasure* to violence is, in her terms, power. Hence there is a fundamental division between disequilibria of power that necessitates violence and a conception of power that stands opposed to it. Power while having a form of ubiquity cannot be generalized. Power is itself the instantiation of differing an incompatible expressions of value. Power has to be understood such that it can be judged.

Within the conflict concerning the status of the *now*, one having an anoriginal quality, one possibility for this *now*, and it is only one possibility, is its location within a naturalized general becoming. The result is that the *now* is defined in terms of a founding irreducibility that contains processes of naturalization as part of it. Naturalization as a constitutive element, thus a possibility, within a conflict cannot be external to it allowing it to be named. Naturalization, which as a process subsumes events, in repositioning them within becoming, is from the start the philosophical attempt to dispel conflict's originality. However, there is no necessity that the potential to be actualized is in fact actualized. Indeed, the present is policed in order that the actualization of the possibility for it to be other is precluded. The naturalization of time and of life stands opposed to a philosophical thinking of this potentiality's actualization.

The second sense of potentiality begins with judgment. Judgment involves potentiality. Judgment is not a simple reiteration driven by the posited inevitable repetition of *sameness*. As a result judgment cannot be thought other than in relation to the concept of potentiality. What this demand on thinking brings with it is the necessity to clarify what is meant by the relationship between judgment and potentiality. Integral to the overall project is the development of this aspect of potentiality, thus linking it to the *othering* of the present as a capacity within the *now*. This will occur in reference to the conception of potentiality that appears in both Aristotle and Arendt. And yet, there will also be a differentiation from the specific way potentiality appears in their work. The limit of both Aristotle and Arendt in this regard, which is a position to be established in chapter 2, is central to understanding the force of potentiality.

It needs to be assumed that a fundamental aspect of judgment is a conception of an occurrence as judgeable. Hence *judgeability* is the recasting of the contingent or the finite as given within a setting created by the already present relation between the conditioned and the unconditioned. Judgment also brings a number of other presuppositions into play. Two that can be identified at this stage are the following: first, as noted, judgment presupposes that which makes it possible. Here what this entails in addition is that there is a capacity for judgment that pertains to the judging subject, moreover that capacity has its own form of necessity. Second, it does not follow from the presence of the capacity for judgment that a capacity's potentiality for actualization will be in fact realized.[6] What the first of these presuppositions entails is that potentiality secures judgment as judgment (in terms of the necessity of its possibility). Equally, judgment brings the unconditioned into play since the unconditioned is integral to any account of what can continue to be called an occurrence's *judgeability*. The connection between the unconditioned and *judgeability* opens up the link to the second presupposition. Namely, that while there is the necessity that both the unconditioned and the capacity for judgment play a determining role in the act of judgment, all that follows from that necessity is a contingency on the level of outcome. In other words, the unconditioned is linked to judgment's possibility, such that there is a necessity in regards to possibility. What is not necessary is the form taken by any specific or determined outcome. In this regard the distinction drawn by Kant in the *Critique of the Power of Judgment* in section 34 between "criticism" and critical philosophy is informative. For Kant the limit of "criticism" (*Die Kritk*) can be located in the way judgment is conceived within it. Even though "criticism" is an important activity, and orientated correctly by a concern with the particularity of the object, the limitation that Kant identifies concerns the actual practice of criticism. For Kant it occurs "without reflecting on its possibility" (*ohne über ihre Möglichkeit nachzudenken*). It is clear that the object, named here in terms of a "possibility," demands a thinking of activity that is orientated by the relationship between the conditioned and the unconditioned. In addition, what is opened by this formulation is the importance of reflection by locating it within the continuity of connection between the unconditioned and the conditioned, which grounds the possibility of criticism in the first place. Kant is referring to what can be described as the object's "criticizability"; that is, the possibility of its being judged. The latter has to be understood as a possibility. Reflection is now an activity that has its own object, namely, in this instance, it uncovers and thinks in terms of the objects' criticizability.[7] This will prove important insofar as central to Kant is the activity of reflection as given by the relation between the conditioned and the unconditioned.

In sum, the distinction between "criticism" and critical philosophy, as formulated by Kant, points to the necessity of "possibility" (*Möglichkeit*). The latter has a twofold quality. In the first instance, it is there as an object for critical philosophy. In the second, it is presupposed without acknowledgment within the activity of criticism. Possibility involves a necessity. It is however a necessity of the possible. The presence of "possibility," however, generates the contingency of any one judgment. However, there is also the larger claim being made here, namely, that once necessity is repositioned in terms of the possibility to act, it then follows that necessity can only ever entail contingency. In other words, there isn't mere contingency. Indeed, central to the ethical when its address is that which *is*, and where the "isness" of existence is its being lived out, is that in terms of both its possibility and its detail, the ethical is no longer circumscribed by establishing obligations to act. As a result law would no longer be thought in terms of its radical separation from life. Rather, life would then be understood as the locus of law, when the latter was itself rethought in terms of the interconnection between the unconditioned and possibility.[8] Restricting the hold of obligation, which is law as pure externality, by repositioning the ethical as given with the project of living, is a position that is already there in Kant's argument—an argument the discussion of which will reemerge later–that "duty" is not located in the realization of an end but rather is there in the striving to act in relation to the moral law. In other words, duty is, is what it is, in the striving to actualize the demands of duty. One cannot be separated from the other. Duty is not therefore given in the content of any formulation that is independent of life such that the question that would then be thought to pertain would concern the relation between the law and life. Striving and actuality cannot be thought other than as life. To the extent that it can be argued that life is commensurate with activity, then duty remains within life as an immanent possibility always to be actualized. It will always have been possible to act in relation to duty's affirmed presence. The fundamental qualification is that actuality is striving rather than a making actual. If the latter prevailed then duty would have to be understood in terms of completion and finality. The end of duty would be its end and as a result finitude would have been separated from its capacity to insist.

The link between the two senses of potentiality sketched above can be located in the formulation: *necessity entails contingency*. Even though this formulation encapsulates part of what has been suggested thus far and which will continue to be worked through in the proceeding chapters, the term *contingency* still warrants further clarification. It should be clear at this stage that contingency is not chance. Rather, contingency names finitude. Moreover, when contingency is defined in relation to necessity, what this indicates is that finitude is an aftereffect of the infinite. Finite being is always an aftereffect. A philosophical thinking of life therefore becomes a thinking of finitude defined in terms of the way potentiality structures, and is structured by, the complex set of relations brought into play by place, commonality, and the unconditioned, that is, between finitude and the infinite.[9]

Hence, the question of judgment can never be effectively separated from a concern with life and its capacity to be lived out. To return to the formulations provided by Wollstonecraft and Hegel, the following can now be suggested. Forming "a just opinion of ourselves," to use Wollstonecraft's felicitous formulation, necessitates understanding that the absence of neutrality evinced by this as a possibility, brings an already present concession into play. First, that relationality is an activity that involves both what Hegel understands by "recognition" and the inevitability of *being-in-relation* and thus what she identifies as the "jostlings of equality." Second, precisely because the content of commonality are always contestable and thus contain, by definition, a capacity for transformation, hence the indispensible nature of potentiality, it then follows that life itself becomes the locus in relation to which these "jostlings" unfold. To which it should be added that life provides the ground in relation to which what calls on judgment can, in fact, be judged. The possibility and the ground of judgment—that is, *being-in relation* and *being-in-place*—have an immanent presence in life. Judgment endures therefore as immanent within life as a possibility. Actualization is the act of judgment. Within this context neutrality, and it would only ever be the feint of neutrality, would be the outcome of both the naturalization of the disequilibria of power and the location of all occurrences within a generalized ontology of becoming. Naturalism and becoming stand against critical thought. Realism once equated with naturalism is nothing other than a form of acquiescence. It is only forms of radical nonacceptance that maintain the possibility of *othering* as a potentiality.

Introductions can preempt a series of arguments by stating conclusions and providing elements integral to their unfolding, in advance of the necessary detail. There can be no escape from this possibility, indeed from its reality. However, the Introduction locates what occurs. It orientates that occurrence in one direction rather than another. Hence, what repetitions there are, and repetitions are an essential part of what follows from any Introduction, have to be read as continuous with the possibility of thinking through the challenge that is given to philosophy once there is a reworking of how the philosophical task is to be understood.

In the lieu of providing reasons for acting, or a set of obligations to be acted out, where both demand forms of policing that will always have to have been extraphilosophical, the philosophical becomes an activity—one with its own history—that is linked to process of judgment. Uncovered with this repositioning of the philosophical is how judgment's possibility is to be understood. Equally as essential is an engagement with the ground of judgment. Between ground and act there are only ever relations of indetermination. Nonetheless, maintaining the centrality of judgment is to allow philosophy to maintain its force as philosophical since to insist on judgment is to mark the limit of the philosophical. Once the ethical demands the extramoral to reinforce it, then such a conception of the ethical, a conception giving rise to such a demand, becomes that form of philosophical thinking that is the abnegation of the philosophical.

CHAPTER ONE

TOWARD THE UNCONDITIONED

Kant, Epicurus, and *Glückseligkeit*

Continuing demands a form of recapitulation. The nature of the overall project, as suggested at the outset, lies in the question: What if life were to be thought philosophically? The question does not pertain to biological life but to human life, namely, to that conception of life that folds biology into it but continues to be present, nonetheless, as that which cannot be reduced to the biological. To which it should be added that the possibility of such a reduction endures as the risk inherent in philosophical accounts of human life. In direct terms, the risk is either life's equation with the biological or the use of the biological as a model for the explanation of human life. Holding human life apart from its biological registration is, from a specific perspective, what inscribes freedom into human life. Freedom depends both on a nondeterministic account of the will and equally on the proposition that one of the defining elements yielding the possibility of the judgment and the evaluation of human actions is the absence of the mechanistic. That absence locates the presence of the world as an indispensible element within judgment. Freedom has to be understood as constrained by the world. Within the "mechanistic" in which the brain figures as a "mechanism," no matter how plastic the brain may be, the mechanistic still needs to be understood as the identification of a setting that refuses the presence of inconsistent and conflicting sets of values. What this means is that the brain as a self-organizing system is inherently apolitical. Though the claim that the brain provides any sort of model for understanding human behavior—a model that in the end obviates the need to engage with genuine conflict since the brain's plasticity posited as a heuristic would not allow it to be thought—is of course inherently political, precisely because values marked by original conflict marks the presence of what has already been identified by the formulation "disequilibria of power." And yet, judgments made in relation to life do not concern life as a given. On the contrary, it is present as a continuity such that life is—is what it is—in the continuity of its self-realization; that self-realization is that in which a distinction between actuality and potentiality is central. Life moves from the simply given or as that which can be incorporated into a biological model, such that as a result of this doubled movement, life has to be understood as inextricably bound up with the continuity of its being lived out. (That continuity is of course articulated within, though importantly is also the articulation of what has already been referred to as a constitutive disequilibrium of power.[1]) Life, therefore, human life, is already worldly once it is identified with life's continuity. However, an integral part of the argument to be developed here is that continuity in harboring a potentiality means that continuity is only ever the possibility for forms of discontinuity. Were this position to be denied, which would be the refusal to think both the necessity and the exigency of discontinuity, then it would depend on the naturalization of continuity. The latter is, of course, the naturalization of the power relations constituting life. The naturalization of life is not just articulated within the retained centrality of an ontology of becoming, it assumes that located articulation. Arising here is a site of engagement. Working through possible forms that could be taken by the link between discontinuity and judgment is an essential element within the development of an ethics of the unconditioned and thus delimiting, by restricting, the hold of becoming.

1.

At the minimum human actions can be judged for two specific reasons: first, because such actions stem from the operative presence of the will, and second because any action could always have been otherwise. Their combination is integral to any definition of responsibility. These two reasons identify the possibility of judgment. And yet, what they don't identify, or at least what they don't identify initially, are the grounds of judgment. Consequently, an initial distinction can be drawn between judgment's possibility and that in terms of which judgments can be made. This distinction is central and thus needs to be noted. To the extent that the distinction between possibility and the occurrence of judgment can be maintained, what then becomes significant is how to understand the relationship between judgment's possibility and that in terms of which judgments occur. As will be seen this distinction and the differing determinations of time within it will continue to play a fundamental role in an ethics of the unconditioned. At this stage, however, it is the second aspect noted above, namely, the ground of judgment, that has to be addressed.

If it can be argued that the ground of judgment is intrinsic to human life, working here with the acceptance of the severance of human life from biological life, what is still to be furnished is any possible unanimity in relation to grounds of judgment. All that can be adduced thus far is that the locus in question is human life; the activity of life, thus the activity that is life. What this means is that the question of life—of human life—were it to be thought philosophically, at the outset, takes on an open quality. There cannot be an automatic response. (In part this occurs as a result of the abeyance of the biological and thus of the determinism of the epigenetic.) As a consequence, the initial element that endures as intrinsic to the question of human life is the maintenance of a certain interrogative force. However, given the presence of questions a space of response or responses is maintained as open.

As a result of the question that was posed at the outset— What if life were to be thought philosophically?—then once life is clarified as "human life," the question can be taken as naming, at the beginning, a locus of contestation as to what would secure and thus establish the "good life" as a potentiality that is intrinsic to life. If the good life is a potentiality that is intrinsic to life, thus to the being of being human, such a setup attests to both the viability and the utility of the formulation, *virtue in being*. In addition, there is the attendant recognition that human being involves living within the presence of an original disequilibria of power. As a result the term *good* should not be identified automatically with the moral. The "good life" is not a life that is lived in one way rather than another (as though the "good life" were simply a matter of choice). *Good* here marks the possibility of that which is proper to life, where that involves both human life and then that life's relation to all other forms of life. Holding to relationality does not exclude thinking the particularity of the being of being human. The possibility of the "good life" still insists within relationality. Given this context, what counts as the good life is to be understood as a locus of contestation, and while there will also be conflict concerning how agency is to be understood, what inheres in attempts within the history of philosophy to think "life," is the recognition that this thinking cannot be separated effectively from a sense of propriety. This is a position that circumvents philosophical nihilism by rendering it impossible. This is even clear in Nietzsche. When Nietzsche argues in *The Anti-Christ* that a "free spirit" is already implicated in a "revaluation of values," what is at work is a sense of propriety. In the case of Nietzsche, however, this is nothing other than the expression of a radical subjectivism that identifies freedom with the quality of a subject who attains this state through individual and individualizing actions. Even if Nietzsche writes *we*, and thus defines a position held by "we free spirits" (*"wir freien Geister"*) the state of "freedom" that results is no more than a grouping of freed individuals.² A position reinforced by his underscoring of the self as the locus of transformation in the ascription of a productive power to a form of "selfishness" ("*der Selbstucht*") in *Ecce Homo*.³

Present as a generalized term, the argument has to be that "propriety" is intrinsic to any thinking of a conception of life that differentiates that conception from an understanding of life as a given and thus as a reiterated generality. (The latter would be the conception of life within the primordiality of "eternal return.") Even if what life is, is still to be discovered and established, it remains the case that what endures is the supposition of there being that which is proper to life. What this means is that there is a sense of propriety that is intrinsic to human being and consequently to the being of being human. As has been suggested at the outset, the result of such a positioning is that there is an anoriginal relation between the ontological and the ethical. The ontological does not precede it in any direct sense, nor should the ethical be added to it, let alone be protected from it. Propriety here depends on the possibility, perhaps the necessity of having to think the being of being human. What is meant by propriety in relation to existence is not mere existence, nor can existence be equated with any one historical or given determination of human being, hence propriety is not normativity, nor can it be reformulated in terms of historical relativity. Rather, the term *propriety* holds open the space in which the question of what it is that is appropriate to and thus proper to human being can be posed. Accepting the question of propriety as a question, and then in positioning the philosophical task as responding to it, has fundamentally important consequences. The most significant here concerns overcoming the way the relationship between the ethical and the ontological is conventionally understood. It is overcome because an insistence on propriety, or perhaps more accurately allowing propriety to insist, means that the philosophical task would never have been reduced to finding ways of connecting the ontological and the ethical. Indeed, the contrary is the case. That relation is always already present. In sum, again, there is *virtue in being*. Part of the overall position to be developed in the course of this undertaking is that the grounds of judgment are already present within the fact of existence when the latter is understood ontologically. There is an important reciprocity here. The ground of judgment cannot be separated from the *fact of existence* or the *worldliness of the world*. The existence of their inseparability, however, does not entail an equation between the ontological and the ethical. As a result of this setup it is their relation that has to be thought; in other words, the always already present relationship between ethics and ontology is that which determines this specific formulation of the philosophical task.[4]

The question then is how to begin to think the relation between the ethical and the ontological. The quality of that which is "already there," understood as the anoriginality of commonality, relationality and place provides a point of departure. There isn't an *arché*. Rather beginning occurs *in medias rei*. In sum, a beginning can be made with that which is already there, namely, the relationship between the affective and the *fact of existence*, since to be in the world is to have been affected. Affect is bound up with worldly being. To be affected is to be a subject of affect within the world. Even though being a subject is to have been affected, there is an additional element here, namely, time. Time, however, is not being adduced. The contrary is the case. Time has an original quality. While its presence can be assumed, time has a greater complexity than that which is revealed by what is given with this assumption. To evoke the world is to evoke the hold of time. Time is not an empty condition. With the advent of philosophical modernity, time is present as that which can be interrupted and challenged. Events occurring within time can be affirmed or disavowed in ways that have an effect on how time is understood. As a result time acquires an ineliminable complexity. Time is revealed to be originally complex. The themes of destruction, progress, recurrence, negation, and so on, each with a project for action that stems from the way these times work, work to denature time by undoing any attempt to identify time with either nature or chronology. (Hence, what is at work is a plurality of times.) Time is now subject to the possibility of both continuity and discontinuity. Within such a setting all that is now settled is the impossibility of time as a locus of contestation ever having a final resolution and thus of there being an image of the future. Time will have always been *times*. The image, to the extent that it is constrained by having to present time as a singularity, is pitted against the plurality of times. In other words, while the politics of time has an inevitability, the outcomes stemming from it are not just far from settled, they are equally the site of genuine contestation.[5] As a result time is more complex than would be indicated by its complete identification with the present, were the latter to be thought as a singularity. Moreover, once destruction and inauguration are connected, and the possibility of finality as event or image is deferred, then the present as a site is defined by a founding irreducibility. Constructing that irreducibility, holding it apart from a setting structured by mere quantitative differences, depends on time harboring a potentiality. The latter, potentiality's insistent presence, becomes time(s) within time. It is times within time that has already been recast as the *now*, where the *now* is thought in terms of a site of anoriginal irreducibility.

As has already been suggested, the potentiality noted above is the potentiality for what "is" to be *otherwise*; to become other than what it "is." There cannot be an *otherwise*, that which will have become other, unless there is both the potentiality for it to occur, and a recasting of the present in terms of locus defined by the possibility of its being other. The present is also, and at the same time, the presence of this possibility. The latter position involves what has to be described as a specific form of recognition. Part of what is recognized are the consequences of holding to a conception of the present as a site whose naturalization is a construct; there are only ever constructions rather than nature. Construction obtains in the place of "nature." Nature can only be posited. The processes of naturalization, differing forms of the positing of nature, appear in different ways. One form involves the incorporation of the present into time as chronology, while another would be to conceive of the present as a singularity within a generalized ontology of becoming. Occurrences regulated by place within becoming. The direct consequence of such processes is that they will have obviated the need to account for the possibility of the present's capacity for its own transformation. (*Othering* as a potentiality.) The distinction between actuality and potentiality is effaced by repetition as continuity and continuity as repetition. As a result judgment becomes both unnecessary and impossible. Again, as noted at the outset, one of the overall contentions of this project is that the processes at work in the naturalization of time, and thus the type of response that necessitates the "denaturing" of this conception of time are implicated, first, in the politics of time and then, second, in the recovery of an ethics of the unconditioned within which judgment has a genuine task.

Once time becomes a site of contestation a different set of questions arise. Rather than being at the end of time, time stages the inevitability of contestation as a contestation over times. This is the time of the present. It is within this setting, thus within this determination of the present, that it becomes possible to respond to those positions within philosophy that posit the possibility of a "good life" as consistent with the time in which that possibility is posed and the realized. The "good life" becomes therefore a type of fulfillment and the *telos* appropriate to life. The relationship between an evocation of fulfillment and the inevitability of confrontation, where the latter has structural rather than mere dispositional force since it cannot be extricated from the disequilibria of power that marks the present, creates the domain in which it becomes possible to respond to differing permutations of fulfillment and different ways of understanding the "end" of time.

There are, of course, other forms of fulfillment within the history of philosophy. The overall point is, however, that fulfillment understood as the actualization of an end (*telos*) has a particular register insofar as once a type of reality is attributed to it, then the presence of an actualized end (putative or not) emerges as a genuine problem for the development of an ethics of the unconditioned precisely because the unconditioned presupposes its own nonactualization (thus it acquires the quality of being un-ending or in-finite). Fulfillment is deferred in advance and, thus, what is opened up as a result is the space in which judgment is possible. An instance of an argument against both fulfillment and fulfillment's actualization can be located in Kant's response to Epicurus. Kant's Epicurus is constructed in opposition to the Kantian philosophical project. That opposition can however be questioned. This does not occur in order to undo its implications, or to show Kant to have been incorrect. Rather, it would be to indicate that the presence of a greater affinity between them than would have been imagined, especially by Kant, furthers the project of developing an ethics of the unconditioned and thus of showing that *virtue in being* had the quality of being already present. Working through Kant's relation to Epicurus is of paramount importance. Moreover, it will be essential to continue to return, almost incrementally, to the presence of Epicurus in Kant. Programmatically what this means is that the structure of this chapter sustains a set of returns. Kant and Epicurus continue to confront each other since what has to be determined is how their relation is to be understood. This necessitates working through some of the different ways in which that relation is thought by Kant. In order to create a setting, a start will be made here with the writings of Epicurus and then with responses to Epicurus, most notably the response made by Cicero. The significance of Cicero is considerable. Kant's access to a great deal of Epicurean and Stoic thought was via Cicero. Moreover, Garve's translation of the latter's *De Officiis* had, it can be conjectured, a profound effect on Kant's own conception of duty.⁶

In Epicurus, "tranquillity" ("αταραχια") is "the goal of the completely happy life" ("του μακαριως ζην εστι τελος").⁷ That "tranquillity" was a state of affairs that was taken to be actualizable and which can be noted in the formulation presented above by the use of the term *goal* (*telos*; τελος) is also clear from Seneca's report of the carving above the entrance to Epicurus's garden. The latter read: "*Hospes, hic bene manebis. Hic summum bonum voluptas est.*"⁸ The reiteration of a specific locus, what can be understood as placed presence, is, of course, carried by the reiteration of *hic*. Even with the advent of Christianity and in a Christianizing response to Epicurus, evident, for example ,in Lorenzo Valla's *De voluptate* (1450), the pleasures that occur in heaven are simply a translation of the earthly. The problematic element occurs in how virtue allows for another sense of happiness. The latter is heavenly happiness; hence, Valla writes that virtue, "is to be desired as a step towards that perfect happiness (*ad eam beatitudinem*) which the spirit or soul freed from its mortal position, will enjoy with the Father of all things from which it came."[9] While this sets up a series of philosophical and theological problems—for example, the nature of the distinction between the earthly and the heavenly—what it provides is an image of the life of pleasure. There is an image and hence there is the literalization of place. A critique of the possibility of ends involves therefore a concomitant critique of the image (of any possible image). Equally it would necessitate breaking with specific conceptions of action. This is especially the case in regards to moral action, in which acting would be a form of emulation. Moral action has to be original and thus not a mere imitation. Moral action has to be both original and exemplary.[10]

Taking up the Epicurean conception of "tranquillity" is as much to question time as it is to question the possibility of identifying one particular affective state with a sense of either an end or a completion and thus with that which has an image (the image of a specific and determined place and to that extent place as an image of an actual place rather than "place" as that in relation to which human being is thought). With this deferring of the image, what is then demanded is a setting within which an "end," the realized *telos*, which is defined in purely affective terms, is able to be judged. Judgment in implicated in the need and thus also in the possibility of discriminating between affective states. (Though it should be added immediately that once this move is made then what will always need to be adduced are concerns defined by delimiting the grounds of judgment.)

There is a difficulty inherent in any thinking that posits an end. To posit an end is to think that time has come to an end; it would be an end in which time continues unendingly as the repetition of what can be described as the *always the same*.[11] (This is a conception of *sameness* in which difference, as has been suggested, is only ever present as variety and therefore defined in purely quantitative terms.) However, such a setting for time—the setting of time—can be contested. The quality of the world, which is the locus of affect and the site where disequilibria of power relations unfold, is such that affect cannot be understood independently of its articulation within a set of relations whose intrinsic quality also demands judgment. Consequently, even if "tranquillity" were thought to be a mere potentiality and not a state whose presence depended on overcoming the differentials of power that may have rendered it impossible and thus not actual, the philosophical question linked to action concerns how the actualization of a potentiality is to be understood. Hence, there is a different question. Allowing for the insistent presence of potentiality means that the *now*, and this will be true of every *now*, is always incomplete insofar as it comprised of the possibility for it to be other. The *now* eschews finality. This *now* will return insofar as Kant defines the locus of the law as that which occurs in a *now* (*Jeztz*). This means that any one now is charged with different possibilities in the precise sense that the *now* becomes a site that has two different yet related qualities.

The first quality is straightforward. The *now* is the site of a founding irreducibility. The *now* is not a point (or not just a point). The *now* is always in excess of the instant and thus the *now* is not the particular within a generalized becoming. More significantly, the *now* in question is constructed by tensions created by the interplay of actuality in the first instance, and the potentiality for the actualization of that which is other, in the second. The elision of a potentiality awaiting actualization would reduce the *now* to the instant in which it then becomes no more than a particular within a generalized becoming. The second quality of the *now* can be discerned as a result of the recognition that what pertains in any "now" is a set of different possible times. Consequently, the "now" is a locus in which there is the constant potentiality for what is other; for what is to be other. Potentiality acquires that which is integral to its force since potentiality allows actuality to be thought. The "now," construed as involving this modality of potentiality, is not a mere occurrence it is a plural event in the precise sense that it is the locus of an irreducibility that is always already there; a setup that has already been referred to as involving *anoriginal irreducibility* which when it takes on a specific form can be understood as a plural event—for example, any one *now* is a plural event.¹²

Returning to Epicurus and the possibility of the actuality of tranquillity, though by extension the argument pertains to the actualization of an already determined end, a specific question arises: Does it mean, as a result of this reconfiguring of the "now" such that tranquillity may not be actual, that it is too early for tranquillity?¹³ As a result would any evocation of tranquillity, of peace, have been precipitate precisely because such an end can only be conceived within a progressive teleology of continuity (a continuity within an envisaged, and envisageable, *telos* and thus a literally imagined end)? Moreover, might it even have been precipitate in advance? Or could tranquillity only ever be belated? At work with these questions are differing modalities of time. A certain modality, for example, is already there in Nietzsche when he suggested that Lucretius's destruction of the very basis of the Christian view of both punishment and hell, namely, the continuity of their presence within the Roman Empire, meant that they "came too early" (*"kam zu früh"*).¹⁴ Christianity stabilized and transformed the belief. Moreover, punishment understood as "eternal torment" continues to return in the guise of either the "life sentence," in the first instance, or the "death penalty," in the second. The latter is an act in which any salvation is *post factum* impossible as justice as a possibility in this life would have ceded its place to the (im)possibility of justice in the next life.¹⁵ If, within this configuration, Lucretius were simply too early, what then of the temporal presence of Epicurus? By the end of paragraph 72 of *Daybreak*, Nietzsche locates in "science" (*"Wissenschaft"*) an Epicurean impulse. With the advent of science there is, for Nietzsche, a sense of having been freed from an oppressive and determining concern with "the after-death" (*das "Nach-dem-Tode"*).¹⁶ As such death and that which occurs after it "no longer concerns us." Having been freed from its hold means that with the emergence of "science" and its account of both life and death, for Nietzsche, there is a return in which "Epicurus triumphs anew" (*"von Neuem triumphirt Epikur"*). This "newness" which occurs within repetition, is the evocation of a certain sense of timeliness; it could be an exaggeration of the present's timeliness, or even the extravagant positing of the timeliness of the untimely. Suffice to say that all such evocations of the present, in remaining oblivious to the complexities of the *now*, are themselves premised on the continuity given within repetition, which can be described as the hold of the *always the same*. Effaced is the presence of the *now* as harboring potentialities for that which is genuinely other. *Sameness* would dictate that its now is always able to "return." It would contain the unity and accord of project for there to be a singularity whose willed return would in fact be possible precisely because it is premised on the retained presence of an ontology of becoming in which every element of the now would be different, one in relation to the other, in terms that were strictly quantitative. Once, however, the *now* is the site of *anoriginal irreducibility*, then its return cannot be willed because the unity of the now is undone in advance. There isn't any one thing to return.

Epicurus becomes the name in both Nietzsche and Kant for a specific mode of thought; a mode, which, even if Nietzsche's path were not followed, is still significant.[17] Ending the fear of death *via* an elimination of any concern with the "after-death" means that with the distancing of death it will be life itself that delimits finitude. As such, time returns. Finitude as the effect of a delimitation attains significance. However, both time and finitude have to be thought in relation to a conception of the "now" as allowing for the presaging of possibilities and thus as containing genuine potentialities, the *now* of *anoriginal irreducibility*. In sum, what has be shown in this instance is the way in which potentiality has the effect of delimiting finitude on the basis that within life what endures as operable is a distinction between the unconditioned and the conditioned. This is the position that Nietzsche's argument demands though which he was unable to furnish. The demand remains. Finitude *qua* finitude has to be thought. What endures as necessary is the effective presence of the unconditioned and the conditioned. The latter is finitude, the former that which delimits it. Hence finitude would be present as an after effect. (The supposition, once again, is that finitude is only ever the *aftereffect*.) Indeed, it is possible to locate the entire tension that exists between a domain of pure affect in which all that is at work are different modalities of affect and thus a version of the naturalization of philosophy in which affect is thought within and as philosophical naturalism and, then, a position involving a ground of judgment as having been given by the relation between the conditioned and the unconditioned. Once the conditioned can be identified with the domain of affect, what then becomes important is understanding what is meant by a ground of judgment in relation to which genuine differences within affect can be both noted and judged. One specific way of approaching this question is to begin, again, with Epicurus. And yet, it needs to be asked again, why begin, once again, with Epicurus?[18] In other words, why start an extended essay the result of which is to secure a reworked version of the Kantian unconditioned as the basis of a philosophical thinking of the ethical, and which moves through Arendt, Kant, and Derrida, with Epicurus? The answer will have been given in advance. Epicurus does not just appear. The name is already there. Indeed, the continual construction of the figure of Epicurus marks a determined set of possibilities within both the history of philosophy and the history of religion. Precisely because of the centrality of Epicurus as figure within the development of those elements of Kant's philosophical project that are central here, his figured presence continues to provide a way into the former's concerns. What matters are the terms within which Kant's critical engagement with this figure is itself staged.

Epicurus endures as one of the philosophers to whom Kant continues to return.[19] His presence is explicit. He continues to be named. There is a continuity of occurrence in which a specific figure of Epicurus is the result. Kant's critical engagement with Epicurus is sustained throughout his writings. While Kant has obvious objections to fundamental elements of the cosmological theories in both Lucretius and Epicurus, in this instance what is central is Kant's project to locate in Epicurus's work a specific and limited philosophical thinking of life.[20] Moreover, what will become the figure of Epicurus is a mode of thought that is, from Kant's perspective, correct insofar as it attests to the ineliminability of a conception of the "greatest good" and thus the possibility of a good life. There is, in other words, the concession of the necessity of thinking the "greatest good." Nonetheless, there is a problem. From Kant's perspective, a limit can be located in Epicurus's inability to provide that thinking and thus the necessity of the "greatest good" with a secure basis.

Epicurus remained an ambivalent figure. In the *Critique of the Power of Judgment* Kant argued that: "Epicurus, who made out all gratification as at bottom bodily sensation, may to that extent perhaps not have been mistaken, and only misunderstood himself when he counted intellectual and even practical satisfaction as gratification."[21] As indicated above for Kant while Epicurus kept on formulating distinctions within life correctly insofar as there were important gradations within the "good," he did not have the philosophical resources to think the "'greatest good," even though the formulation— τὸ μέγιστον ἀγαθόν—appears in the *Letter to Menoeceus*.[22] Integral to this identification of a limit to thought appearing as a demand for thought that cannot be realized, is the term *eudaimonia*, which appears in its translated form in Kant's writings as *Glückseligkeit*. It is both the perceived centrality of *eudaimonia* in Epicurus and the impossibility of its grounding a sense of moral worth that is essential to the limitation, for Kant, of Epicurus. Again this is a formulation that stages the severance of happiness from moral worth and to which a return will continue to be made.

Kant's engagement with Epicurus, his construction of the figure of Epicurus, needs to be understood as occurring within the setting established by the set of philosophical exigencies established by the difference between the conditioned and the unconditioned. As indicated above, Epicurus names a limit condition. Even within this limit, however, there are moments that complicate the surety of the division between Kant's project and Epicurus's. Part of what can be argued, an argument that complicates the possibility of clear divisions, is that Epicurus's critique of superstition coupled to Kant's advocacy of the Enlightenment as leaving superstition to one side and thus as having the courage to think, an act named by Kant in terms of *sapere aude*, brings them into a far closer alliance than Kant may have imagined. Moreover, the argument posed in relation to what Kant calls "legality" would itself be close to an Epicurean mode of argumentation. Kant argues against an identification of the moral with a simple following of the law. His claim is that while the "letter of the law (legality)" would be found in such "actions" what would be missing is "the spirit of it in our dispositions (morality)."[23] The key point here is not what is meant by "spirit" per se, but in how the difference between "spirit" and "law" is itself to be understood. What would difference mean in this context? It is in the nature of this difference that the continuity of the relation (or nonrelation) between Epicurus and Kant needs to be presented.

Once the name Epicurus is allowed greater extension such that it is present as a figure within philosophy's history, then it can be argued that the "name" stands as much for the identification of pleasure (hedonism) taken as an end in itself, as it does for a refusal of the import of divine law. For Maimonides, as well as within other significant instances within the history of Jewish philosophical and religious thought, in addition to a range of Greek and Roman philosophers, "Epicurus" named the apostate. In the *Mishnah Pirkei Avot*, for example, the study of Torah has a necessity for a range of different reasons. One is that studying Torah, it is argued, equips the reader to respond "to Epicureans" ("תא סורוקיפא"). However, what is meant by "סורוקיפא" is "heretics." A position that is also clear from references to the same figure in the *Babylonian Talmud Sanhedrin* (cf 96b–100a). Maimonides in *The Guide to the Perplexed* bases his evocation of Epicurus on the Talmudic tradition, even if his knowledge of Epicurus's actual writings, and hence the construction of the figure in that particular context, will have come more directly from Arabic translations of Alexander of Aphrodisiensis.[24] As Maimonides argues the Epicureans, "did not recognize the existence of God, but believed that the existing state of things is the result of accidental combinations and separation of the elements."[25] It is clear that for Maimonides the ethical and cosmological theories of the Epicureans intersect. The further supposition was that this name—"Epicurus"—named not just a form of atheism but also the denial of the divine nature of divine law. It is of course possible to keep compiling examples which, when taken together, indicate that Epicurus, now the name of a figured presence, names from a differing set of perspectives, the refusal to think the active presence of God and equally the refusal of a conception of the good that was transcendent in relation to finitude. The good had been actualized and therefore was from the start an actualizable possibility. Hence, the earlier reference to the interplay of "tranquillity" and place.

This construction of the figure of Epicurus can, of course, be subjected to questioning; a process that can only occur by referring to the extant writings. As a beginning, it is complicated by the claim that can be found in the writing of Epicurus concerning "God." In the *Letter to Menoeceus*, he argues that integral to a sense of "the beautiful life" ("τοῦ καλῶς ζῆν") is the recognition that "God" is "a blissful and immortal being" ("τὸν θεὸν ζῷον ἄφθαρτον καὶ μακάριον").[26] That this conception of the divine is also evident from the writings of the pre-Christian Epicureans is also significant.[27] The latter position combined with a critique of superstition locates both Epicurus and subsequent Epicureanism as having a specific relation to both God and religion. He was not as writing and thinking contra God or even religion, but rather against a certain form of religion. Within that process a space for the philosophical, as a philosophy of life, is being cleared; a space with a space for God. Whether this occurs in the name of atheism or necessitates atheism are separate questions. Indeed, it can be more plausibly argued that the critique of religion only occurs to the extent that religion is equated with superstition.[28] To maintain religion, in the wake of this critique, would be to define it in relation to both reason and judgment.[29] Part of what has to be argued in this regard is that in Epicurus the object of critique was a not religion per se. Rather, what was subject to critique was the presence of religion as superstition thus leading to what might be described, as a result of that critique, as the repositioning of religion such that it can be located within the "bounds" of reason. This will account for why as Diogenes of Oenoanda's inscriptions attest, it is not as though Epicurus was a figure attracting public disdain.[30]

Equally, it accounts for why Gassendi, writing in an ostensibly Christian garb, in his *De vita, et moribus Epicuri*, will also take up, as part of his defense of Epicurus, an examination of what is at work in Epicurus's identification of certain religious practices with superstition.[31] Again, it is possible to continue to cite other instances in which both Epicurus's commitments to civility and to God (and thus via extension to religion) endure as central. However, precisely because Kant's knowledge of Epicurus, if both the content of his library and the texts to which Kant had direct access can be taken as setting the measure, will have come from Cicero, Seneca, and it can be conjectured from the first volume of J. J. Brucker's *Historia Crtitica Philosophiae*, rather than from a detailed study of the extant texts which at the time were only to be found in Diogenes Laertius, a return needs to be made to the presence of Epicurus in Cicero. In this instance to the *De Finibus*.[32]

In the *De Finibus*, Cicero's critique is specific. It stems from the identification by Epicurus of the "greatest good" (*summum bonnum*) with "pleasure" (*voluptas*). It should be noted that the difficulty lies in the identification. As a way into Cicero's concerns it is important to note the actual terminology deployed in the following line, which is presented by Cicero as a citation from Epicurus: "the Wise Man (*sapienti*) is but little interfered with by fortune (*fortunam*) the greatest concerns of life, the things that matter are controlled by his own reason (*ratione*)."[33] While Cicero goes on to locate reason in relation to sensation, which is a position that is clearly not opposed to the project that can be located in Epicurus's own writings, it remains the case that what is identified is a distinction between "fortune" and "reason." This distinction needs to be recalled.

In *De Finibus*, Book 11, Cicero's form of argumentation does not pertain to the presence of the "greatest good" within Epicurus, as though its status could be posed as a question in its own right. What the absence of this specific form of questioning means is that there isn't an argument against the presence of the "greatest good" as such. The argument is against its identification with a particular construal of "pleasure."[34] There is a direct correlate here with Kant's own argument in the *Critique of Practical Reason*, where he suggests that Epicurus along, "with many morally well disposed men of this day ... do not reflect deeply enough on their principles" ("über ihre Principien nicht tief genug nachdenkende").³⁵ Note of course that Epicurus is "well disposed," hence, the question is how the process of "reflection" would be understood in this context and what would be its object? A way in has already been provided since, as was made clear in the *Critique of the Power of Judgment*, "critics" as opposed to the critical philosophers did not "reflect." The terminology is the same. The process of reflection will return because Epicurus will also use a related term. Consequently, it is essential to underscore the presence of "reflection" here. Remembering that for Kant in the *Critique of the Power of Judgment* reflection is not determined by a concept but occurs in relation to one.

The formulation of the relationship between the "greatest good" and "pleasure" in Cicero, however, warrants attention. Cicero's claim is that for Epicurus the assertion that "the chief good is pleasure" gives rise to a specific philosophical project. Namely, that it necessitates, for Cicero, an examination of "what pleasure is." The identification of one with the other creates the framework of investigation. Arguments continue within the text. They mirror arguments taking place elsewhere within both Greek and Roman philosophy as to the definition of pleasure and thus whether any one definition is adequate to the "greatest good." A similar position can also be found, for example, in Seneca's Letter 90 where it is suggested that the Epicureans "bestowed virtue on pleasure" ("*virtutem donavit voluptati*").³⁶ However, what remains undiscussed in Cicero, and equally in Seneca, is the nature of the "greatest good" itself. While in the *De Finibus* there may be a tentative conclusion in terms of an identification of the "greatest good" as involving a relationship between the "conduct of life" and the operation of "natural causes" (Book III, ix), what continues, as a question, is how the greatness of the "greatest good" is to be understood (to the extent that "greatness" is not thought in merely quantitative terms). The questioning is orientated by a search for a definition of the "greatest good" that results from an identification (i.e., a definition of X in terms of Y). What remains undiscussed, as has been suggested, is the presence of the "greatest good" as an end in itself. While this question remains unexamined by Cicero, such that all that would seem to be of concern is a description of pleasure that allows a certain definition of pleasure to be identified with "the greatest good," there are elements in the earlier citation from *De Finibus* concerning the connection between wisdom and reason that opens up another significant domain of inquiry.

Prior to noting that positioning, one that will bring a concern with "reason" into consideration precisely because of the evocation of "wisdom," another presentation of Epicurus within the writings of Cicero needs to be taken up. In the *Academica* (I.ii, 6) Cicero asserts that the Epicureans, "think that the good of cattle is the same as the good of human being" (*"pecudis enim et hominis idem bonum esse consent"*). In other words, it is as though the nature of the "good," for the followers of Epicurus, can be transferred unproblematically across the animal/human divide. What needs to be noted here is that in the case of Cicero, even though this is not the case with Kant, there is the failure to engage the problem of human animality. For Cicero the nonrelation to the animal is decisive; a position mirrored at the same time in Greek, if the arguments of Plutarch's *De Pythiae Oraculis* are followed, and in which the language of prose overcomes the possibility and the necessity of attributing sense to sounds made by animals.[37] Not only therefore is the separation of the animal from the human already complete and consequently there is a projected relation of nonrelation between them, it can also be argued that what is put out of any consideration is the possibility that the question of what "the greatest good" is would have to take up the problem of how the relation between the "greatest good" and human animality is itself to be understood. Allowing that relation to maintain a problematic status means maintaining it as a relation that demanded negotiation rather than excision. (This, as will be seen is fundamental to the argumentation of Kant in *Religion within the Bounds of Mere Reason*, in which the ineliminable presence of human animality—a positioned named in the *Critique of the Power of Judgment* in terms of "socially determined creatures" [*"die Gesellschaft bestimmten Geschöpfs"*] establishes the site of engagement.[38])

In the *De Finibus*, and in the passage cited above from the *Academica*, the problem is not that of the correct identification or definition of the "greatest good," this is simply Cicero's concern. The problem, in fact, is the failure to define and thus to think "the greatest good" outside any form of identification at all. Despite the critique of Epicurus that is taking place in his writings, Cicero is still resisting the possibility that the identity of the "greatest good" is *ab initio* unconditioned. Doing no more than establishing the correct identification, or at least taking it as that which determines the nature of the philosophical task, opens the space in which it becomes possible to respond to Cicero; a response engendering a limit. The limit arises simply by insisting the clear presence of the failure to think "the greatest good" in the only way it can be thought, namely as the unconditioned, and then as a consequence to think its relation to the conditioned. While this set up may seem to give rise to a type of Platonism, such a conclusion is not inevitable. Indeed, the dramatic strength of the arguments made by Kant in relation to Platonism opens the possibility for another thinking of the unconditioned. Moreover, it is a thinking which, in establishing the limits of one way through the tradition of idealism, opens up the need to engage with the question of what is at stake in holding to what can only be described as the unconditioned nature of the unconditioned. In others words, Plato's delimitation of the unconditioned as that which, while it is differentiated from the conditioned (e.g., the argument in the *Euthyphro* in which "piety" is there, and has to be there, in its differentiation from any one pious act) nonetheless has a causal relation to the particular's identity, is not the only way of thinking that relation.[39] The project demanded by this limitation has two interrelated elements. First, thinking the unconditioned without causality and then, second, thinking the relation between the unconditioned and the conditioned beyond the hold of quantity and thus of mere quantitative difference.

In the *Critique of Pure Reason* Kant calls Epicurus the "foremost philosopher of sensibility."[40] The contrast is of course, albeit only initially, with Plato. As philosopher of sensibility Epicurus held, according to Kant, to the proposition "that reality [*wirklichkeit*] is in the objects of the senses alone."[41]

Earlier Epicurus, again in the guise of a form of empiricism, is taken as denying the existence of "whatever lies beyond the sphere of intuitive cognitions."[42] Kant's own response to this version of empiricism is initially to concede the general truth of empiricism, namely, that objects are linked to corresponding intuitions, but then to go on and argue that what empiricism cannot grasp is that the condition of appearance is not itself an appearance. Empiricism rather than ending philosophy simply serves as its limit. However, it does not delimit the philosophical. Speculative reason as reason's own self-engagement uncovers that limit. This was a possibility, so the argument runs, that would have been open to Epicurus. The correlate is that Kantian transcendental idealism has to incorporate a fundamental difference between the conditioned and the unconditioned. In other words, the totality of what there is, where that totality absorbs the conditioned and the unconditioned, needs to be thought in a way that undoes a possible co-implication; a co-implication that would then mean that there could no discernible difference between the contents of what there is other than that of intensity. (The latter is, of course, equally a version of Spinozism.[43])

As is already clear Epicurus was a continual presence in Kant's writings. In the *Dissertation* (1770) (*De Mundi Sensibilis atque Intellegibilis Forma et Principiis*), in a position that will attain a certain familiarity as the critical project develops, Epicurus is named explicitly and then criticized for "reducing the criteria of moral judgment to feelings of pleasure or pain" (*"criteria ad sensum voluptatis"*).[44] What is significant in this formulation is not the identification of pleasure or pain, since there was always a concern with feeling and its philosophical significance, even in the *Vorkritische Schriften* there is still a detached treatment of the aesthetic. Rather what is important is that with the argumentation of the *Dissertation*, a text whose ostensible concerns are cosmological, there is the need to establish "criteria" that hold in their differentiation from the domain feeling. Deploying a terminology that will be used through his writing, this position—that is, the domain of feeling—is contrasted to what is named in the *Dissertation* as "*Philosophia pura.*" There is a twofold determination here. While *pure* identifies what is held apart from feeling, more significantly, in this context, *pure* also means independent of any form of calculation.[45] *Philosophia pura* becomes therefore an early way of indicating both the presence of the unconditioned and the way in which the unconditioned furnishes criteria of judgment.[46] (This position has to hold to the extent that what is precluded is not just the possibility that feelings alone could furnish these criteria but that feelings gave rise to forms of abstraction that established such criteria.[47]) To which it should be added that what then emerges as the philosophical question as a result is the necessity to think the relationship between the conditioned, where the latter is the locus of feeling and thus finitude, and the unconditioned since *philosophia pura* here names the unconditioned. The consequence of this way of conceiving of the unconditioned is that as a result finitude has to be thought in terms of its having been delimited by the infinite; here the unconditioned. This overall position is reiterated, first, as a structuring force in the separation of "happiness" ("*Glückseligkeit*") from "moral worth," and then, second, in the way the argument was advanced that reason recognizes the limits of "happiness."

The identification of that limit, does of course, occur throughout Kant's writings. In the *Groundwork*, for example, it is formulated in a more emphatic way. Not only is "happiness" linked to "misology"—the latter being the misuse of both reason and argumentation—it is also the case that morality cannot be based on one's "own happiness" ("*Glückseligkeit*"). The overall structure of Kant's argumentation in this regard is clear:

> making someone happy is quite different from making him good, or making him prudent and sharp-sighted for his own advantage is quite different from making him virtuous; it is the most objectionable because it bases morality on incentives that undermine it and destroy all its sublimity, since they put motives to

virtue and those to vice in one class and only teach us to calculate better, but quite obliterate the specific difference between virtue and vice.[48]

Accepting the formulation of the *Groundwork* means that the project is then to think the nature of the difference between "virtue and vice." Again, differences cannot be posited, they have to be thought. What was lacking in Epicurus and equally in Spinoza and what will come to be lacking in Nietzsche is the capacity to think difference as difference.[49] Consistent, therefore, with what has been argued thus far, difference cannot be a matter of degree. Before broaching the nature of that difference, it needs to be recalled that what is at stake in this approach to Epicurus is the "problem" *Glückseligkeit*.[50] The question that remains is clear: What is *Glückseligkeit*?[51]

This question opens in at least two directions. While being circumscribed continually by a third. First, there is the question of the way Kant understands *Glückseligkeit* and thus how within his writings its presence is thought, and then second, the way the presence of this term, now of course as *eudaimonia*, figures within Epicurus. The translation problems while considerable can be justified by noting the ease with which these terms were "translated" in the eighteenth century. Nonetheless, what is at work each in term demands careful attention. It is not simply the identification of a vocabulary of *Glückseligkeit, eudaimonia* (happiness) in texts by both authors. Of equal significance is the continual evocation of aspects of the worldliness of the world. The introduction of the world introduces worldly being and thus opens up the connection to *being-in-relation*. To evoke the world is equally to evoke the place of *being-in-relation*. In sum, therefore, this constellation of terms names activity and in so doing names, implicitly, the world in which activity occurs. In occurring activity brings the already present connection between the ethical and the ontological into play. To evoke either *Glückseligkeit*, or *eudaimonia* is to concede that what is in play, axiomatically, is the question of the "good life" as that which occurs in place. Evoked therefore is the worldliness of the world.

―⋄―

The third and final aspect inhering in the question—What is *Glückseligkeit?*—is that what *Glückseligkiet* also names is the continuity of the affective. For Kant the continuity of affect is the continuity of that which invites judgment while simultaneously not being able to provide judgment with any effective criteria to secure its project. In broader terms judgment can only be effective when it overcomes the problem of subjectivism, on the one hand and, on the other hand, the restrictions that emerge from the location of both the condition of judgment and equally what calls on judgment within a generalized ontology of becoming. Becoming cannot sustain judgment. Judgment interrupts. Hence becoming undoes in advance the possibility of judgment since the continuity of becoming would always attempt to incorporate the conditions allowing for judgment within the process itself. As a result judgment would be impossible. Hence, part of the answer to the question What is *Glückseligkeit*? is that what is named within it is the problem of the relationship between judgment and affect. In one of the texts that makes up the fragments within Kant's *Nachlass*, he states the following in relation to Epicurus: "Epicurus was concerned only with the value of the condition, he knew nothing of the inner worth of the person." ("*Epikur sahe blos auf den Werth des Zustandes, er wuste nichts vom inneren Werthe der Persohn.*")[52]

―⋄―

What has to be pursued of course is not just the viability of this specific estimation of Epicurus but rather how what Kant identifies as the "inner worth of the person" is to be understood. In a way it is not the direct presence of Kant's critique that is to be questioned. Rather, what endures as important is the way in which the concession of a form of worldly being can be located within it. What returns is the question as to how the presence of the world, as it figures both implicitly and explicitly in passages of this nature is to be understood.

———◆———

Occurring in both Kant and Epicurus is a conception of the ethical understood as a philosophical thinking that is already located within a formulation of the world as the place of human being; a formulation, which as will be suggested, allows for a presentation of place as delimiting human being. Commonality is *being-in-place* with others and where being with others which can itself be understood as *being-in-relation*, demands the place in which relations are lived out. In other words, being with others is always placed. This is a state of affairs that needs to be understood as evoking more than a conception of the world were the latter is thought as mere physical geography. What is demanded is a thinking of place as involving the worldliness of the world.[53] The force of this formulation is its capacity to sustain the world's presence as a locus of philosophical thinking. If the world cannot be equated with the mere description of physical places, then how is its worldliness to understood? The latter—worldliness—is a quality of the world and thus of being in the world understood as *being-in-place*. As will emerge in the engagement with Arendt, her argument is that violence in its denial of speech and action has the consequence of reducing those who suffer the effects of violence to a state in which they are, in her terms, "literally dead to the world."[54] This has to be understood as the elimination of worldliness. The elimination of worldliness—the effect of violence—is the reduction of life to "mere life." The latter, "mere life," is living on in the world without worldliness. While it cannot be pursued the impact of such a conception of worldliness on the formulation *virtue in being* should be clear. Being, where being is deprived of virtue, can then be equated with existence in the world without worldliness. Both are the effects of violence. Both demand another thinking of power, namely that conception of power that sustains worldliness. That demand underscores the philosophical significance of Arendt in this regard, since it is her understanding of "power" that stands opposed to violence.

The setting of the world as the locus of human being, a locus that is not just a setting but plays a significant role in how the being of being human is thought and thus how human beings think, can already be identified as present in the writings of Epicurus. It emerges once living comes to be articulated with living justly, that is, life with the potentiality to become the "good life." In other words, where life cannot be equated with mere natural life. Epicurus continues to return. This is the setting in which he argues the following:

> Practical wisdom is the foundation of all these things and is the greatest good. ["τούτων δὲ πάντων ἀρχὴ καὶ τὸ μέγιστον ἀγαθὸν φρόνησις."]) Thus practical wisdom is more valuable than philosophy and is the source of every other excellence, teaching us that it is not possible to live joyously without also living wisely and beautifully and justly, or to live wisely and beautifully and justly without living joyously. ["ἡδέως ζῆν ἄνευ τοῦ φρονίμως καὶ καλῶς καὶ δικαίως οὐδὲ φρονίμως καὶ καλῶς καὶ δικαίως ἄνευ τοῦ ἡδέως."] For the excellences grow up together with the pleasant life ["τῷ ζῆν ἡδέως"], and the pleasant life ["τὸ ζῆν ἡδέως"] is inseparable from them.[55]

In order to begin to understand what is at work in this passage it is vital to note the precision with which Epicurus writes. While it may be the case in the passage cited above that there is a sense of "pleasure" or "tranquillity" as a possible *telos*, it is also the case, first, that the *"arché"* (ἀρχὴ) and the "greatest (or highest) good" is *"phronesis"* and that, second, neither can be separated from *"eudaimonia."* There is then, for Epicurus, an original relation. The importance of that relation is its integration into life. Taking Epicurus's formulation as a point of departure the project then is thinking the continuity of life philosophically within the constraints established by the effective centrality of *"eudaimonia"* and in relation to *"phronesis"* as the "greatest good." This entails working with the already present status of that relation. Given the presentation of the connection between *"phronesis"* and *"eudaimonia,"* the question that has to be asked concerns the presence of that in terms of which judgment—here named as *"phronesis"*—actually takes place. (Questions arise at this very point: Does judgment just occur? Or is there a ground of judgment?)

At this point it is essential to recall the position that has already been advanced in relation to Cicero's summation of aspects of Epicurus's argumentation in the *De Finibus*. Namely, that *sapientia* (wisdom), which is of course *"phronesis,"* in its combination with reason works against *fortuna*. The complexities at work here are many. (Especially as there is an important link between *fortuna* and *Glückseligkeit*.) However, the straightforward conclusion that can be drawn is that for Cicero in his formulation of Epicurus's philosophy and then Epicurus's *Letter to Menoeceus* is that it is clear that *sapientia/phronesis* comprise "the greatest good." There does need to be a form of equivocation introduced at this point as Cicero in *De Officiis* (III, 13) will argue that "moral goodness" in the "true and proper sense of the term," is the exclusive possession of "the wise" (*"sapientibis"*) where the term *the wise* refers exclusively to an elite, rather than to a property or capacity of human being. Despite what Cicero might be suggesting here, it is much more plausible to argue against this interpretation, which particularizes wisdom. Hence *pace* Cicero it can be argued that Epicurus along with Aristotle and Sophocles see wisdom as a capacity—to be exercised or not—rather than then province of the few. In other words, it is an integral component of a generalized philosophical anthropology. Following this path of argumentation the claim would then be that "wisdom" is a component integral to the being of being human and is at work within the activity of life.

What is important therefore about the formulation in both the *Letter to Menoeceus* and in Cicero's presentation of

Epicurus, rather than in his own deliberations on "wisdom," is the way that, while not checking Kant's assertion that "the inner worth of the person" (*inherent Werthe der Persohn*) was not considered and that all that endured within both Epicurus's cosmological and his ethical writings depended uniquely on the senses, what it opens up as a question is what the presence of *sapientia/phronesis* actually entails. In other words, consistent with the argumentation already developed the problem may not be the senses per se, but that what is lacking in Epicurus is the possibility of securing judgment. This "lack" can be rephrased. What it highlights is the problem of holding judgment apart from mere subjective assertion. While there may seem to be points of rapprochement between Kant and Epicurus the difficulties with any evaluation of Epicurus that may align him too quickly with aspects of Kant's thought have already been identified. As is clear from the preceding for Kant there are two reasons to hold to a fundamental division between their projects. Both have already been noted. The first is the apparent absence of a distinction between the conditioned and the unconditioned in Epicurus, and then, second, there is the argument that Epicurus does not have the philosophical resources to think an engagement with distinctions within affect other than in purely affective terms. However the centrality of *sapientia/phronesis* would seem to challenge such a position. Before pursuing both these presuppositions a return needs to be made, to another formulation of what Kant objected to in his version of Epicurean thinking.[56]

While the following passage from the *Critique of Practical Reason* states the problem posed by the presence of Epicurus with great clarity, what is important is what Kant takes Epicurus to be arguing. Again, it needs to be remembered that at stake in this setting is the continual construction and reconstruction of the figure of Epicurus. Here the figure's construction needs to be approached in relation to the presence and force of what Kant refers to in the passage cited below as "the *whole highest good*" ("*das ganze höchste Gut*").

> The Epicurean maintained that happiness is the *whole highest good* [*Glückseligkeit sei das ganze höchste Gut*],

and virtue only the form of the maxim for seeking to obtain it, namely, the rational use of means to it.

Now, it is clear from the Analytic that the maxims of virtue and those of one's own happiness [*die der eigenen Glückseligkeit*) are quite heterogeneous with respect to their supreme practical principle; and, even though they belong to one highest good, so as to make it possible, yet they are so far from coinciding that they greatly restrict and infringe on each other in the same subject.[57]

The problem therefore, as posed by Kant, concerns first the ineliminability of "heterogeneity" and then second the necessity to distinguish between the "highest" and the heterogeneous. What Kant is identifying, and thus what generates the problem of "heterogeneity," or rather what yields the presence of "heterogeneity" as a problem, does not pertain to the presence of heterogeneity, as though it occurred as an end in itself. Rather, what is of concern is the nature of the relationship between "heterogeneity" and the "supreme practical principle." Once again, the question to be addressed concerns how the connection between the conditioned and the unconditioned is to be understood. Implicit in the very structure of the distinction between "heterogeneity" and the "supreme practical principle" is the recognition that the conditioned, which can be understood as finitude, cannot be thought other than in relation to that which delimits its presence as finitude: that is, the unconditioned or the infinite. The question concerning the conditioned and the unconditioned noted above continues to return. The "supreme practical principle" is the unconditioned. However, what should be clear from the ways in which Epicurus presents his position is that he did not argue that the "*whole highest good*'" is *eudaimonia*. This is the point that has to be pursued.

In the *Letter to Menoeceus* Epicurus exhorts his reader to "reflect on" or "meditate upon" ("μελετᾶν/μελεταω") what produces "*eudaimonia.*"[58] While the vocabulary is different insofar as Kant identifies a failure in Epicurus "to reflect upon" ("*nachdenken über*") "principles," it is not as though Epicurus is resisting that activity. While the "end" may be defined in terms of both "pleasure" and "tranquility," it is also clear, as is indicated by the lines cited above, that neither "pleasure" nor "tranquility" can be disassociated from the interplay of "beauty," "justice," and "wisdom." Indeed, if it can be argued that their interrelation constructs the "highest good" insofar as their presence can be named as "practical wisdom" ("φρόνησις") then it is also the case that whatever it is meant by *Glückseligkeit* in Kant's formulation, for Epicurus it cannot be divorced from "virtue," as though "virtue" is transcendent in relation to the individual, while *Glückseligkeit* itself would then only be defined on the level of the individual.[59] For Kant, on the other hand, it would have to have been a sense of individuation—the sense in which the individual is taken as primary and thus whose relationality pertains to relations between individuals—that could not have been incorporated into forms of cooperation or processes of universalization. This is, after all, why Kant uses the specific formulation, "one's own happiness" ("*die der eigenen Glückseligkeit*"). Not only is *Glückseligkeit* a site of "heterogeneity," for Kant, it can only ever pertain to the individual. As a result there cannot be a sense of commonality defined by the unconditioned presence of *Glückseligkeit*.

The problem is always going to be that "*ataraxia*" is, for Epicurus, "the goal of a completely happy life" ("τοῦ μακαρίως ζῆν ἐστι τέλος").[60] On its own the proposition is simply too general. What has to be indicated is that such a claim brings with it the attendant problem of how the subject position appropriate to it is to be understood. In other words, the problem now is the nature of the subject position that is proper to "*eudaimonia*." And given this setting what emerges is the problem to which, implicitly at least, allusion has already been made, and which is at the heart of the presence of *Glückseligkeit*. Namely, the relation between the conditioned and the unconditioned. On one level, it can always be argued that the subject position appropriate to the "good life" is the abstract individual. The *telos* of *ataraxia* depends on the *arché* given by the interplay of "practical wisdom," the "greatest good," and a "joyous life" pertain to the individual alone. Thus what would be central is the presence, or possibility, of anyone individual's "tranquillity." This is a possibility that can never be excluded. Leaving aside its detail, this is what Kant interprets Epicurus as arguing. And for this reason it has to be understood as a possibility that is antithetical to a version of the Kantian project that sees a sense of the communal or the "cooperative" as fundamental.[61] Hence, the formulation that "a good that is the *highest good* in the world" would only ever be possible, to use the formulation of *Religion within the Bounds of Mere Reason*, "through our cooperation."[62] The move from the individual, to individuals being given, and thus only existing within "cooperation," is central. There is an interesting parallel here with Hegel's interpretation of Epicurus in his *Vorlesungen über der Geschichte der Philosophie*, in which he argues that even though Epicurus identified with the position that holds to the claim that "Being is not being above all" ("*das Sein nicht als Sein* überhaupt") and that as a result Being is thought simply as "sensation" ("*Empfundenes*"), it is still the case "pleasure was sought through thought as a universal." As such this universalizing move allows "pleasure" a sense of commonality that would have not been possible if Epicurus's thought were orientated purely by sensation.[63] It can be argued that what Hegel discovers is the tension that inheres in Epicurus between a subject position defined in terms of the individual and one that necessitates the move to *being-in-relation*. (To which it can be added that this is also the tension that pervades Kant's entire philosophical project: the tension that exists between two concepts of the subject; first, the subject position given within *being-in-relation*, and then second, the individual and autonomous subject.)

If the second of these possibilities is given predominance, that is, the position in which a sense of commonality or *being-in-common* is attributed priority, then a different position emerges. With the emergence there has to be the recognition that what is named by Kant as, for example, "cooperation," allows for its incorporation into the following argument: While *ataraxia* may indeed be a *telos*, once it is viewed as too early, or precipitate, where that state of affairs is a result of the quality of the world (note the move from the individual to the world, a move that has to incorporate a concern with the worldliness of the world into it), then, rather than return or reduce *ataraxia* to the merely individual, it would become an "end" (*telos*) for which cooperative practices would then be orientated. It would be an end, moreover, one that cannot be divorced from a thinking of the highest good and for which relationality would be the only viable subject position. The move to this subject position and away from the individual subject would reflect the quality of the world. Knowledge and judgment made in relation to the world's insistent worldliness would take the link between a given *telos* and the interplay between the highest good and the set of complex possibilities that are named by the term *Glückseligkeit* as furnishing both the ground and therefore the possibility of those judgments. To the extent that the communal is emphasized then not only is the domain of pure affect to be put to one side because worldliness predominates, the possibility of the critical project continues to depend on the impossible possibility of that which in the continuity of deferring its own actualization the unconditioned can be taken as demanding.

Where the development of the overall argument has to go next is *via* a consideration of what is meant by *phronesis*. The reason for this development is clear. *Phronesis* stages a continual interplay worldliness and the world. This will need to be linked to the identification of reason and judgment thought in relation to what has been called the worldliness of the world. What this means is that the question of the greatest good is *not* the Platonic question but one that both invokes and demands criteria of judgment. This move from Platonism toward another thinking of the unconditioned is clear from the following passage from the *Critique of Pure Reason*:

> ... we are all aware that when someone is represented as a model of virtue [*als Muster der Tugend vorgestellt wird*], we always have the true original [*das wahre Original*] in our mind alone, with which we compare this alleged model and according to which alone we estimate it. But is thus that the idea of virtue [*die Idee*

> *der Tugend*] in regards to which all possible objects of experience do service as examples . . . but never as archetypes [*aber nicht als Urbilder*]. That no human being will ever act adequately to what the pure idea of virtue [*was die reine Idee der Tugend enthält*] does not prove in the least that there is something chimerical in his thought. For it is only by means of this idea that any judgment of moral worth or unworth is possible. [*Dennes ist gleichwohl alles Urteil, über den moralischen Wert oder Unwert, nur vermittelst dieser Idee möglich*]; and so its necessarily lies in the ground of every approach to moral perfection [*mithin liegt sie jeder Annäherung zur moralischen Vollkommenheit notwendig zum Grunde*], even though the obstacles in human nature . . . may hold us at a distance.[64]

What is significant here is twofold. In the first instance there is recognition that the ground of judgment is the presence of the "the pure idea of virtue" [*die reine Idee der Tugend*]. While what is meant by the "pure idea of virtue" stands in need of greater clarification Kant's position still needs to be noted. The claim is that any calculation, and calculation here means any judgment made in relation to a specific determined act is itself only possible because it is made in relation to the unconditioned. Here, and consistently with Kant's writings as a whole, the presence of the unconditioned can be located and identified by the use of the term *pure* (*reine*). Recalling therefore the passage from the *Dissertation* that has already been noted and where Kant evoked what, in that context, was called *Philosophia pura*.

The second point that has to be brought into play opens a separate domain of concerns; separate but related. It hinges on the centrality of movement. Note Kant wrote of "every approach to moral perfection" ("*jeder Annäherung zur moralischen Vollkommenheit*"). Fundamental to any understanding of the sense of movement at work in this formulation and thus of its possibility has to begin both with the absence of causality between the idea of virtue and acting, and then second the sense of nonadequation, thus the nonidentity, between them. There is therefore the creation of a space of activity. A space that is held open and which makes activity possible precisely because of the impossibility of there ever being an identity between action and "the pure idea" where the object of any action was the actualization of the "pure idea," or that any action was causally determined by that "idea" (or even depended on the idea's actualization). This sense of movement toward (*Annäherung/annähern*) therefore is a process that, following Kant and the vocabulary he will come to deploy, can be rethought in terms of "striving." *Striving* is the term that will be used to name the active relation between the conditioned and the unconditioned. Precisely because it is activity positioned in relation to the unconditioned, an activity that is of necessity acted out within and as a part of life, striving can be understood as integral to life. Life that in its being lived out continues to differentiate itself from "mere life," is life as *vita activa*. When movement, is understood as incorporating different senses of striving, it indicates that that the structuring force within a dynamic process is premised on a form of impossibility. Here impossibility has a precise meaning. It is an impossibility of actualization, where impossibility is that which holds the unconditioned apart from the conditioned. There is the incorporation of the unconditioned and therefore what might be described as *unconditionality* as the basis both of activity, on the one hand, and judgment, on the other.

The figure of Epicurus and the problems posed by *Glückseligkeit* have significance far greater than that which would be delimited by the relationship between affect and judgment. What they stage is a twofold concern. First, it is the problem of how the nature of the relationship between the conditioned and the unconditioned is to be thought. Again, it is of central important to underscore that was it at work here is not just the presence of a relationship, but that relationship emerging as an object for thought. (Perhaps it should be recalled here that Kant delimited the project of critical philosophy in terms of its attention to "possibility.") Second there is the way subject positions are constructed. Addressing the question of the creation of subject positions, and thus questions of agency posed in relation to the "good life" is of fundamental importance if what is at stake is a philosophical thinking of life. In this context life is understood as an activity, and the ethical as not given in its differentiation from life, a differentiation demanding that the connection then be established, entails that what continues to insist is the presence of *virtue in being*.

Left open in Epicurus therefore is the status of the relationship between *phronesis*, *eudaimonia* and reflection. Once this relationship is positioned beyond the individual then what has to come into play is the prospect of a universal ground of judgment. The tension in Epicurus as Hegel identified is between sensation, which is the domain of the individual, and commonality. The latter opens up the locus of the unconditioned; it allows for its work. What continues as the task therefore is to think through how the already present status of the unconditioned is to be understood.

CHAPTER TWO

ARENDT AND THE TIME OF THE PARDON

Allowing for *virtue in being* means holding to its quality as anoriginally present. Recovering its presence is the recovery of a philosophical thinking of life that is structured by the relationship between the conditioned and the unconditioned. In addition, that allowing involves the recognition that what hinders and restricts the project of recovery and affirmation are different modalities of philosophical naturalism. What can be added here is that naturalism stands opposed to thought precisely because it is simply the positing of feeling or of the natural as that which serves as a condition for reflection while simultaneously failing to think the very grounds of reflection itself. Naturalism fails within the terms of what makes it possible. Hence, naturalism is an attitude. It is not thought. Let alone thought as reflection. Again, the project of this book is to try and move a concern with thinking the ethical away from generalizations based on affect and feeling, while simultaneously noting their ubiquity and importance, by moving toward that which grounds the philosophical. As has been suggested, this is an undertaking that involves recognizing that the basis of both the conditioned and the conditional, thus finitude, stems from the exigency instantiated by the already present hold of the unconditioned. Recognizing, in addition, that this is an instantiation marked by its own fragility.

Precisely because of the centrality of the unconditioned and its effect on how the being of being human is to be thought and thus a philosophical thinking of life undertaken, in sum the development of a philosophical anthropology, this entire project could be viewed as a commentary on a formulation deployed by Derrida in his book *Pardonner*, in which the relationship between the conditioned and the unconditioned is pivotal. In writing about the philosophical problems posed by the demands for forgiveness, he states the following:

> ... the distinction between unconditionality and conditionality is shifty enough not to let itself be determined as a simple opposition. The unconditional and the conditional are, certainly, absolutely heterogeneous, and this forever, on either side of a limit, but they are also indissociable. There is in the movement, in the motion of unconditional forgiveness, an inner exigency of becoming-effective, manifest, determined, and, in determining itself, bending to conditionality [*se plier à la conditionalité*].[1]

What needs to be taken up and developed is a detailed understanding of what is entailed by a conception of the unconditional as that which in its realization is there "bending to conditionality" ("*se plier à la conditionalité*").[2] Unconditionality, as it appears in this formulation, provides the conditions of possibility for any one conditioned act. Derrida's formulation stages that necessity. (It is also a version of the position in which a form of necessity entails contingency.) Hence the demand that what is meant by "bending" be understood. This will be the case even though it will lead to an eventual distancing of Derrida due, it will be argued, to the failure of the latter to grasp implications and perhaps the radical force of his own undertaking.

Proceeding with this project involves addressing the question of how to approach the complex setup that has emerged concerning the relationship between the unconditioned/condition, on the one hand, and a philosophical thinking of life, on the other. While there are clearly a range of ways into this relation the approach taken here involves concentrating on how the fragility that inheres in life provides an understanding of life. Indeed, the formulation that has already been deployed, namely the *worldliness of the world*, opens up the already noted possibility that what can always be effaced is worldliness such that life is reduced, as a result, to "mere life." This is a life without dignity. The latter attends life and inheres in worldliness. In other words, the locus of dignity is worldliness. It is also, now to use Kant's language, a life in which the anoriginal potentiality for "holiness" has been effaced.[3] Moreover, the threat to worldliness which will be taken up in the context of this chapter in relation to the work of Hannah Arendt on "violence" and then on the "pardon" introduces a number of other themes and concepts that are fundamental to the project as a whole.

1.

Violence strikes at language. Language is spoken. The latter, namely speaking, brings the presence of worldly being into play, being's worldliness. At the beginning, though equally as a beginning, the mutual implication of speaking and violence has to be attributed a central place. Precisely because of its centrality coupled to the resonance of its continuity it is vital to note Arendt's formulation of this intertwined presence. Arendt's recognition is that life and speech are not just connected they are implicated *ab initio* in worldliness. Arendt presents this position in the following way: "A life without speech without action . . . is literally dead to the world; it has ceased to be a human life because it is no longer lived among men."[4]

From Arendt's perspective, therefore, life, action, and speech are defined in terms of each other. Life is from the start relational. This is the power already there in the formulation "among men." Violence can be understood, therefore, as that which breaks or seeks to break the link between life and speech and as a result may undo an already present sense of relationality. To reiterate the formulation already used it can be argued that such a severance would be the reduction of life to "mere life," hence, a projected undoing, as a result of violence, of the anoriginality of *being-in-relation*.[5] Mere life is the life that can be made "superfluous." She writes to Jaspers that evil is "making (*zu machen*) human beings as human beings superfluous."[6] A position reiterated in *The Origins of Totalitarianism* in the following terms: "Radical evil emerged in connection with a system in which all men have become equally superfluous."[7] Speech, however, is more than *logos*. As will become clear *logos* cannot be thought independently of its already present interarticulation with the place of speaking. This is the correlate of the identification of human life with relationality. Working on from Arendt means that as a result of this correlation thinking life philosophically takes as its point of departure the already present interarticulation of speech and place. The incorporation of place as a contested site, where contestation involves value and thus enjoins judgment renders problematic any attempt to secure an identification of place with the natural. The critique of naturalism occasions another possibility for nature. Now, while the argument of this and subsequent chapters continue to turn around Arendt's fundamental insight concerning the relationship between life and speech, that turning will be as much a form of separation as it will be a turning back.

As is clear from the outset worldliness is voiced and continues to have presence as being voiced. And, precisely because it is voiced and where that voicing implies the presence of others, there is an already existent set of relations that the voice positions and within which it occurs. What is common therefore cannot be identified with the voice as though the latter existed as an end in itself. (Taking the voice as comprising such an end would be, by definition, one of the most resilient forms of logocentrism.) Rather, what is common are the relations in which the voice can itself be located (albeit positively or negatively). Moreover, these relations are either actual or potential.[8] To recapitulate the position being worked out, the claim is that once relations and relationality are attributed a primordial status it then follows that singularities are always aftereffects of relations. Equally, because that voicing is worldly, the voicing of worldly being, which is the voice of being in the world, the voicing of the necessity of placed relationality, becomes the voicing of *being-in-place*. In sum, *being-in-place* is lived, thus it is voiced. The voice is retained within a setup in which any possible centrality of logos is mediated in advance by the primordiality of relationality and place. As is already becoming clear, the development of a philosophical anthropology, a philosophical thinking of life, one eschewing both anthropocentrism and logocentrism depends first on maintaining while explicating the terms *being-in-relation* and *being-in-place*; second, on the continually attempted realization of the task of thinking human life apart from its biological registration. Both of these positions pertain from the start.

Violence, the violence that attends this anthropology and thus the violence whose threat is that from which human being can never be freed, has a twofold quality. First, it is defined in relation to speech and the voice. Second, it is a violence that calls on judgment. Demands for judgment have, of necessity, forms of contingency built into them. However, the contention here is that the ground of judgment has to be thought in regard to the being of being human, namely *being-in-relation* and *being-in-place*. Within that setting necessity will continue to entail contingency, and there is the already noted distinction between the ethical and the ontological. They are not identical. Rather there is an anoriginal relation. The ethical therefore is continually present as ground in the being of being human. Activities that have the structure of a decision can be judged because of the anoriginality of this relation. As will be see it is the retention of the structure of the decision that allows both for an account of "evil" and its relation to judgment.

What matters and therefore what counts with judgment is as much the act as it is its possibility. Indeed, the act takes on the quality of an act precisely because of its possibility.

Ontology, as a consequence, will have already been related to the ethical. Moreover, for the ethical to have force it needs to be ground in the ontological. Judgment can be understood therefore as that which interrupts the continuity of becoming insofar as judgment is the act that resists the naturalization of activity or activity's naturalization in which activity is, as a consequence, nothing other than variety within *sameness*. Value is originally implicit in being. Again, there is *virtue in being*. The naturalization of activity is the absorption of events into the continuity of the given. As has been noted, judgment interrupts. Judgment therefore is a *countermeasure*. And yet, countering is not a mere play of forces. The *countermeasure* must come from the outside. It comes from that which is proper to the world. It must come therefore from what gives credence, then force, to Arendt's claim that a "life without speech without action . . . is literally dead to the world."[9] Finally, there is the additional point that judgment is both possible and can only have purchase because of the presence of *being-in-place* and *being-in-common*. The terms, *judgment*, *being-in-place*, *being-in-common*, and *being-in-relation*, continue to circle around each other.

Acts and decisions have an inevitable contingency. Judgment therefore takes place in relation to finite contingent acts. It responds to such acts. It is the response. Equally, however, judgment is itself both finite and contingent. Responding to the inherently contingent brings both mutability and fragility into play. Within this setting agency remains a complex problem. Its problematic status is clear once a term such as *responsibility* is taken as providing a way in. Responsibility, which is also defined in relation to the responsible agent, when the term and any ensuing formulation describe actions that call on judgment, pertains with equal force whether the locus of agency is an individual or whether it is a public or private organization. Noting of course the necessity of the difference between these locations of agency. Taking this further involves recognizing that the structure of the decision in which agency is inscribed brings at the very least a twofold set of concerns into play. They pertain to time and to abstraction. A beginning will be made here with abstraction. Indeed, taking up abstraction opens up the complexities inherent in the question of time.

Abstraction emerges because judging the finite and the contingent takes place in relation to abstractions. Judgment, as has already been intimated, is, in terms of its possibility, inextricably bound up with both *being-in-relation* and *being-in-place*. Any judgment, therefore, will have already brought them into play, positively or negatively. This intricate setting provides judgment with its force. While the terms *being-in-place* and *being-in-relation* (recognizing, again, that relationality is *being-in-common* precisely because what is there *in-common* is relationality) will always stand in need of greater elaboration, what is initially important about both is that they are abstractions. Moreover, they are abstractions in relation to which finite and contingent acts of judgment occur. As a consequence what has to be taken up is what is meant by *abstraction*. Equally, what also has to be brought into consideration is the position of these abstractions. In sum, what obtains with the finite moment is the ground of judgment and the presence of a form of abstraction, in part delimiting its finitude. This is the case whether the moment is the act or the judgment. Here, there is an intimation of what Derrida refers to as "bending."

The presence of the ground of judgment is significant precisely because it takes place simultaneously with the act. It attends the act. At the same time therefore acts bring with them that in terms of which they are to be understood and explicated. This is a mode of simultaneity that is another iteration of the temporality of *at-the-same-timeness*. As will be seen it is a specific determination of *at-the-same-timeness* that is fundamental to the way that Kant positions the relationship between abstraction and particularity. In that context what marks out *at-the-same-timeness* is that it is the site of an original form or locus of irreducibility and thus a form of anoriginal difference. It marks the presence of a founding irreducibility that cannot be formulated adequately in terms of epistemological, moral, or semantic relativism. Relativity and, therefore, relativism, as with perspectivism, is difference within the quantitative. What stands opposed to relativity is both anoriginal difference and the continuity of its actualization that characterizes the *plural event*. The latter names, and continues to name, the particularity of anoriginal difference.

Abstraction arises as a genuine philosophical problem once both naturalism and empiricism which in the end involve similar philosophical commitments are put to one side. Indeed, the philosophical exigency established by abstraction exposes the philosophical vacuity of both naturalism and empiricism as philosophical positions. In part this is of course Kant's response to Hume.[10] Fundamental to the Humean conception of abstraction is not just the insistence that abstractions are useful "fictions," nor is it merely their necessity; a necessity that arises despite the absence of a corresponding object that could sustain the "impression" of an abstraction. These aspects are important. However, central to both is how the relationship between abstractions and particulars is understood and, therefore equally, how the conceptions of abstraction and particular entailed by it are then discerned and their qualities noted.

One of the central presentations of this position emerges in the *Treatise*. It arises at the end of a longer argument. Hume writes that: "since all ideas are derived from impressions, and are nothing but copies and representations of them, whatever is true of the one must be acknowledg'd concerning the other. *Impressions and ideas differ only in their strength and vivacity*" (emphasis added).[11]

While the point of departure is that which grounds both Hume's epistemology and consequently the subject/object relation that structures his work, namely, a conception of representation thought in terms of a theory of impressions, the key moment is the way the difference between "impressions" and "ideas" operate in this formulation. Hume's term *idea* will be extended such that it also names that which appears under the heading of *abstraction*. Hume's language is precise. "Ideas" and "impressions" "differ," one in relation to the other. With regard to the connection between particulars and abstractions there is, in the *Treatise*, a thinking of their difference. As always with difference what matters is not its presence. Difference is not given. What counts, and thus what difference actually is, cannot be separated from the way it is thought. Hume continues by describing the nature of the difference. Again Hume's language is precise. He writes that they "differ only in their strength and vivacity." What this means is that difference is thought in in terms of quantity. To which it should be added that while it would not be Hume's formulation, difference is located in terms of the continuity of becoming. Abstraction, therefore, is held apart from particulars in terms of the intensity of affect. The latter term, *affect*, is deployed here as the generalizable term necessitated by the interplay of feeling and the epistemological staged by Hume's terms *strength* and *vivacity*. Difference, as it occurs in Hume, is linked to a difference within the affective. Even conceding that there are different ways that such a position can be understood and the affective adumbrated, it remains the case that the identification of the ubiquity, ineliminability, and homogeneity of the affective is such that difference is always difference within the continuity or the becoming of *sameness*. This is the setup that will be countered by Kant. However, it is essential to be exact. The *countermeasure* in question, insofar as it pertains to these concerns, involves a thinking of difference that cannot be assimilated to the Humean conception. As a result once this conception or thinking of difference is possible then it counters a thinking of difference as defined by the quantitative and held within the continuity of becoming. Difference is to be thought otherwise. Difference can itself be articulated in the process of *othering*. *Othering* is the process in which simple quantity—the play of forces defining difference within the registration of affect—is checked by that moment whose nonassimilability is the registration of value.

Given this opening the problem at hand, therefore, concerns the way or ways in which the abstract differs from the particular. The Humean version, and Hume's version has a longevity that is yet to be accounted for adequately, locates difference within an overlapping of the quantitative and the affective. Countering this position demands another thinking of abstraction and, therefore equally, another thinking of the relation between abstraction and particularity. This other thinking, which needs to be understood as a way of opening a break with naturalism as well as with empiricism and their recourse to forms of pragmatism, on the one hand, and, on the other, the reduction of the event as located within the continuity of becoming, for the project of this book continues with Kant.

2.

While Kant continues to figure, the passage to which emphasis will be given in order to construct an opening, an arbitrary though decisive move that is another beginning with Kant, comes from the latter's essay: *On the Common Saying: That It May Be Correct in Theory, but It Is of No Use in Practice*.[12] The passage in question occurs at the start of his critical engagement with Hobbes. Kant is clarifying what he means by "external right." In this context he writes that

> . . . the concept of an external right as such proceeds entirely from the concept of *freedom* in the external relation of people to one another and has nothing at all to do with the end that all of them naturally have (the aim of happiness) [*und har gar nichts mit dem Zwecke, den alle Menschen natürlicher Weiser haben (der Absicht auf Glückseligkeit)*] and with the prescribing of means for attaining it; hence too the latter absolutely must not intrude in the laws of the former as their determining ground [*als Bestimmungsgrund*].[13]

As a way into the concerns of this passage what has to be noted is this specific instance of Kant's evocation of "nature" and its interconnection with an "end" that is defined in relation to the natural (thus construed). Kant's position as it emerges from such a setting is pitted, for Kant, against the figures of Aristotle, Epicurus, and Stoicism.[14] While it is not cited, it is nonetheless not difficult to imagine that one of the passages from Aristotle to which Kant can be read as responding is the famous line from Aristotle's *Politics* (1253a) in which "nature" is incorporated into a thinking of a specifically Aristotelian version of the being of being human.

Aristotle writes in a line whose centrality, despite its ubiquity, cannot be overstated: "Human being [ο ανθπωπος] is by nature [φυσει] a polis dwelling creature [πολιτικον ζωον]." For Aristotle human being is by "nature" ("φυσις") the life of a "polis dwelling creature." Fundamental therefore to Aristotle's position is a thinking of the being of being human as *being-in-place*. This is *a* version of the affirmation of what was identified at an earlier stage as the always already present placedness of human being, that is, *being-in-place*. In this context, "place" is named as the *"polis."* It can also be argued that the distinction that Aristotle draws between the city and the "house" sets in play two different modalities of organization and thus two different senses of governance. The government of the city, at least in its initial iteration, differs from the government of a house. The distinction resides in the nature of the city versus the house. However the house — the *oikos* — quickly becomes the economy in the precise that it is attributed a form of a singularity. What needs to be brought in here is not just the distinction staged in Aristotle between the economic and the political, but also the nature of the distinction. This occurs in another key line in the *Politics*. At work in the distinction is the relationship between place and power. The latter is present in terms of how governance is understood.

> Yet it is clear that if the process of unification advances beyond a certain point, the city will not be a city [ουδε πολις] at all for a city by nature [την φυσιν] consists of a multitude of persons {πληθος], and if its unification is carried beyond a certain point, city will be reduced to family [οικια] and family to individual [ανθροπος].[15]

What is important about this passage is that the distinction concerns a relationship between "the many" named here as the πληθος, and thus what might emerge as the regulation of the many, and then, the *oikos*. The governance of the latter demands a unity of local, project and the singularity of the now of its occurrence. What is important here is that it sets in play an analogy in which the home (*oikos*) in the process of becoming the *oikonomeia* sets the measure for an understanding of the economic and then the economy as a unifying force. There is in Aristotle an important distinction between the *polis* and the *oikos*. A critique of the Aristotelian conception of the *oikos* and thus *oikonomeia* and the conception of place project and "now" that they entail would be located in the way that another understanding of place is at work in his thinking of the *polis*. Place in Aristotle admits of a fundamental division. The *polis* cannot be regulated as though it were a singularity. Politicizing the economy demands refusing its identification with the *oikos*. This could only occur in the name of an ethico-political project stemming from the anoriginality of *being-in-place*. The latter is of course is a possibility that is already there in Aristotle. This accounts, in part, for the enormous value of recovering of thinking of place from Aristotle even though that conception admits of an important and productive divide.

However, even though the naming and renaming of place is important, what matters is not place per se, rather it is the evocation by Kant, in the passage quoted above, of an "end" (*Zweck*) as one that is given by nature or that can be accounted for in terms of natural being. While it is possible to interpret Aristotle in ways that do not equate his position with a reductive naturalism—indeed the way in which a thinking of the *polis* has to draw the distinction between the city and *oikos* into consideration is a way of beginning such an undertaking—what is important to note is that Kant's own argument is positioned against the identification of the "end" of human being with that which can be accounted for in terms of nature or the natural. This is reinforced by noting once again that in the setting in which Kant is writing the term *Glückseligkeit* can be understood as the translation of *eudaimonia*.[16] As has already been shown in chapter 1, Kant interprets *eudaimonia* in terms of a mode of abstraction that is taken from life and then applied back to it.[16] Hence Kant's claim that, "Epicurus placed the ends of all virtuous as well as vicious actions merely in the relationship of the objects to sensibility, i.e., to the satisfaction of inclinations, and he distinguished virtue only through the form of reason with regard to the means."[17]

For Kant life cannot be thought within the terms that it presents, where that presentation is understood as a naturalization of the given. Even though, for Kant both Aristotle and Epicurus are thinkers of the "highest" or "greatest good," and yet neither has, nor could have had, the philosophical resources to think adequately such a conception of the good.[18] (The "highest" cannot, for Kant, be thought merely in quantitative terms.) The accuracy of this estimation of Epicurus has already been taken up. Focus here needs to be given to how Kant would go on to think "the highest" or "the greatest good." Hence, the question: What is at stake in their being thought?

The problem for Kant then is how to think both abstraction and subsequently the way "abstraction" and "particularity" come into relation. Thinking what elsewhere will be named the "highest good" is a problem that is only resolvable, in the context of the passage cited above, to the extent that the concept of freedom is held apart from *"Glückseligkeit."* Hence, to the extent that *"Glückseligkeit"* is understood in terms of means/ends calculations, it cannot be understood as the determining ground precisely because any determination has to have the force of universality. As has been seen what is necessitated is a conception of a ground that is "pure," that is, a ground that can be thought independently of any form of utility and therefore any calculation in terms of means and ends. There is, therefore, a fundamental division. This division, which recurs throughout Kant's writings, generates a specific sense of abstraction. The attendant problem, the one to which it will be necessary to return, is the definition of the "pure" as disjunctively related, that is, held apart from while also being held in relation to means/ends calculations.

Moving on from here demands recourse to the precision of Kant's actual formulation. Kant is arguing that there cannot be a relation between the means by which "happiness" is implemented, and in this context "means" names the mediating force of the means/end calculation, and the "laws" that obtain in the relationship between freedom and right. *Glückseligkeit* (happiness), names the positive formulation of the affective, a position that as has already been shown, can neither found, nor attune nor determine the link between freedom and right in exactly the same way that it cannot ground a sense of "moral worth." However, it names more. *Glückseligkeit* names the affective as the only locus of possible differences. While Kant's argument's are well known in regard to the position that *Glückseligkeit* (happiness) has to proceed from the recognition of moral worth rather than grounding it, what has to be taken up here is the question of how that relation is understood. In other words, if the Humean position can be generalized such that what is at stake is a relation between abstraction and particulars that can be accounted for such that difference is only ever quantitative, then the question that has to be asked is how does Kant think relationality such that the endlessness of the becoming of affect can be either suspended or interrupted? While the answer is, on one level, quite straightforward, what occurs within it is a formulation of difference in terms of quality rather than quantity. It is only this move that can have the effect of ending the hold of becoming, understood as the continuity of *sameness*, and which yields a thinking of the "pure" as the incalculable and therefore as standing opposed to the finite and determined nature of calculation, while, of course, being that which allows finitude genuine insistence (i.e., its insistence *as* finitude). Even though it is a position that becomes more complex insofar as that which is problematic within it has to emerge, at this stage it is essential to turn more directly to Kant to begin to understand that what is at work within the problem of abstraction is twofold. It is both the thinking of difference and the thinking of time. Working on (and through) abstraction while continuing to evoke the writings of Kant has to be understood, therefore, as continuous with the attempt to present the conditions in terms of which it becomes possible to think the interruption of becoming where the latter is the ontological condition of naturalism, that is, naturalism's address to being.

One of the demanding aspects of the argumentation of Kant's *Critique of the Power of Judgment* concerns what is meant by the "free play of the faculties." Part of the difficulty arises due to the presence of what can be described as relations of indeterminacy. An essential element of the overall argument takes the following form. There is an experience of an object that is accompanied by the feeling of pleasure. There is an immediate simultaneity at work. And yet, a mistake is made if a quality—that is, beauty—were then to be predicated of an object. The judgment of taste has the form of a logical judgment. The judgment of taste mimes the latter's presence within a separation sustained by the "as if." Nonetheless, despite the basis of the way they are distinguished, the distinction between them is fundamental. The passage in section 9 of the *Critique of the Power of Judgment* that is central to the overall argument is the following:

> The powers of cognition that are set into play by this representation are hereby in a free play, since no determinate concept [*kein bestimmter Begriff*] restricts [*einschränkt*] them to a particular rule of cognition [*eine besondere Erkentnissregle*]. Thus the state of mind in this representation must be that of a feeling of the free play of the powers of representation in a given representation for a cognition *in general* [überhaubt]. Now there belongs to a representation by which an object is given [*ein Gegenstand gegeben wird*], in order for there to be cognition of it *in general* [überhaupt], imagination for the composition of the manifold of intuition and understanding for the unity of the concept that unifies the representations. This state of a free play of the faculties of cognition with a representation through which an object is given must be able to be universally communicated, because cognition, as a determination of the object with which given representations (in whatever subject it may be) should agree, is the only kind of representation that is valid for everyone.[19] (Emphasis added)

What is communicable universally is the generalizable "free play of the faculties." This generalizable state occurs at the same time as the "object" is "given" or presented. And yet, the object's presence is not causally related to the faculties' "free play." Nor is the "free play" particularized such that it pertains to that object and to that object alone. There is an indeterminant relation. Hence, the demanding formulation that what is occurring pertains to the "free play of the powers of representation in a given representation for a cognition in general." The given is linked to the general. How is this giveness to be understood? What is meant here by the term *in general* (überhaupt)?

There are two elements involved in the answer to this question. The first concerns the meaning of this formulation given by the place of the passage within the *Critique of the Power of Judgment* as a whole. The second has greater extension since it refers to the way distinctions of this nature are at work in Kant's larger project. In regard to the first, it can be suggested that the conception of "free play" occurs in relation to concepts, though without the latter's determination. More broadly, however, what is at stake is best expressed in terms of bringing the relationship between the "conditioned" and the "unconditioned" into play. While it is a relation that will be central at a later stage, it is worth noting both the provisional nature of its formulation while at the same time underscoring its necessity. In a Fragment dated from the 1790s, Kant wrote that:

> The proposition that if the conditioned is given, the whole series of all conditions through which the conditioned is determined is also given is, if I abstract from the objects or take it merely intellectually, correct. The unconditioned can never be given but must always exist in thought (*Das Unbedingt kan niemals gegben warden, muß aber iederzeit in Gedanken sehn*). Hence ideas. (*Daher Ideen.*)The absolute totality of the conditions is the only unconditioned. Unity of principle for reason. Approximation. Rules of the synthesis of the subordination of empirical concepts.[20]

While the complex question is what is meant by the "absolute totality of the conditions" arises and must be addressed (a formulation that is found elsewhere in Kant's writings, most notably in the *Critique of Pure Reason*), what is significant in this specific presentation is the form of presence that is staged. The "unconditioned" as both term and concept does not have a single determination, indeed it has a threefold quality. In the first instance, it is present; then in the second, it is necessary; and then, finally, in the third, it is also the case that the "unconditioned" is neither given nor at hand. As Kant writes in the *Critique of Pure Reason*, the "unconditioned is that to which all experience is subordinated but which cannot itself be experienced."[21]

When Kant writes in the Fragment cited above—"(H)ence ideas" ("*Daher Ideen*")—while this underscores the role of the idea, the idea is nonetheless thought outside relations that are causal. For Plato the idea is the "cause" ("αιτια") of the identity of the particular. In addition, integral to that causal relation is the idea's presence or "participation" ("μετεχειν"), in the particular. Causality occurs through "participation." It is this setup that establishes the particular's identity.[22] Hence, there is an identity giving mode of causality that involves a form of presence. The idea is present. Here, however, the "unconditioned" and the "idea" are terms implicated in a rethinking of the "absolute," the unconditioned as the "absolute" (noted here is Kant's use of the terms *absolute*), as occurring with (and within) modes of relationality that are necessary and indeterminate (and yet not structured by a causal relation to the transcendent). Moreover, the *unconditioned*, as the term appears in Kant, marks the interruption within affect. *Glückseligkeit* (happiness) cannot function as an end because it is always a condition. Thus it can only ever entail determinate relations. The "principle of morality" is unconditioned. It is not the totality of all conditions but rather is "absolute" in the precise sense that it is unconditioned in relation to the totality of conditions. Nonetheless, and here it is vital to introduce a point of fundamental importance, namely, that the unconditioned cannot be equated with a totality, if that totality is thought in additive terms. While it is a formulation to which it will be necessary to return, the way in which the unconditioned and by implication a thinking of the unconditioned as the absolute occurs in *Critique of Practical Reason* when they are taken together form a fundamental part of these concerns. Kant writes,

> ... that unconditioned causality and the capacity for it [*unbedingte Kausalität und das Vermögen derselben*], freedom, and with it a being (I myself) that belongs to the sensible world but **at the same time** to the intelligible world (*zur Sinnenwelt gehört, doch **zugleich** als zur intelligibelen Gehörig*), is not merely *thought* indeterminately and problematically (speculative reason could already find this feasible) but is even *determined with respect to the law* of its causality and *cognized* assertorically; and thus the reality of the intelligible world is given to us, and indeed as *determined* from a practical perspective, and this determination, which for theoretical purposes would be *transcendent* (extravagant), is for practical purposes *immanent (ist in praktischer immanent)*.[23] (Boldface emphasis added)

Again, it needs to be noted that this is a passage that contains a range of fundamental motifs and brings with it its own important interpretive difficulties. For these current concerns what needs to be taken up is the force of what Kant means by the "immanent" presence of the "intelligible world" (in its differentiation from the "transcendent"). The "unconditioned" within the realm of the practical is "immanent." Hence the question: What is the "immanent"? As a beginning what this question dramatizes is a mode of presence: it refers to the immanent presence of the unconditioned. *Immanence* is a term that demands to be thought in a way that allows it to be differentiated from the Platonic heritage by showing that it brings into play a mode of presence and a form of relationality characterized by irreducibility, on the one hand, and the absence of both causality and determinacy, on the other. The unconditioned, therefore, is already held apart from the conditioned, though in being held apart is held in relation to the conditioned. (The reciprocity here is inevitable. The immanent allows the unconditioned to be both *a part* and *apart*. Recalled here is the complex logic of the *apart/a part* that has already been noted.) There is therefore an originally present and constitutive spacing that enables the relation between the conditioned and the unconditioned to be thought as operative. Here there is a spacing whose temporal presence and thus whose own possibility is defined and sustained by the temporality of *at-the-same-timeness* which is, of course the temporality of the *a part/apart*. What this means is that there is a complex structure of interrelated elements at work. Spacing is an effect of time, while the temporality of *at-the-same-timeness* figures as an irreducible spacing.[24] At work here therefore is an already present intrication of the temporal and the ontological.

As this passage opens what continues is Kant's commitment to the inscription of freedom as a form of causality into that which is fundamental to human being. This becomes a claim concerning what it means to be a human being: in sum, what can be understood as Kant's response to the question of the being of being human. A position identified in the passage in terms of the proposition that there is "a being" ("*ein Wesen*") in whom this principle is operative and this "being" is "I, myself" ("*Ich, selber*"). It comes to be named as the "I, myself." Despite the apparent oddness of the formulation it needs to be insisted on. Two elements are central. The first moment that Kant identifies is the thinking of "a being." Then, that this "being" has both a "capacity" and the presence of "unconditioned causality." The two need to be thought together. Even though the first, namely, the "capacity" refers here to the presence of that which allows the unconditioned to be operative, part of the argument to follow is that this "capacity" is not just interconnected with immanent presence, more is at play. What has to be noted as fundamental to this set up is that the realization of a capacity, which is a capacity for actualization, brings a twofold demand into play. The first is that its presence be immanent. The second is that underscoring the already present and ineliminability of the "capacity" entails that operativity is defined in terms of potentiality. There is a capacity to act. Furthermore, and even though it cannot be addressed, what emerges with the immanent is a way of circumventing an identification of that which is external with that caricature of the transcendental that ends up identify the transcendental with forms of Platonism.

In the passage under consideration causality is present in a way that is not determined in advance. It pertains, however, not in its differentiation from the sensible such that any form of relation is excluded. Rather, the condition of relationality is the premise of a simultaneous nonrelation. Hence, the being that is held apart from the sensible world because it belongs to the "intelligible world" is one that also belongs to the sensible world. The name of that being is "I, myself." What is involved therefore is not just a relation between the conditioned and the unconditioned but the uncovering of a "being" in which that relation can in fact be staged. If this "being" is determined in this specific way, then the results of that determination are necessarily indeterminate. To deploy, again, a motif that remains fundamental, what this means is that necessity entails contingency. In other words, there are outcomes that are open as much to "pathology" as they are to "holiness." These are the terms that Kant uses in the *Critique of Practical Reason* to stage the difference between the sensible and the intelligible in ways that allow for their necessary copresense to be a continual site of negotiation. Negotiation however depends on irreducibility. If a further example were needed then it can be located is the distinction between "enthusiasm" and "true enthusiasm" (*"wahrer Enthusiasm"*) that presented with stark clarity in *The Contest of the Faculties* in terms of spectators of the French Revolution.

The "spectators" fail to understand the event if they think "this event" (*"diese Begebenheit"*) is reducible to a set of "deeds" (*"Thaten"*).[25] Rather, "true enthusiasm" moves "only ever towards what is ideal and indeed purely moral" (*"nur immer aufs Idealiche und zwar rein Moralische geht"*), such that what is set in play is the necessity for both a protracted form of negotiation between them and thus the inescapability of judgment.[26] This is what constitutes the "event." Judgment cannot be avoided as it is only in terms of this irreducibility that judgment becomes both possible and necessary. Moreover, this divide between the sensible and the intelligible, a divide that reappears in different guises, is the fundamental though constitutive split within the subject. It is a divide that opens up the possibility of a form of indeterminate and thus potentially endless negotiation. Negotiation necessitates anoriginality. That it is negotiation, as opposed to a predetermined sense of eventuality, flows from the location of necessity in the presence of freedom and a related "capacity" as opposed to necessity being located in the results of activities based either on that capacity's own actualization or the immediate determination of the concept. There is the inscription of the necessity for action defined in relation to a form of indetermination at the centre of the project. Hence, there is the presence of, for example, both the "pathological" and "holiness" or "enthusiasm" and "true enthusiasm" that indicates the absence of necessity. At this stage what is important is to recognize that there is a founding irreducibility that is held in place by the conception of temporality that is defined by this determination of the temporality of *at-the-same-timeness*.

The temporal quality of *at-the-same-timeness* holds together while holding apart the sensible and the intelligible (the *a part/apart*). Moreover, it is a temporality that cannot be thought other than in terms of the inscription of a defining and constitutive opening and thus marks the presence of an anoriginal spacing. *At-the-same-timeness* is as much spatial as it is temporal. Equally, the irreducibility that is the spacing opened up by the relation of nonrelation between the sensible and the intelligible is as much temporal as it is spatial. *At-the-same-timeness* has the effect of introducing the possibility of thinking that which allows for the interruption of the affective while simultaneously allowing for affect. It holds in place the setting in relation to which any conditioned encounters the unconditioned. This does not occur as the result of the creation of two domains such that the affirmation of one is premised on either the disavowal or negation of the other. What occurs is the copresence of both, given as held apart within and by the temporality of *at-the-same-timeness*. It can be added here that the necessity to introduce this temporality is that it underscores the way in which this spacing and its accompanying temporality—and again their actual separation is impossible—needs to be understood as a deconstruction of the opposition between the sensible and intelligible.[27] The argument for this conclusion is that as a result of this ontologico-temporal configuration the sensible and the intelligible are no longer positioned in term of their mutual exclusion. Not only are they copresent in their difference; it is the effect of that difference that interrupts the continual becoming of affect as a result of the immanent yet effective presence of the unconditioned.[28]

At work here, therefore, is a thinking of the relations between time and being that is not simply constitutive of the subject it is also that specific relation that locates time as a condition of subjectivity. That relation's particularity is thought in any one instance as a plural event. Moreover, the question that then emerges is the relation between the temporality of the subject, where being a subject is in part constituted by *at-the-same-timeness* and the way in which it figures within developing an understanding of the relations between subjectivity, judgment, and the world. Time plays a determining role within this network of relations. Equally, were it not for the possibility of interrupting and taking a stand within time, which is a positioning, a stand that refuses time's naturalization, then modalities of activity such as promising and forgiving would not be able to emerge. Taking these concerns a stage further occurs here via an engagement with the way the promise and the pardon are already acts that can be understood as implicated in processes of undoing the naturalization of time. They have the further effect of defining the ethical and thus judgment as occurring to the extent that it is possible to take a stand within time and thus to take a stand against the simple flow of becoming. The ethical stands against nature.

3.

A stand is a position in time. Taking a stand is both to undo the flow of time while what can be described as *stand taking* brings both place and a specific modality of being into play. Taking a stand, in part through its link to *stehen* from *sto, stare*, involves the copresence of existence and *being-in-place*. A stand therefore is a mode of existence that occurs within time. Both the "promise" and the "pardon" can be understood therefore in terms of *stand taking*. They are determinations of being. Note in this context the way time figures in Arendt's formulation of both the "promise" and the "pardon."[29] She writes the following in *The Human Condition*:

> The possible redemption from the predicament of irreversibility—of being unable to do what has been done though one did not, and could not, have known what he or she was doing is the faculty of forgiving. The remedy for unpredictability, for the chaotic uncertainty of the future, is contained in the faculty to make and keep promises.[30]

This passage occurs toward the end of chapter 5 of *The Human Condition*. And note that when she writes *faculty* she actually means *Vermögen*, and thus the "remedy for unpredictability" lies in the "capacity to make and keep promises." In other words, it lies in a potentiality. This particular section of *The Human Condition* can be understood as staging what can be described as the necessity to think interruption. Toward the end of chapter 5 she writes: "The life span of man running toward death would inevitably carry everything human to ruin and destruction if it were not for the faculty of interrupting it and beginning something new, a faculty which is inherent in action like an ever-present reminder that men, though they must die, are not born in order to die but in order to begin."[31]

Taken on its own this formulation is far from sufficient and yet at its core there is the evocation of interruption where the latter is defined in terms of a capacity and thus the potentiality for interruption. And yet, interruption is not present as a random act. On the contrary, interruption stages the presence of a capacity that is linked to the creation of the new that is itself ground in the immanence of place and relationality. The new, and here there will be a link to the pardon that also takes on the quality of the new, interrupts that sense of continuity that can be located in what Heidegger identified as "being-toward-death."[32] This is, of course, the possibility that is integral to her formulation that the project of human being is inextricably interarticulated with beginnings (thought more broadly in terms of "natality"). The question that attends this formulation is that if this possibility can be recast as a potentiality that defines human being, which is a potentiality precisely because of her use of the term *faculty*, understood as a "capacity," it then follows that the question to be addressed concerns how the actualization of that potentiality is to be understood. What is the actualization of a potentiality?

The setting in which these questions are asked is held in place by a complex relation between space and place, on the one hand, and, on the other hand, a conception of potentiality. However, there is an additional element in Arendt's formulation. It is as though she is intent on both defining and then locating an original condition that is both prior to any sense of collectivity while simultaneously providing collectivity with its conditions of possibility. In other words, there is an implicit thinking of both anoriginality and immanence. As will be noted, such a move is also fundamental both to her conception of "power" and in addition to the way power's necessity as well as its fragility, stands opposed to violence. In *The Human Condition* she writes of the "space of appearance" that underscores the presence of the anoriginal: "The space of appearance comes into being wherever men are together in the manner of speech and action, and therefore *predates and precedes* all formal constitution of the public realm and the various forms of government, that is, the various forms in which the public realm can be organized"[33] (emphasis added).

If what is meant by "formal constitution of the public realm" refers to historically determined forms of government whose histories can be written and whose internal relations can be examined, then *preceding* and *predating* such pragmatic determinations, to recall her formulation, is that which makes such constitutional arrangements possible. Hence, the reference in the passage noted above to that which both "predates" and "precedes" needs to be understood as a form of reference to states of affairs that have to be thought as anoriginal conditions. The question to be addressed, however, concerns how the presence of such conditions is to be understood and then how an already present relationality is to be understood. What is at work here, thus harbored within these questions, is a claim that there exists that which is both a precondition and a potentiality. Indeed, such a formulation accords with what she writes a few lines later concerning "the space of appearance," which is the space in which human being in its anoriginal irreducibility obtains. That space while present as a "potentiality" is neither "necessary" nor permanent.[34] Not only does this potentiality have to be realized, that which appears as a threat both to its actualization and the continuity of its presence has to be acknowledged. What enables the "space of appearance" to be maintained is what she identifies "power." Hence she writes that, "without power, the space of appearance brought forth through action and speech in public will fade away as rapidly as the living deed and the living word."[35]

"Power" for Arendt provides the essence of government. Moreover, power is linked to a conception of human being that is positioned, as has been noted above, within a founding sense of collectivity. (Arendt's word will be *concert*.) That sense is already the site of a founding legitimacy. In this regard she writes in *On Violence* that: "Power springs up whenever people get together and act in concert, but it derives legitimacy from the initial getting together rather than from any action that then may follow."[36] The way into this sense of legitimacy is provided by the implicit temporality at work in the formulation of the 'initial getting together." It has to be argued that there is an important accord between this temporality and her earlier discussion of what she identifies as the "structure of power." That specific "structure" is different from those pragmatic instances in which power is at work. The reason is that the presence of the "structure" "precedes and outlasts all aims, so that power far from being the means to an end, is actually the very condition enabling a group to think and act in terms of the means-end category."[37] "Power," therefore, is pure. Its "purity," it can be argued, recalls both Kant and

Walter Benjamin in the precise sense that it is located outside any determinable calculation. And yet violence can destroy power.

The importance of Arendt's thinking in this domain can be located, initially, in her recognition that anoriginal relationality—for example, the "initial getting together" that is always already at work—is equally a thinking of the insistent presence of place. In the argumentation that establishes her position, the thinking of anoriginality is not only linked to a thinking of potentiality, it is thought as a modality of place named as "the public realm." The latter becomes clear when she writes that:

> Power is what keeps the public realm, the potential space of appearance between acting and speaking men, in existence. The word itself, its Greek equivalent *dynamis*, like the Latin *potentia* with its various modern derivatives . . . indicates its "potential" character. Power is always, as we would say, a power potential . . . While strength is the natural quality of an individual seen in isolation, power springs up between men when they act together and vanishes the moment they disperse. Because of this peculiarity, which power shares with all potentialities that *can only be actualized but never fully materialized*, power is to an astonishing degree independent of material factors, either of numbers or means.[38] (Emphasis added)

It is important to note that the actualization of power is what power is. Moreover, it is power that keeps the "space of appearance" in play. What stands opposed to power's capacity to actualize, to continue to be actualized, is violence. As she argues in relation to violence it "can destroy power."[39] While the recognition of the fragility of the "space of appearance" and thus of the link between speech and the "actualization of the human condition of plurality" is fundamental, if there is a problematic element within the overall argument then it does not inhere in the use of the concept of potentiality. Rather it inheres in the way that potentiality is understood. This is the concern to which a turn must be made.

Speech and potentiality have an interarticulated presence. Indeed, if a precursor for this position is needed then it can found in a recasting of the dramatic opening of Kant's essay on the Enlightenment in terms of the finding of voice. The move from "self-imposed immaturity" (*"selbst verschuldeten Unmündigkeit"*) to "maturity" is the acquisition of voice.[40] The finding of voice, *being-in-place* as the uncovering of the mouth, should be understood as the actualization of a potentiality or a "capacity." However there is a question here: What would stand in the way of speech understood as the finding of voice? Even if the answer is not specified such a hindrance has to be thought in terms of the refusal to allow for a potentiality to be actualized. This is the point that has to be pursued through the way in which Aristotle figures within Arendt's argumentation. This point arises in her discussion of Aristotle's use of the terms *eudaimon* and *eudaimonia*. In this regard she argues the following: "To be *eudaimon* and to have been *eudaimon*, according to Aristotle, are the same, just as to live well (εὖ ζῆ) and to have 'lived well' are the same as long as life lasts; they are not states or activities which change a person's quality, such as learning and having learned, which indicates two altogether different attributes of the same person at different time."[41]

"Learning" and "having learned" have beginnings and ends. If there is a capacity to learn then its actualization is "having learned." Arendt's point is that for Aristotle being a *eudaimon* is importantly different. In making this point her reference is, of course, to the discussion of the modal identity of "living well" and to "have lived well," as it is presented in *Metaphysics* 1048b25. The entire passage reads as follows:

> We are living well and have lived well, we are happy and have been happy [εὖ ζῆ καὶ εὖ ἔζηκεν ἅμα, καὶ εὐδαιμονεῖ καὶ εὐδαιμόνηκεν], at the same time; otherwise the process would have had to cease at some time... but it has not ceased at the present moment; we both are living and have lived [ἀλλὰ ζῆ καὶ ἔζηκεν.][42]

The argumentative basis of this position can be found in the use of the preposition ἅμα (which means "at the same time," and yet is a radically different formulation of *at-the-same-time-ness* than the one found in Kant). Here, however, in Aristotle, *at-the-same-timeness* in this specific instance, is a thinking of identify and confluence rather than providing the conditions of irreducibility and therefore a thinking of genuine difference. In others words, it is a conception of *at-the-same-timeness* that stands apart from the need to think the insistent of anoriginal presence. What this outlines, therefore, is a sense of simultaneity that precludes both "living well" and *eudaimonia* from ever being an actualized potentiality. Again, this is a position that can be reinforced by making use of another formulation from Aristotle that is deployed by Arendt, namely, that the polis is there in order for the continuity of the good life and not for its potential actualization.[43] Indeed, it possible to argue that Aristotle did not think of the "good life" or "*eudaimonia*" as potentialities. This is not, however, to argue that Aristotle's engagement with potentiality and capacity is not equally a sustained thinking of that which endures as unactualized (and thus as an incapacity). In the famous passage from the *Metaphysics* 1046a30, in which this position is presented, what is clear is that linked to every "capacity" ("*dynamis*") is a contrary "incapacity" ("*adynamis*"). Aristotle's formulation is the following: "Incapacity and the incapable (ἡ ἀδυναμία καὶ τὸ ἀδύνατον) is the privation contrary to capacity (δυνάμει) in this sense; so that every "capacity" has a contrary incapacity (τὸ αὐτὸ πᾶσα δύναμις ἀδυναμίᾳ) for producing the same result in respect of the same subject."

At work in this formulation is the affirmation of the absence of necessity within potentiality. Were it to be the case that potentiality entailed actuality of necessity then the Megarians would have been right.[44] If they are not right then there has to be an account of what is present when there is the absence of actuality that is not an argument against potentiality. If it is the case that any potentiality allows for the possibility of its *nonactualization*, then the question to be addressed to any potentiality is the question of its actualization. For Aristotle once the path opened by the *Metaphysics* is followed, then neither the good life nor the state of being a *eudaimon* are potentialities or capacities that await their actualization. While existence is delimited as divided between the actual and the potential, and this can be said to be inherent in "things," it is also the case that "change is always in accord with the categories of Being" (*Metaphysics* 1065b5). While Aristotle will not generalize across the categories, it would still appear to be the case, if the argumentation of the *Metaphysics* is followed, that there is no room for the realization of a potential through action when it pertains to the ethical. There would need to be a different ontological configuration were this to be a possibility.

What is emerging is the problematic place of potentiality within Aristotle, and equally within Arendt, when what is of direct concern is the ethical. In order to take this mode of argumentation a stage further, a return needs to be made to both the promise and the pardon. That return is based on the fact that for Arendt they are modalities of interruption. As such the question that needs to be addressed concerns their presence as interruptions and the possibility that the actualization of a potentiality involves, if not necessitates, an interruption within the continuity of becoming.

4.

In the context of *The Human Condition* the distancing of "love" occurs in the name of "respect." While its use allows for the reverberation of the presence of "respect" ("*Achtung*") in Kant to continue, Arendt links it to the Aristotelian conception of *philia politiké*, which she goes on to describe as: "a kind of 'friendship' without intimacy and without closeness; it is a regard for the person from the distance which the space of the world puts between us, and this regard is independent of qualities which we may admire or of achievements which we may highly esteem."[45] Respect "prompts" forgiving, where the latter is a state of affairs, which here is to be understood as occurring in relation to others. As she intimates, no one can forgive themselves. Forgiveness and respect as forms of speech necessitate, therefore, both the presence of others as well as the place of forgiveness. Respect in the Arendtian sense is linked to the "space of appearance." The threat to the latter is violence. Violence would not be aimed at the abstract individual. Rather, the individual would suffer violence as a result of the movement in which violence and evil combined in rendering either the individual or groups of individuals "superfluous." Superfluity becomes therefore the refusal of speech and the worldliness of the world: place becomes simply the world, *being-in-place* is refused. This amounts to the reduction of the individual to "mere life." What this means of course is that speaking is a potential in the precise sense that its actualization is not necessary even though its presence as a capacity is necessary. Even if the potentiality for the finding of voice is there, this does not mean that a voice is always found or always maintained. The totalitarian impulse links the rendering superfluous to processes of silencing. Speech has to be understood in terms of a potentiality whose continual actualization while not necessary becomes a version of freedom in which freedom is structural rather than the predicate of a given individual. It becomes the latter only as an aftereffect of the former. Arendt has already indicated that speech is held in place by a conception of power that is subject to its own intrinsic form of fragility. However, it is in the formulation of this position that difficulties begin to emerge.

At an earlier stage in her argument potentiality is located in what is defined as the human "capacity to act." This is then defined with great exactitude in the following way: "In acting and speaking, men show who they are, reveal actively their unique personal identities and thus make their appearance in the human world."[46] The actualization of potentiality is defined in terms of the presence of "unique personal identities." And yet, violence and the totalitarian always threaten more than specific identities, even though they also threaten specific identities. While violence is always directed against named identities, the refusal of violence has to be in excess of a claim simply about these identities. As such it would need to be more complex than both the space of appearance and presence within it. It has to be what brought the ground of judgment into play. If there is a problem here then it pertains to the impossibility of reconciling the Kantian and the Aristotelian conceptions of *at-the-same-timeness*. Indeed, what is problematic is the retention by Arendt of that which is intrinsic to the Aristotelian conception of potentiality—*dynamis* and *energia*—namely, the impossibility of thinking that which is proper to her understanding of natality. The pardon and the promise both demand an understanding of interruption and the inevitability of linking *at-the same-timeness* to anoriginal difference. It is this possibility that Aristotle's metaphysics, insofar as the discord between *eudaimonia* and potentiality is concerned, will jeopardize. The elucidation of this point will form the final part of this chapter.

In *On Revolution* the promise is linked to the continuity of the original bond that defines human being. She begins in the following way: "The hope for man in his singularity lay in the fact that not man but men inhabit the earth and form a world between them. It is human worldliness that will save men from the pitfalls of human nature."[47] The question of course is what is "human worldliness"? Clearly, it is what stands opposed to violence. Moreover, it is that which is undone by violence. However, there is more involved than just a form of undoing. It is also the case that violence undoes the work of power. It ends speech. It individualizes and renders superfluous. Not only, therefore, does power have a specific type of fragility what emerges is the obvious question of what would count as a *counter-measure* to violence. There are two levels on which the response to this question can be posed. Prior to taking them up it is essential to note what is being asked.

Violence has a specific definition and locus of activity. It is pitted against power as that which maintains the space of appearing. Equally, violence works against worldliness and therefore against anoriginal relationality (thus, *being-in-relation* and *being-in-place*). What then is the *countermeasure* to violence? As noted there are two domains of response. The first is the recognition that what counters violence is judgment. To which it should be added that if judgment is to be operative then what counters violence is power. However, precisely because in Arendt's argumentation violence undoes power there needs to be another though related conception of power. Or rather, what is meant by power needs both greater extension and equally greater precision.

First, Arendt is right to argue for the centrality of speech. Equally fundamental to the argument is the position that what she terms the "space of appearance" is to be thought in terms of potentiality. However, it can also be suggested that she makes the same mistake as Aristotle insofar as she precludes the possibility that *eudaimonia* is a potentiality and as a result is necessarily bound up with the possibility of its nonactualization. If *eudaimonia* is there as a potentiality then what has to be opened up is both the possibility and thus the eventual reality of its actualization and equally the possibility of its nonactualization (the latter is of course inextricably connected to violence). In other words, if there is a *countermeasure* to violence, then it has to be that speech and the space of appearance are there as potentialities in their own right ground in that which is proper to the being of being human. It might be argued that what is at play here is a conception of potentiality within potentiality; a presence that has the effect of reworking potentiality. A position of this nature, thus another conception of potentiality, is already implicit in Kant. Understanding maturity as the finding of voice it to recognize that voicing and speech and therefore *being-in-relation* as well as the demands for place that accompanies them are potentialities the actualization of which, while not necessary, is nevertheless possible; that is, necessity-sustaining contingent possibilities.[48] While Kant may not have given an adequate account of processes of actualization, indeed it could be argued that the conception of history that privileged progress over revolution was incapable of so doing, it is still the case that it is in terms of Kant's use of "striving" that the possibility of actualization can be thought.[49] Striving recalls here what has already been noted in terms of the sense of movement occasioned by the necessarily unactualized presence of "moral perfection." This is the striving that takes the immanent presence of the unconditioned as its condition of possibility.

For Kant "striving" is a process. Kant writes that "striving" has a constant though "unattainable goal" (*unerreichbaren*

Ziele).⁵⁰ And yet, it is not just the case that the goal of striving is unattainable. The position is more emphatic. That goal has to be necessarily unattainable. In other words, the unconditioned cannot be actualized as such. Nonetheless, implicit in the structure of striving is the recognition that it is a setup whose continuity is imposed, self-imposed, and is thus one that is there in its being allowed. (And yet, of course, the negative possibility also exists. Striving can either be suppressed or it can be misdirected. There is an inherent ambivalence in striving precisely because it names the dynamic rather that a locus of intrinsic value. That can be seen, for example, in relation to the moral law where there can be "striving [*Bestreben*] to resist respect for it."⁵¹) Despite this ambivalence, there has to be what can be called an *allowing* for striving. It is essential that term *allowing* is maintained, since at work here is an occasioning whose contents are not determined in advance. Equally, allowing for the "space of appearance" is to sustain modalities of power that stand against violence. However, they are modalities of power the thinking of which sets in play a rethinking of Arendt's conception of potentiality.

Striving becomes a way of naming a relation to the unconditioned, in the exact sense that it is relation both to the immanent presence of the unconditioned in the domain of the practical and then the way the unconditioned provides the only possibility for judgment. As has been noted earlier, Kant defines duty not in terms of actualization but in terms of a process positioned in relation to the unconditioned. While the content of duty may have a necessity, the exigency that it sets in play obliges necessity to fall away from it. Hence Kant's description of what pertain to duty take the following form.⁵⁰ Duty, in Kant's terms, "is only the striving to produce and promote the highest good in the world" ("*Zur Pflicht gehört hier nur die Bearbeitung zu Hervorbringung und Beförderung des höchsten Guts in der Welt*"). While there are other formulations of duty what is significant here is that it cannot be separated from processes that hold the unconditioned in place, and therefore processes that demand the presence of the unconditioned. Moreover, in regard to actions occurring in relation to duty they must be understood as involving a specific form of recognition. Again Kant argues that in regard to conditioned acts, the actor "can become aware of a maxim of striving for such purity; that he is capable of, and that is also sufficient for his observance of duty." ("*mithin der Maxime zu jener Reinigheit hinzustreben sich bewust zu werden; das vermag er; und das ist auch für seine Pflichtbeobachtung genug.*")[53] Striving for "purity" ("*Reinigheit*") is not striving for moral purity, if the latter were thought in terms of purity's actualization. Rather, what is occurring here is a conception of striving that is set in play by a thinking of the unconditioned located beyond the hold of the calculable; namely that which occurs in relation to the immanence of the unconditioned and whose locus of registration is the world. Actions occur and enjoin judgment. They point, however, is that judgment is only possible because of the necessity of the unconditioned. It provides finitude with its insistence.

The full force of the promise and the pardon as interruptions, once taken beyond merely individual concerns, is that they interrupt the "prevailing" order. The promise and the pardon as figures of interruption have to be thought in terms of the actuality of speech and action and, therefore, in terms of potentialities within (and as) life. Restrictions within and of life are violence as a response to power. For judgment to be possible, its possibility occurs as a result of the retention by Arendt of the presence of forms of *anoriginality*. What, for example, "predates" and "precedes" is that which can be "actualized but never fully materialized." It is this state of affairs that is possible only if action is recast in terms of an interconnection with striving and that the promise and the pardon are rethought in terms of that conception of *dynamis* that does itself have to bring with it what can be described as the continually present possibility of its own nonnecessity. In other words, that it continues to allow for contingency. Contingency understood in this setting is finitude. Finitude insists precisely because of its relation to necessity. Contingency therefore can also be thought as the *insistence of finitude*. The pardon moves beyond the ethical if the latter were to be understood in purely pragmatic terms. The sense of movement necessitates underscoring again the sense in which the pardon attests to what has been called the *anoriginal* relation of the ontological and the ethical.

In lieu of a sustained conclusion it will suffice to note that what will always need to be addressed is the relationship between the pardon and the continually reworked presence of *virtue in being*. What has to be identified is a relation that is structured neither causally nor in terms of dependence. There are many ways of arguing for the presence of the *anoriginal* relation of the ontological and the ethical. In this instance one of the most germane to this project is to insist that *eudaimonia* as a possibility can be undone by what Arendt has referred to as "violence." Equally, and though it complicates Arendt's argumentation in ways that have been pointed out, to the extent that *eudaimonia* exists as a potentiality there is a specific entailment, namely, that its actualization is not necessary. There is no obligation as such. Hence, there is no direct connection between the necessity of its presence and the necessity of its presence as actual. Moreover, its nonactualization, a state of affairs that have pragmatic and specific determinations, indicates that an already present disequilibria of power may refuse its actualization. Rather than have recourse either to moralism or to mere affective preference, Arendt's conception of the pardon can be taken as indicating, albeit in generalized terms, the presence of judgment's possibility. Moreover, it is conception of judgment that restricts the work of violence, as it is grounded in the presence of the being of being human, that is, *being-in-place* and *being-in-relation*.

CHAPTER THREE

KANT, EVIL, AND THE UNCONDITIONED

If the unconditioned as a philosophical term finds its fundamental point of orientation in the writings of Kant, and goes on to have a contemporary register both in the writings of Derrida as well as in attempts to formulate the ethical in terms of an infinite demand, then it is essential to remain with Kant. Remaining and continuing to work through those writings occurs here in order to uncover the force of the distinction between the conditioned and the unconditioned and its presence within the development of a philosophical anthropology. The latter, as stated at the outset, is a philosophical thinking of life. It is not as though a direct concern with the formulation of a philosophical anthropology was an undertaking distanced from Kant's own. Kant wrote a text with the title *Anthropology from a Pragmatic Point of View*, thus there is a work whose concerns are delimited by an engagement with what he describes as the "human being as citizen of the world" (*"des Menschen als Weltbürger"*).[1] While this text forms a fundamental part of Kant's own development of a philosophical anthropology and coincidently marks the presence of a specific thinking of place in Kant's overall corpus, essential at this stage is the way is locates the possibility a philosophical anthropology as given by the anoriginal relation between the ontological and the ethical and the various forms of human being that have been presented by formulations such as *being-in-common* and *being-in-place* as they are themselves present in Kant's work. As will be clear from the engagement with *Towards Perpetual Peace: A Philosophical Project* staged below, with this particular turn to Kant, the point of departure is a specific thinking of place. *Being-in-place* has an original presence. Moreover, it is a thinking of place in which the place as a literal presence cedes its priority to Kant's implicit positioning of the intrinsic placedness of the being of being human within a setting structured by the relation between the conditioned and the unconditioned. This complex weave of concerns is central. Within it what has already been identified in terms of the relationship between movement, which has a sustained presence as "striving," and then the interplay between finitude and judgment comes to play a central role.

1.

In a remarkable passage in *Towards Perpetual Peace: A Philosophical Project*, Kant draws a distinction between the "right to be a guest (*Gastrecht*)" and the "right to visit" ("*Besuchsrecht*"). What is at play within this distinction emerges once it is recognized that these two modalities of "right" are defined in terms of the rights of "a foreigner" ("*eines Fremdlings*") when she or he arrives on what is then described in the text as "the land of another." (A formulation whose emphatic literalism can always open to a generalized understanding of place in which this "land" and thus all places, place in general, thus *being-in-place*, would be "the land of another" and the condition of "foreigner" also acquires a pervasive ubiquity such that one is always already "a foreigner.") Kant's opening move in this section of the text is to argue that as long as the one who arrives does so "peaceably," then such a person cannot be treated other than in a friendly manner. Before noting the detail of the distinction between the "right to be a guest" ("*Gastrecht*") and the "right to visit" ("*Besuchsrecht*"), it is essential to point out that arriving peaceably has a specific meaning in this setting. Such a mode of arrival means nothing other than arriving in a way that is "pure" ("*reine*"). In others words, consistent with the identification of the "pure" ("*reine*," "*pura*") as outside any sense of calculation, the arrival is unconditioned in the precise sense that it is not located within a setting defined by utility and thus by means/ends relations. To that extent therefore the response to such a setup must itself be immediate (i.e., without mediation or determination in advance) and consequently already located in relation to the unconditioned.[2] While what is meant by 'unconditioned', especially in terms of its setting in this context, still stands in need of detailed clarification, this can only occur after having turned to the philosophical issues raised by the passage in question.

The passage begins with a reiteration of the opening point that characterizes the presentation of "peace" within the text as whole, namely, that specific distancing of "hostility" that allows peace to be thought of as other than that which would occur were peace to be equated with the simple abeyance of hostility. The latter is no more than a positioning that still defines peace in terms of war. The suspension of war, to the extent that it retains a setting in which that suspension, be it immediate or continuing, is defined by a relation to hostility, still holds to the primacy of war. Moreover, that suspension would be the result of a calculation. What has to be worked out, therefore, and this is Kant's project, is the possibility of their abeyance. Within the context created by the distinction between the "pure" and that which demands forms of calculation, Kant writes of the arrival of "the foreigner" in the following terms:

> as long as he behaves peaceably where he is, he cannot be treated with hostility. What he can claim is not the *right to be a guest* (for this a special beneficent pact would be required, making him a member of the household for a certain time), but the *right to visit*; this right, to present oneself for society, belongs to all

human beings by virtue of the right of possession in common of the earth's surface on which, as a sphere, they cannot disperse infinitely but must finally put up with being near one another; but originally no one had more right than another to be on a place on the earth. [*ursprüngliche aber niemand an einem Orte der Erde zu sein mehr Recht hat, als der andere.*]³

The *"right to visit"* is differentiated from the *"right to be a guest."* What is important about the latter is twofold. In the first place, it involves what Kant describes as a "pact" ("*Vertrag*") which can be understood as the necessity for a form of calculation. Second, it obtains for a specific a determined period of time. Time here can only be thought within the domain of calculation. Here, therefore, what is meant by a "right" is mediated in advance by the existence of conditions. What this entails is that the state of being a "guest" would not be possible were it not for the presence of such conditions. Central to these conditions is a form of temporal constraint. As noted above, the force inherent in the possibility of a *"right to visit"* introduces a fundamentally different setup. In the case of this second "right." and it should be noted that Kant maintains the term *right*, what is involved is of necessity that which is unconditioned in advance. And yet, precisely because the "right to visit" is described by Kant as a "right," then the question of its ground has to be posed. The answer that can be located in the passage cited above is that this ground is given "by virtue of the right of possession in common of the earth's surface" ("*vermöge des Rechts des gemeinschaftlichen Besitzes der Oberfläche der Erde*"). It is worth staying with this formulation, since it introduces what allows for the possibility of the "right to visit." A ground is provided. The anoriginality of *being-in-place* is affirmed.

There are two interrelated aspects of this formulation that are pivotal to the overall argument of this book, namely, the location of *virtue in being* as a setup thought within the both difference and the relation between the conditioned and unconditioned (the a part/apart). In the first instance there is an evocation of commonality and then, in the second, there is the related evocation of place. One is defined in terms of the other. *Place*, as the term is presented here, has an important connection to Locke's discussion of property in *The Seconds Treatise on Government*. Even though Locke moves on to an argument for the acquisition of individual property, the concerns of the individual are still defied in connection to the work an individual may undertake in relation to the common. Commonality has a specific definition. It is a form of collectivity created by the gift. In terms of the "common" Locke's claim is that: "God, who has given the world to men in common, has also given them reason to make use of it to the best advantage of life and convenience."

Place exists in relation to the sense of commonality already at work in *being-in-place*. It is named as "the world." However, place, the "world," is there as an aftereffect of God's gift. Place, in other words, loses its anoriginality. Kant's arguments are importantly different. There is another thinking of place and therefore a different conception of both *being-in-place* and *being-in-relation*. What returns in Kant is a thinking of *being-in-place* and *being-in-relation* that has force independently of the incorporation of place within a specific determination of the logic of the gift in the first instance, and, in the second, of the actuality of any place and any determined sense of commonality's actualization. Both *being-in-place* and *being-in-relation* are present, immanently present, for "practical purposes" and both identify what is essential to the being of being human in the sense that they both underscore the presence of what for Kant, as the argument unfolds in this context, is the inherently unconditioned nature of the "right to visit." Visits do not condition the unconditioned. It is rather that they allow it to be staged. Equally, the unconditioned would be present as the ground of judgment. Moreover, the presence of the unconditioned is immanent and thus not actualized. As such, the effective presence of the unconditioned is that it occasions and sustains judgment. Given a specific occurrence judgment is not caused by the unconditioned, it is rather that judgment takes place in relation to it.

The refusal of the right to visit would be judged in relation to that which was proper to the being of being human and where the evocation of a sense of propriety is to stage the anoriginal relation between the ontological and the ethical. Here the formulation the "being of being human" thought in terms of *being-in-place* and *being-in-relation* stages the unconditioned. It is the unconditioned for any conditioned. The important consequence of this setting is that judgment, when it is understood as a finite act, would always be preceded by a particular determination of the ontological. The presence of a judgment as occurring in an indeterminant relation to the unconditioned accounts for why judgment is neither arbitrary nor contingent even if the precise content of any one judgment is itself not necessary. If the question of its ground is posed, then the answer is *being-in-place* and *being-in-relation*. As has been suggested, this has the quality of the unconditioned. The problem that continues therefore concerns the nature of the link between this sense of the unconditioned and what might be described as the more directly metaphysical conception of the unconditioned. (The latter can be located in Kant's specific use of the term *unconditioned*, and where it is defined in terms of the relationship between Reason and the Understanding. [4]) The presence of the link can be assumed. Its quality is the question. As always, the correct setting needs to be created.

In the First Appendix to *Towards Perpetual Peace: A Philosophical Project* Kant writes a sustained critique of that philosophical thinking of the political that turns the latter into what he describes as no more than the work of "politically prudent men" ("*diese staatskluge Männer*").[5] Their project is specific. As a start it is possible to give a negative formulation of their self-appointed task: it is not to think the political philosophically. Rather, all that occurs within this version of political prudence is the identification of the political with a particular sense of the "practical" ("*gehen sie mit Praktiken um*"). And it should be added that it is a sense of the practical where the nature of the practical is misconstrued as a result of the practical's identification with what may be thought as involving nothing other than the merely pragmatic. This conception of the practical is in the end no more than a type of acquiescence to the prevailing order of what Kant defines as "operable power" ("*Gewalt*").[6] In the same passage Kant goes on to identify the limitations of such an approach. The most significant of which arises from the fact that intrinsic to this conflation of the prudent, the pragmatic, and the practical is a resulting claim about the knowledge of human beings. However, this knowledge, despite its own internally motivated aspirations, is both fundamentally and definitionally inadequate. The limitation, its already present inadequacy, and then its possible overcoming of it, are all formulated by Kant in a way that introduces a dimension that complicates any claim about human being where such a claim would be based on nothing more than an extrapolation from a set of observations, and which would then oscillate between completion and that sense of finitude in which finitude is defined in terms of the pragmatic; in other words, the finitude of naturalism. (And thus, it will be argued, is not finitude at all.) Hence, the need for a conception of finitude that is defined in relation to the unconditioned's inevitability. (Finitude as the after effect of the infinite [the unconditioned] acquires an insistent rather than a merely pragmatic quality.) Kant writes of those implicated in such a project that, "they make much of their knowledge of human beings. . . . but without knowing the human being and what can be made of him [*und was aus ihm gemacht werden kann*] (from which a higher standpoint) [*ein höhere Standpunkt*] of anthropological observation is required)."[7]

There are three decisive elements at work in this passage. The first is the presence of a formulation of human being; here an interpretive concession has to be made, namely, that Kant's distinction between two modes of human existence allows the second to be interpreted in terms of the being of being human. (The setting of that anoriginal sense of propriety that is captured, for example, by the term *worldliness*.) In addition, the "making" in question, recalls that Kant wrote, "'the human being and what can be made of him" ("*und was aus ihm gemacht werden kann*") is defined in relation to the inscribed presence of the relationship between potentiality and actuality. The second element, and one to which it will be necessary to return toward the end of this chapter, concerns the evocation of "a higher stand point." The question to be addressed is clear: What is meant by *higher* in this context? Is this "higher" the "highest"? A question the relevance of which is straightforward insofar as Kant defines the "highest good" in the *Critique of Practical Reason* as "the unconditioned totality of the object of pure practical reason."[8] The third element is less directly relevant even though its overall significance is considerable. If a philosophical thinking of the political cannot be identified with purely pragmatic concerns, and moreover it must sustain the complementarity between theory and practice, then it becomes clear that a philosophical thinking of the political is a thinking orientated by the presence of the universal. Within Kant's philosophical project presented thus far, universality is the absolute presence of the unconditioned. Differences therefore between genuine political philosophies pertain to how the question of the already present nature of universality is answered (and thus the absolute as the unconditioned is thought). What this indicates is that a philosophical thinking of the political demands a repositioning of metaphysics in order to allow for this possibility.

Now, in regard to the first two elements, there is in this passage a description of human being and thus by extension the being of being human as it pertains at a given point in time. The knowledge of which, or at least this is the pretension, can be completed within that point in time. Repeated here is of course the temporality of the "pact." Namely, the incorporation of time within calculation such that time is always already calculable. The pragmatic would be present as that which sought to defy the hold of the unconditioned. (To recall Arendt this could take the form of the response to "power" that appears as "violence.") That would be its putative philosophical role. Pragmatism sustains a conception of human being as that which can be represented in its entirety in the moment and whose actions are incorporated both as actions and as objects of judgment within the enacted presence of the calculable. Knowledge, within this setting, would be linked either to the completeness of representation or the equation of the finite with the pragmatic. The implicit suggestion here is of course that such a conception of finitude, a conception in which the finite becomes the merely pragmatic occurrence, is premised on the effacing in any one instance of the plural event insofar as what is effaced is anoriginal irreducibility, that is, the centrality of the presence of the unconditioned as holding sway within the activity of calculation while remaining independent of any conditioned act. A position sustained by the temporality of *at-the-same-timeness*.

A further point concerning this conception of human being needs to be made, namely, that, this observed human is positioned within the naturalization of historical time; a setup thereby reinforcing the equation of time with the calculable. However, as Kant precedes, it is clear that this is a conception of knowledge that has, within the terms Kant has already established, failed from the start. A failure that is defined by the nature of the object that is constructed to be known; an object located at the intersection of the naturalization of the movement of historical time, representation, and the projected completion of knowing (where that latter is working within the definition of knowledge suggested by Kant's own contrastive formulation). At this limit there is that which is not delimited by it, hence, it is what fails to be known, precisely because it is not completely present, nor could it have ever been present. This is the point at which Kant's description of human being that was advanced in terms of what can be made of that "being," is to be located. Recall, again, Kant wrote: "what can be made of him" (*"was aus ihm gemacht werden kann"*). What is identified in this formulation is not a contingent property of human being. The argument has already been advanced that the presence of the term *making* underscores both the presence of potentiality and the repositioning of that potentiality in terms of the possible actualization of what is proper to human being. As formulated here, the latter is a potentiality that while not actualized as such is nonetheless always already present. (Here, of course what has already been identified in terms of "immanence" returns.) Implicit in the formulation of this position is the recognition that the naturalization of human being once it is articulated within the naturalization of historical time cannot sustain the interconnection that allows for the actualization of what human being is when the latter is thought, not in terms of direct or simple presence, but in terms of the actualization of a potentiality. While the formulation "what can be made of him" evokes the Kantian formulation of "hope" that occurs in the *Logic* in terms of the question: "What may I hope?" ("*Was darf ich hoffen?*"), what the structure of the question brings to the fore is a dynamic process and therefore an implicit thinking of potentiality.[9] (And it should be recalled that this project as a whole, the project of developing a thinking of the ethical delimited by the presence of *virtue in being*, continues to be defined both by the necessity of potentiality as well as by the modes of necessity it stages. The modes in which contingency's inevitability is itself necessary.)

There are two specific points that have to be added here. They follow from the general claim concerning the centrality of potentiality. In the first instance this identification of potentiality is intrinsic to the Kantian formulation of the being of being human. The second point is that such a process cannot be separated from what has already been identified as the effective presence of the temporality of *at-the-same-timeness* (indeed, part of the implicit project of this Chapter is to establish this interconnected presence.) Potentiality as a mode of being is articulated within the temporal structure its presence both demands and maintains.

2.

In the "General remark on the exposition of aesthetic reflective judgments" in the *Critique of the Power of Judgment*, Kant brings potentiality into connection with both a thinking of the unconditioned in the first place, and then in the second, with the version of *at-the-same-timeness* that is specific to this particular part of this overall project, namely, the component that is concerned with the continual development of the anoriginal implication of the ethical and the ontological. He writes the following:

> The absolutely good, judged subjectively in terms of the feeling that it instills (the object of the moral feeling) [*das Objekt des moralischen Gefühls*] as the

determinability of the powers of the subject by means of the representation of an absolutely necessitating law [*als die Bestimmbarkeit der Kräfte des Subjekts durch die Vorstellung eines schlechthin-nötigenden Gesetzes*], is distinguished chiefly by the modality of a necessity resting on concepts *a priori*, which contains in itself not merely a claim [*Anspruch*] but also a command [*Gebot*] that everyone should assent, and belongs in itself not to the aesthetic but to the pure intellectual power of judgment; it is also ascribed, not in a merely reflecting but in a determining judgment, not to nature but to freedom. But the *determinability* of the subject by means of this idea [*die Bestimmbarkeit des Subjekts durch diese Idee*], and indeed of a subject that can sense in itself obstacles in sensibility but at the same time [*zugleich*] superiority over them through overcoming them as a modification of its condition, i.e., the moral feeling, is nevertheless related to the aesthetic power of judgment and its formal conditions to the extent that it can serve to make the lawfulness of action out of duty representable at the same time as aesthetic [*zugleich als ästhetisch*], i.e., as sublime, or also as beautiful, without sacrificing any of its purity [*ohne an seiner Reinigkeit einzubüssen*]; which would not be the case if one would place it in natural combination with the feeling of the agreeable.[10] (Emphasis added)

The "absolutely good," which in the context of this passage is the presence of the absolute (or the universal) as the "unconditioned," needs to be understood as incorporating within it the ineliminability of the affective. The "absolutely good" is felt. The "feeling" in question is not necessary since it does not pertain to an already present determination, that is, to the identification of a given feeling at a given time, but to "the determinability" ("*die Bestimmbarkeit*") of the "subject's powers." The determination takes place by "means of the representation of an absolutely necessitating law" ("*durch die Vorstellung eines schlechthin-nötigenden Gesetzes*"). As a result the subject awaits determination. The subject is determinable. The term *Bestimmbarkeit* does not announce a determination as that which is has already taken place. On the contrary, what it introduces is the possibility of determinations. As a term, *Bestimmbarkeit* names potentiality. As a possibility it sustains its presence. The "powers of the subject" are able to be determined. Elsewhere, of course, Kant has argued the same point in a formulation that despite reiterating a similar mode of argumentation has a slightly different inflection. The argument takes the following form: "if the moral law commands that we *ought* to be better human beings now [*wir sollen* jetzt *bessere Menschen sein*], it inescapably [*unumgamglich*] follows that we must be *capable* of being better human beings [*wir müssen es auch können*]"[11] (emphasis added). Note the way the law commands in a "now" ("*jetzt*"). Law's conditioned presence occurs in time. While the significance of this "now" and the temporal determinations it allows will return, it should clear be from the above that the force of law is always actualized charging a "now" with both a sense of obligation and possibility. As a result, this sense of now becomes the *now*. Thus, it was always both. Necessity entails contingency. Within it the "inescapable" endures. The force of law, however, takes as integral to its possibility the interrelated claim that the being of being human is always already "capable." This capability is a potentiality whose actualization defines the now of its happening; with the *proviso*, of course, that this potentiality continues. Actuality, actualization, cannot still potentiality. The latter always survives. Here again there is a radically different sense of the event than would be found if the actuality and thus the status of the event where either attributed no more than a pragmatic quality or contained the structure in which what called for judgment and then the act of judgment had to be one and the same. This would be "mere enthusiasm." Reiterated here is both the impoverishment of the event were it to be equated with the directly pragmatic or the effacing of the space of judgment. Distancing both introduces the possibility if not the necessity of affirming, as judgment's possibility; a setup that can be expressed in terms of the already present status of the plural event. In other words, the presence of an event whose force cannot be equated with anyone singular determination. The "now" is reconfigured beyond the instant. This is the "now" that has already been cited by Kant. It is the "now" harboring the necessity of a possibility whose actualization is itself not necessary precisely because the "now" is the locus of anoriginal difference. The "now" is an event of plurality. Kant's "now," as noted above, takes on the more generalized quality of the *now*.

Potentiality introduces its own form of necessity. It is both necessary that the determinability of the "subject's powers" is always already there, and hence it has an anoriginal quality, and yet it is also the case that it is not necessary that any determination take place. It should be added that, as indicated by the argumentation of the passage from the *Critique of the Power of Judgment* that such a state of affairs is representable. Representability has the following form: the effect of determinability's actualization is a recognition that the "moral feeling" can be represented since it is "at the same time" aesthetic. Representation in this sense occurs without the diminution let alone "sacrifice" of "purity." (This will become a central point in forming a response to Derrida's interpretation of the "unconditioned," which is structured in terms of impossibility, loss, and guilt.) Again the latter stands for a definition of an act without determination by either utility or means/ends calculations. Here this becomes a version of the unconditioned. To which it should be added that what allows for the actualization of the subject's determinability, in general terms this is the actualization of a potentiality, is the nonactualizability of the unconditioned. It is held apart; a holding of that which is anoriginally apart; an apart in which elements cohered insofar as each is a part.

At this point a return can be made to what has already been identified as valuable in Aristotle's thinking of potentiality namely his location and explanation of the presence of "impotentiality" within any thinking of potentiality. Here it needs to be added that the negative within potentiality, the already noted relation established by Aristotle in the

Metaphysics between "*dynamis*" and "*adynamis*" is, as Aristotle goes on the argue, a very specific form of "privation." Bringing potentiality, which in this context is to be understood as bound up with the Kant's term *capacity* (*vermorgen*) into a form of defined relation to "incapacity" does not mean, as has been argued elsewhere, "to be in relation to one's own 'privation.'"[12] Indeed, as has been suggested, the contrary is the case. Allowing for the interplay between potentiality and potentiality, that is, between, in this context, "*dynamis*" and "*adynamis*," means that potentiality has to be thought in terms of what can be described in a way that recalls the formulation all ready used—that is, *necessity entails contingency*—as bringing with it the always already possibility of the nonnecessity of its actualization. This is the sense in which any potentiality is at the same time an "impotentiality." To recall the passage from the *Metaphysics* that has already been noted: "Incapacity and the incapable [ἡ ἀδυναμία καὶ τὸ ἀδύνατον] is the privation [στέρησίς] contrary to capacity in this sense; so that every capacity has a contrary incapacity [τὸ αὐτὸ πᾶσα δύναμις ἀδυναμίᾳ] for producing the same result in respect of the same subject." What this reinforces is both the already present nature of potentiality and the nonnecessity of its actualization. Equally, however, it underscores that what inheres as fundamental to any original form of potentiality is the possibility for its actualization as well as the inscribed presence of the nonnecessity of that actualization. Hence, it is possible for the same subject that an occurrence not happen. This nonhappening is the nonactualization of a potentiality. The latter, as already noted, is thought by Aristotle in terms of "privation" ("στέρησίς"). What is of interest in this regard is the possibility that the immediacy of recognition, for example,. that specific form of immediacy in which the subject sees itself as subject to the law, can be understood as a form of actualization, and that crucially the subject must be defined in terms of this potentiality, namely, a potentiality that is there to be actualized. This, it can be argued, is precisely what Kant means by the subject's "determinability." And why this term must be interpreted in terms of the inscribed necessity of potentiality within a philosophical anthropology that take this aspect of

Kant as fundamental. It thus follows that one of the attending arguments has to be that the presence of a definition of the subject and thus the definition of the being of being human in terms of potentiality, a subject by both *being-in-place* and *being-in-relation* sets in play a specific group of philosophical demands.

As a beginning, there must be a thinking of process and movement as integral to any adequate account of the subject's constitution. Activity is not a secondary quality. Being is what it is, in its being acted out. What this means is that the *actative* and the substantive have to be thought together.[13] Being is an activity that will always have the imposition of nonactualization attending it as a threat. This is the threat of violence that when exercised means that the worldliness of the world would have excised rendering life as no more than mere life in the world. A world reduced to the world of life. What must continue to be uncovered, therefore, is the language appropriate to this thinking as it occurs in Kant. The subject and subjectivity are processes whose work and thus whose activities are constitutive of the subject's self-definition. Subjectivity, therefore, cannot be differentiated from the processes of its own enactment. However, that enactment has to be thought in terms of the complex modalities of potentiality. In other words, what "determinability" stages is the need to account for processes of determination. Precisely because Kant is critical of mechanistic accounts of duty, the move from "claim" to "command" needs to be accompanied by both a generalized as well as a specific language of "striving." The earlier discussion of "striving" and thus of movement return here with emphasis having now been given to the actative. What this means is that there has to be a further development of the argument outlined in chapter 2, namely that "striving" was present and possible precisely because of the immanent presence of the highest good and as a consequence "striving" (and cognate terms) names the staging of the relationship between the conditioned (thus also the conditional) and the unconditioned.

Allowing for the centrality of the dynamic means that it can be argued that there is a strong sense of potentiality that inheres in what the subject comes to experience. If there is a move from naturalism to that philosophical project that includes Kant, then it takes potentiality and its related language as central to it. Note in the same section of the *Critique of the Power of Judgment* the way the sublime is formulated. Kant writes that the sublime is orientated around process and thus activity. Integral to it is the presence of

> an object (of nature) the representation of which determines the mind to think of the unattainability of nature as a presentation of ideas. [*es ist ein Gegenstand (der Natur), dessen Vorstellung das Gemüt bestimmt, sich die Unerreichbarkeit der Natur als Darstellung von Ideen zu denken.*] . . . This striving and the feeling of the unattainability of the idea by means of the imagination [*Diese Bestrebung, und das Gefühl der Unerreichbarkeit der Idee durch die Einbildungskraft*], is itself a presentation of the subjective purposiveness of our mind in the use of the imagination for its supersensible vocation [*für dessen übersinnliche Bestimmung*], and compels us to think nature itself in its totality, as the presentation of something supersensible [*als Darstellung von etwas Übersinnlichem*], subjectively, without being able to produce this presentation objectively.[14]

"Unattainability" ("*Unerreichbarkeit*") recalls the use of the "'unattainable" that has already been identified; namely, a definition of striving as that which occurs and can only occur in relation to an "unattainable goal" ("*unerreichbaren Ziele*").[15] Striving is linked to "unattainability."[16] This is not a privation in any straightforward sense. On the contrary, finitude is the recognition of a limit. It is not a doing without. Rather defining a "goal" in terms of its "unobtainability" reinforces the effective hold of potentiality insofar as "unattainability" holds to the presence of striving as a continuity whose continual actualization reinforces the necessity to continue striving. (It can be added here that it is this precise setup that will allow for a response to what might be described as Derrida's failure to grasp the force of the unconditioned. Not its necessity but its *force*.¹⁷) Kant's insistence on striving and the necessity of the link between striving and potentiality yields a philosophical account of action that depends on and yet maintains the effective presence of the unconditioned. The latter is integral to the force of the actative. What Kant opens therefore is both the possibility and the necessity of thinking the unconditioned as effective, immanently effective. Striving both affirms the inscription of value within being while defining the possibility of a life which affirms the irreparable presence of an anoriginal divide that constitutes the subject. Affirming that divide as irreparable and thought beyond the hold of either synthesis or sublation is to affirm both finitude and the possibility of the ethical by establishing the necessity of a site if negotiation and thus judgment.

The "feeling" to which "unattainability" gives rise is linked to the recognition of a "vocation" ("*Bestimmung*") that does of course depend, and continues to depend, on the subject's "determinability" ("*Bestimmbarkeit*"). Again the subject is "determined." *Bestimmbarkeit* leads here to a specific determination, occurring in the "now" of its happening; allowing for an opening in which this "now" becomes the *now* as plural event. Determinability becomes an orientation. It is a potentiality. While there are clearly a number of different ways to interpret this passage, the most compelling is that what sublimity in the Kantian sense opens up, is a thinking of finitude that is delimited in the sense that it the result of the recognition of that which cannot be actualized and yet which has a productive presence. Finitude occurs in the movement toward the supersensible. It is only in that movement as a possibility that finitude is disclosed. This movement is an original orientation. What is brought to the fore is the inscribed necessity of (and for) a capacity. Precisely because the unconditioned, named here in terms of ideas and the unpresentable, cannot be actualized, there is the recognition that the unconditioned is that which is deployed and which, moreover, has to be deployed within the possibility of acts of judgment. This is another version of the move from "claim" to "command." As has already been suggested the "supersensible vocation" ("*übersinnliche Bestimmung*") necessities the "determinability of the subject" (*"die Bestimmbarkeit des Subjekts"*). The "vocation," therefore, depends on the actualization of its possibility. To which it needs to be added that this "vocation" is a result intrinsic to the being of being human. This is the vocation of determinability. Within both what continues is potentiality.

3.

In order to develop the way in which potentiality has emerged as an element that is integral to the conception of subjectivity within the Kantian project, and thus to the way it is interconnected to the presence of both forms of the unconditioned and the temporality of *at-the-same-timeness*, the next element in staging this attempt to work through Kant, and thus in thinking through the possibility of recovering *virtue in being*, involves what can most directly be described as a commentary on defining elements of Part One of Kant's *Religion within the Bounds of Mere Reason*.[18] This celebrated discussion of "radical evil," where the latter means no more than the "indwelling" (*"der Einwohnung"*) of "the evil principle 'alongside' ['*neben*'] the good," such that the questions of what "indwelling" (*"der Einwohnung"*) and "alongside" (*"neben"*) means have to be taken as central, allows for the development of an account of the implicit anthropology at work in Kant's overall argumentation.[19] Part of developing that account is the identification of the way a language and a thinking of the dynamic is indispensible to that development. Allusion has already been made to the latter *via* the invocation of the necessary inscription of modalities of striving within the Kantian project where striving defines a conception of finitude, namely, the conditioned in its relation to the unconditioned, that is itself positioned by the presence of a spacing that pertain anoriginally, and which is held in place and occasioned by *at-the-same-timeness*. Within the setting created by this set of related and interdependent elements, what has to be noted is the effective presence of the unconditioned and thus the infinite. The latter, as will be suggested, becomes a formulation of the inescapability of the plural event. Again, if there is a summary position, it is that finitude is always an aftereffect of the recognition of the infinite nature of the infinite. Finitude is disclosed by the latter. Moreover, it is a disclosure given within and as consciousness, which is itself the oscillation between the immediacy of recognition and that which occurs as the result of reflection. Reflection is that in which the positing of mere doctrine is displaced and consequently critique occasioned.

The problem of evil, the presence of evil, and thus its already present status, when taken together means that there needs to be an account of evil, which even though the actuality of evil is assumed, nonetheless accounts for evil in terms of its possibility. In other words, a beginning cannot be made with the presence of evil acts or even the presence of the continuity of movement between good and evil acts as though they were simply given. The account of evil (and therefore equally of the good) would have to be given in relation to that which is "original" in both instances. In more general terms what this means, of course, is a recasting of the ethical in relation to possibility and thus the larger question of potentiality. The direct result is a consequent sidelining of the language of obligations, and so on. Within this setting evil can be neither mere contingency or there as a result of an evil nature. Kant is not involved in writing a theodicy.[20] There is therefore at the very basis of Kant's thought an important relation between "originality" and "possibility." What has to emerge is a thinking of the determinations of the force that is already at work within this relation. Within the thinking of those determination what emerges is another way into the question of origins; "origins," defined in terms of "possibility," and thus as "an-origins," and therefore the anoriginal. The move is from an originating *arché* that is static to the presence of an origin as an already present potentiality. A move of this nature, it can be argued, sets the measure for Kant's entire vocabulary. Of equal relevance therefore, placed alongside terms such as *originality* and *possibility*, is the terminology of "incentives" ("*Triebfeder*") in their connection to but differentiation from "natural drives" ("*Triebe*"). Established thereby are the limits and the necessity of what Kant names as the "the drive to society" ("*der Trieb zur Gesellschaft*"). (A formulation that has profound effects on post-Kantian philosophy; e.g., central to Fichte's argumentation in his *Some Lectures concerning the Scholar's Vocation* is what he refers to as "the social drive" ["*der gesellschaftliche Trieb*"]). Kant goes on to note that the "drive to society" is "one of human being's fundamental drives." Force is at work elsewhere. Included in the domain in which forms of force are at work such as the "power of choice" ("*Willkür*"), "propensity" ("*Hange*"), "dispositions" ("*Gesinnung*"), and "predispositions" ("*Anlagen*") are all central. Finally, added to this setting is the reworking of human nature such that what is of importance is not its presence as that which is given to be thought. Rather, in eschewing the given, Kant reformulates the presence of "human nature" in terms of the "possibility of human nature." Human nature, therefore, is that which is realized. And thus is that which comes to realize itself as itself. Here necessity meets contingency. "Human nature," as already noted, is not a mere given. For Kant the "dispositions" in "human being" are "original," since "they belong to the possibility of human nature" ("*sie gehören zur Möglichkeit der menschlichen Natur*").[21] At work in this web of possibilities is the general supposition that there is a domain of necessity in which there is the inevitability, thus the necessity, of contingency.

The disposition for the morally good is a complex formulation of which Kant writes that while this "disposition" may be "innate" ("*angeborne*") this does entail that it "has not been earned ["*erworben*"] by the human being who harbours it."[22] In other words, there is a distinction between the presence of this disposition and the ensuing recognition that this disposition's actualization is that through which, to rework that language of the *Critique of the Power of Judgment*, human being discovers its "vocation." "Vocation," understood as an orientation, is defined by that which is proper to the being of being human. (Again it is an ontological configuration that precedes action but which is then acted out. Necessity precedes contingency. Value is inscribed in being.) However, to reiterate the point made above, while the "vocation" is there of necessity, its discovery and thus its actualization is a contingent possibility. Earning or acquiring that to which human being is disposed is taking over what is open as a possibility for human being. This is an opening where the presence of acting entails that a potentiality is actualized (or in the negative that this actualization has been refused or suppressed both of which will have determined contingent conditions.[23]) This is a state of affairs that has its own set of consequences. While they are defined in terms of the positive and the negative, where the negative can be thought in terms of a relation between "pathology" in the Kantian sense and "privation" in the Aristotelian (and *in extremis* the "superfluous" in Arendt), it remains the case that of greatest significance is that the actualization of a potentiality had to have been possible in the first place. This relation between necessity and contingency is precisely what Hegel in the *Phenomenology of Spirit* fails to understand. Hegel asserts that: "This contingency of the content has universality merely in the *propositional form* in which it is expressed; but as an ethical proposition it promises a universal and necessary *content*, and thus contradicts itself by the content being contingent."[24] It is the presence of *at-the-sametimeness* and thus the construction of the subject as in each and every instance a plural event staging both the ineliminability and the necessity for negotiation that underscores that what is stake is precisely not a contradictory state of affairs emerging as a result of contingency's necessity. Content is by necessity contingent. Contingency brings reflection and judgment into play. And as a result contingency becomes the sign of the ethical.

Now, in order to account for what Kant describes as the "originality" of a "disposition to good" he identifies, within *Religion within the Bounds of Mere Reason*, three defining modalities of human being. There are three "predispositions." They pertain to the location of the "good" within "human nature," and are presented in a way that are implicated in the already present interarticulation of both the being of being human and the temporality proper to human being's anoriginal complexity; in other words, the presence of human being as a locus of anoriginal irreducibility. The three "predispositions" becomes modes of orientation. They are formulated as the "elements of the determination (*der Bestimmung*) of human being," the determinations that already presume "determinability." They are presented thus:

1. The predisposition to the *animality* [*die Thierheit*] of the human being, as a *living being*; [*als eines lebenden*].
2. To the *humanity* [*Menschheit*] in him, as a living and at the same time *rational* being; [*als eines lebenden und zugleich vernünftigen*]
3. To his personality [*Persönlichkeit*] as a rational and at the same time *responsible* being [*als eines vernünftigen und zugleich der Zurechnung fähigen Wesens*].[25]

The evocation of the "animality" identifies human being's biological life. This is human being understood in terms of its biology. As has already been suggested, it is what comes to be named by Walter Benjamin and reformulated by Arendt is terms of "mere life." (The latter is of course the conception of life in which speech and worldliness have been effaced by the enacted presence of violence.) While it opens a path that cannot be pursued here implicit in Kant's formulation, and the movement beyond it, is the recognition of both the inherent animality of human life as a quality of human being, and, then, the subsequent impossibility of equating human being with "mere life"—that is, either biological life or the life created as the result of violence having undone what Arendt called "the space of appearance." The reduction to "mere life" would return, for example, in a philosophical account of slavery in which replaceability and the superfluous would define life. Potentiality linked to contingency would have been replaced by that potentiality that is there as the counter possibility. The "impossibility" of the equation of human being with "mere life"—or indeed the all to ready possibility of the same—underscores the presence of a mode of thinking in which the specificity of human being is to be maintained as a project. And yet, Kant makes an important concession here. He introduces on the level of animality the already noted formulation, "the drive to society" ("*der Trieb zur Gesellschaft*"). Animality is present as a drive that has to be thought in terms of an ineliminable and already present movement toward relationality. (Mere life present in terms of the inscribed possibility of its own self-overcoming. Indeed, it has to be added here that it is the anoriginal spacing held in place by *at-the-same-timeness*, which functions as the condition that precludes the possibility of an absolute and thus final equation of human being with mere life. Even though the presence of that reduction attends human being as an ineliminable threat.)

The "drive to society" is not present as already accomplished. It is there as a "drive," and as a "drive" what has to be held in place is the possibility of its actualization (and thus what is opened up as a question is what is involved in the drive's own transformation in order that its end is obtained). The refusal of this form of relationality becomes therefore the refusal of human animality and thus the refusal of the designation of human being as "a living being" ("*eines lebenden*"). Again this accounts for the force of Arendt's formulation that those who are "without speech" and "without action" are "literally dead to the world." In other words, the most elementary of "drives" would not have been actualized. A further sense of both the limits of animality and yet the location of those limits within the space created by *at-the same-timeness* is also evident in the *Lecture on the Philosophical Doctrine of Religion*. What needs to be noted is that this space becomes spacing. Namely, it moves from the positing of space as a given and thus as only having a singular quality to the presence of space as that which is there being created and re-created in the continuity of its being lived out. In the *Lecture* he writes that

> This predisposition to good, which God has placed in the human being, must be developed by the human being himself before the good can make its appearance. But since *at the same time* the human being has many instincts belonging to animality, and since he has to have them if he is to continue being human, the strength of his instincts will beguile him and he

will abandon himself to them, and thus arises evil, or rather, when the human being begins to use his reason, he falls into foolishness.[26] (Emphasis added)

While God is acknowledged as its source, the originality of the "predisposition to the good" provides this "predisposition" with a location that is the activity of life. Fundamental to this position is the claim that at no point is this prior to life. It is positioned as immanent within life and is thus there in its being lived out. The good is always present as a possibility because of the "predisposition." "Animality" and this disposition when taken together structure a site of negotiation because both pertain "at the same time." (Parenthetically, what this means is that "animality," "humanity," etc. are not retained as "superseded forms." They live on within the spacing opened and sustained by *at-the-same-timness*. The interplay of the *a part* and the *apart* endures.) The centrality of the "predisposition" announces, to recall the terminology that has already been used, what has been described as the anoriginality of the actative. "Foolishness" is avoided to the extent that the incalculable endures. It is a form of endurance that resides in the recognition of the limits of reason.

While the details of what is meant by *humanity* (*Menschheit*) and then *personality* (*Persönlichkeit*) as presented in *Religion within the Bounds of Mere Reason* would always have to be taken up, at this point it is essential to note what is intrinsic to the formulation of the second and third of these "predispositions." Each involves two elements. In the first instance there is the equation of "humanity" with the combined presence of "animality" and "rationality." In the second, "personality" is equated with the combined presence of rationality and responsibility. The question posed in both instances is straightforward, given that these elements are not mutually excluding: How is this combined presence to be understood? Answering this question demands having recognized that present in both formulations is the temporal marker *zugleich*. What is at work therefore is a particular determination of the temporality of *at-the-same-timeness*.

In the *Critique of Pure Reason* in the formulation of the relationship between generalizable conditions of possibility for experience and then the specificity of a given experience, Kant writes of the necessity of this distinction in the following terms: "The *a priori* conditions of a possible experience in general are *at the same time* (*einer möglichen Erfahrung überhaupt sind* zugleich) conditions of the possibility of the objects of experience"[27] (emphasis added). In a different domain, this time in section 28 of the *Critique of the Power of Judgment*, as part of an attempt to think and then formulate the particularity of the sublime, insofar as the concern is what sublimity reveals about the capacity of human being, he notes of the sublime's power that, "the irresistibility of its power certainly makes us, considered as natural beings [*als Naturwesen*], recognize our physical powerlessness [*Ohnmacht*], but *at the same time* it reveals a capacity [*aber entdeckt* zugleich *ein Vermögen*] for judging ourselves as independent [*unabhängig*] of it and a superiority over nature [*eine Uberlegenheit über die Nature*]"[28] (emphasis added). These are not examples of simple forms of differentiation, that is, different modalities of *sameness*. The contrary is the case. What they underscore is the role within Kant's philosophical thinking of importantly differing forms of what has been called the temporality of *at-the-same-timeness*. It is essential to realize that *at-the-same-timeness* cannot be reduced to a single determination since it is not a time that has an essential or singular nature. In the case of the first iteration, which is located in the *Critique of Pure Reason*, what *at-the-same-timeness* stages is a state of affairs in which one component of what occurs is given with the other in such a way that simultaneity opens and closes a space "at the same time."

However, an importantly difference conception of *at-the-same-timeness* emerges in the case of the passage from the *Critique of the Power of Judgment*. In that instance what *at-the-same-timeness* allows is the copresence of the recognition of "natural being," and thus an essential form of limitation occurring at the same time as that what is also revealed is a "capacity" that has a specific effect; namely that it delimits further "natural being." That "capacity" lifts human being above nature to the extent that the latter is understood as the domain of mechanistic laws in which what occurs is coterminous with the conditions of possibility for its occurrence.[29] Or equally what occurs is coterminous with the conditions of its intelligibility. Here, in the domain demarcated by the sublime, there is a form of *at-the-same-timeness* that creates a spacing to which reference has already been made. A setting of anoriginal difference: hence, a spacing that is held in place by *at-the-same-timeness* while of course being its place. What is brought into play is not a static setup. Again there is the anoriginality of the actative. What pertains here is a "capacity" for judgment. The latter is a potentiality. As the passage makes clear "natural being" becomes the definition of human being defined by the presence of animality and mere rationality, such a conception of human being is known to be limited. This recognition occurs from a position that is "independent (*"unabhängig"*) of it." There is a holding apart. However, for this apartness to be effective it must be present at the same time as that from which it is held apart. Finitude can only be recognized as finitude if that which yields it as such, which must be the infinite or the absolute as the inherently unconditioned, occurs at the same time that finitude takes on an insistent presence. A setup already identified by the formulation—the *insistence of finitude*—is finitude as continually delimited. Here there is a thinking of finitude beyond acquiescence and which thus has to be understood as a severance of the finite and the pragmatic. In that severance finitude takes on another quality. (Moreover, as will be argued in the next chapter, it will be a rethinking of finitude within the setting created by finitude's recasting in terms of its insistence—hence, again, the *insistence of finitude*—that sets in play a rethinking of Derrida's formulation of the unconditional, thus the presence of the unconditioned, as "bending to conditionality.")

What has been designated above as "holding apart," within the construction of a Kantian philosophical anthropology, where the latter once again accounts for the implicit and explicit presence of Kant's thinking of the being of being human, finds one of its clearest formulations in the move from "animality" to "personality." It attains its clarity because of the retention of *at-the-same-timeness*. (A positioning that means that the thinking of the being of being human is not defined either as a singularity or by a simple form of progress let alone by the inherently misleading nature of a logic of negation. The latter misleads because it misconstrues time by failing to think the now in terms of its occurrence as a *now* and thus as a plural event. *At-the-same-timeness* both eschews and distances the work of negation.) "Personality" is not distanced from the possibility of forms of negotiation, even the presence of protracted forms. "Personality" is not an end in itself, rather it is a predisposition that is "rooted in reason practical of itself, i.e. in reason legislating unconditionally [*unbedingt gesetzgebende*]."³⁰ Personality is bound up therefore with a form of necessity even though actions taken in relation to it are not necessary. Once the moral law and respect are involved then what is at stake is personality itself even though personality is never present as itself. Kant's formulation is the following: "The idea of the moral law alone, together with the respect that is inseparable from it, cannot be properly called a *predisposition to personality*; it is personality itself (the idea of humanity considered wholly intellectually)."³¹ The above is a position that is reinforced in the *Critique of Practical Reason* in which "personality" is understood as "freedom and independence from the mechanism of the whole of nature."³² While that is a state of affairs that is reiterated in a way that underscores the independence of human being from nature, what it in fact creates, in disallowing an equation of human being and nature, is the continuous presence of a site of negotiation with nature. The retained presence of this site occurs precisely because of the already present status of *at-the-same-timeness* as well as its inevitable and therefore necessary continuity. A position allowed by the continuity of space having become spacing. The retention of this site indicates that freedom is always a form of relation, namely, a relation to freedom as the unconditioned. In other words, what this means is that freedom has it be thought in terms of the relationship between the conditioned and the unconditioned. Freedom, understood as located within negotiation both emerges and takes place, because of the impossible possibility of maintaining this setting. This will be integral to the argument that evil, what can be understood as the reality of evil, a reality that forces on Kant (and thus philosophy) the need to respond to the presence of evil in terms of its possibility, is a "propensity." In more precise terms it is for Kant a "propensity" that is attached to what he identifies as "the moral capacity of the power of choice" (*"dem moralische Vermögen der Willkür"*). In other words, it is a propensity that is linked to a form of potentiality. Potentiality, both here and in general, has to be thought in relation to freedom. Nonetheless, what is important about this formulation is the inescapability of potentiality. Recognizing, as has been argued from the start, that the presence of the term *capacity* (*vermögen*) is already a thinking of potentiality.

———◆———

For Kant "life" is not to be understood as a mere singularity; as though there were just life, as though life could never be more than "mere life." The term *life* lends itself to forms of differentiation. There is a distinction between three differing determinations of "life." The distinction sketched by Kant in the lecture course known as *Metaphysik L* repeats to a significant degree the distinctions that have already been noted in *Religion within the Bounds of Mere Reason*. "Animal" and "human" life, which while they can be distinguished from each other, are themselves to be differentiated from what is described by Kant in the lectures as "spiritual life." The latter defines, from within this frame of reference given by his lectures, that which yields its own sense of propriety. (The already noted force of the "proper" needs to be recalled.) There is a "pleasure" within "spiritual life." Kant continues,

> this pleasure is an intellectual pleasure. One has satisfaction with it, without its gratifying one. Such intellectual pleasure is only in morality. But from where does morality get such pleasure? All morality is the harmony of freedom with itself. E.g., whoever tells lies does not agree with his freedom, because he is bound

> by his lie. Whatever harmonises with freedom agrees with the whole of life. What agrees with the whole of life pleases. However this is only reflective pleasure; we find here no gratification, but rather the approval of it through reflection. Virtue thus has no gratification, but instead approval, for a human being feels his spiritual life and the highest degree of freedom.[33]

"Reflective pleasure" is the pleasure that occurs in the recognition, first, of what exists in and for itself and thus, second, of that occurs neither as a result of calculation's necessity nor of utility's apparent exigency. The second is purposive in relation to a determined end. The former is purpose in relation to its being what it is. The "spiritual life" is a thinking of the possibility of the unconditioned. And yet, even if "morality is the harmony of freedom with itself," it does not follow that morality can be actualized. All that can occur are moral acts. Hence, spiritual life remains as immanent within the practical as part of life's own self-definition. Precisely because there will be an important affinity with *holiness*, which is a term deployed by Kant to define the subject position constructed by the nature of the continuity of the encounter between the conditioned and the unconditioned, a return still has to be made to the language of the "spiritual."

Holiness and the *spiritual* are terms that for Kant are fundamental to a reworking of the being of being human. They are terms that, despite any appearance to the contrary and thus despite the reductive possibility of locating within them a merely theological or pietistic impulse, work in the opposite direction. What both terms enact is the set up that locates the ethical within the being of being human and, therefore, which has to be thought in terms of *being-in-place* and *being-in-relation*. And thus when these elements are thought together continue to allow for the formulation *virtue in being*. (Here, perhaps despite all intimations to the contrary there is a genuine affinity with both Epicurus and Aristotle.)

In a complex formulation in the *Groundwork of the Metaphysics of Moral* there is another staging of life. While it forms part of the critique of *Glückseligkeit*, a critique enacting a critical distancing of *Glückseligkeit* from "morality," Kant locates that staging within what he identifies as "organized being." He then goes on to describe that entity as one which is "constituted purposively for life" (*zweckmäßig zum Leben eingerichteten*).[34] Life's purpose is defined internally. What is essential to such an entity is that which is appropriate to that "end" ("*Zwecke*"). Here of course "end" has to be thought in terms of its realization, rather than as an end to be reached such that the "end" did not orientate the nature of the reaching. The latter would be a thinking driven by utility and the pragmatic. While the question that has to be addressed concerns the way that "end" is to be understood, what has to be noted at this stage, is that this entity is organized such that its capacity to realize its own end is a property that is integral to it. The purpose of life does not have an end that can either be located outside it, or fail to have the potential to orientate it. This does of course have to be linked to what is described in the *Critique of the Power of Judgment* as the subject's "feeling of life" ("*das Lebensgefühl*").[35] In the latter what is involved is a feeling that lifts or elevates the subject beyond its equation with mere feeling.

4.

Life becomes itself, becomes what it is, through the force of law. Remembering that law's force cannot be separated from its "purity." It should be added here that the recognition of the recasting of how the force of law is to be understood, a recasting that begins with "purity," would be integral to a critique of law in the name of law. A critique the result of which would be the development of a conception of law in which law was positioned beyond its reduction the domain of calculation.[36] The argumentation of this section of *Religion within the Bounds of Mere Reason* works through a number of important points prior to the introduction of the "purity" of the law. The first demands noting what Kant describes as the "irresistibility" ("*unwiderstehlich*") of the law's imposition.[37] Again, this has to be understood as a formal claim. What imposes itself is the form of the law. Its "irresistibility" brings the connection between the form of the law and the "moral disposition" ("*moralischen Anlage*") into play. Given this setting evil emerges because human being makes "incentives" that are not moral—in the sense that they are mere conditions or non-universalizable particulars—into those which then orientate the range of responses to the moral law. In other words, there is a failure to recognize that what exerts its hold is the incalculable and thus the unconditioned. Both have an effective presence. To deploy the formulation of *Metaphysic L*, this failure of recognition also occurs on the level of reflection. This is the locus of "radical evil," which is radical because what has been corrupted is what Kant describes as the "ground of all maxims" ("*den Grund aller Maximen*"). What this means of course is that the calculable has undone the incalculable. Evil is another name for actions that work on the fragility of the unconditioned's presence and thus the attendant possibility to undo it. In Arendtian terms this is the continual threat of violence. The essential point, however, is that evil can be judged.

Judgment, which would be the precondition of any engagement with evil, has two dimensions. The first is that it can be judged since it is ground in the human being "acting freely." Evil is neither mysterious nor strictly incomprehensible. Evil acts may appear incomprehensible insofar as the reason for such acts cannot be universalized. Nonetheless, evil acts are comprehensible because they can be judged. The second dimension of judgment is the recognition that formally it is impossible to resist the presence of law's unconditioned presence. (Even though one response to that "impossibility" shows itself in varying pathological forms.) Given these two aspects of judgment evil can then be reformulated in terms of a relationship between the *now* of action and the setting that equates this *now* with the already calculated moment in time (the pragmatic moment in which the now is taken as singular). Kant writes in this regard:

> However evil a human being has been right up to the moment of an impending free action (evil even

habitually, as other nature [*als anderer Natur*], his duty to better himself was not just in the past: it still is his duty *now* [*jetzt*]; he must therefore be capable of it and, should he not do it, he is at the moment of action [*in dem Augenbliche der Handlung*] just as accountable, and stands just as condemned, as if, though endowed with a natural predisposition to the good (which is inseparable from freedom), he had just stepped out of the state of innocence into evil.[38]

Prior to noting the details of this formulation Kant's earlier clarification of how a "propensity" is to be understood must be brought in. The "propensity" involves a particular determination of the act or deed: "And yet by the concept of a propensity is understood a subjective determining ground of the power of choice [*dem Begriffe eines Hanges subjectiven Bestimmungsgrund der Willkür*] that precedes every deed [*jeder That*], and hence is itself not yet a deed [*noch nicht That ist*]."[39] What is significant is that the "deed" is defined in relation to a "subjective determining ground," which is itself formulated in terms of a specific modality of force, namely, "the power of choice" [*der Willkür*]. Deeds, therefore, where the deed is understood as finitude, and thus as both finite and particular, are always aftereffects. Here it is the aftereffect of its possibility. When read together what the two passages can be taken as arguing is that there is a constitutive space that creates its own structure. A space defined in terms of the temporality of *at-the-same-timeness*. Duty endures in every *now* (thus, in every instant precisely because every instant is always more than one). It is an immanent presence. Duty, because it is staged in relation to the form of the law, from within a Kantian perspective, cannot be differentiated from the force of the law. There is both a structural and a dynamic coalescence between force and form. Again, this is the presence, the privileged though now assumed presence, of the actative. Indeed, it is possible to go further and suggest that in Kant form is always tied up with the actative. Even the claim that the "beautiful" pertains to the "form of the object," which while it means that what is at stake is the object's generalizable conditions of intuitability, form is what allows the relation—the subject/object relation—to have force and thus for there to be aesthetic feeling ("pleasure" and "unpleasure").[40] The *now* is charged with a possibility. Possibility contains two elements. There must be a space in which to act and acting must itself be possible. These two dimensions have an anthropological aspect since a philosophical anthropology has to involve both *being-in-place* and *being-in-relation*. What this entails of course is that an insistence on the actative and thus on a response to the force of law brings determinations of place into consideration. These considerations are not contingent. They are inscribed into the structure of duty insofar as duty demands modes of response. Duty is the demand that finitude be acted out. Duty is acted out, striving occurs in place with others. Finitude is life and yet life's finitude cannot be reduced to pragmatic determinations. Finitude is always the aftereffect of the unconditioned's effective presence. Finitude is enacted in place. Taken together at work here is the affirmation of the actative that is commensurate with the *insistence of finitude*.

Propensity, as the term is used in this setting, has an important relation to what is described later in this section of *Religion within the Bounds of Mere Reason* as "the original predisposition to good" (*"der ursprünglichen Anlage zum Guten"*). While the terms are different each is involved in a conception of process and thus a version of the dynamic. Any account of act or a "deed," both can be subsumed under the heading of the actative, is allowed by that which attends the deed or accounts for its "possibility." The presence of an "original predisposition" means that an account of evil cannot be given in terms of the loss of that which inhered "originally." Hence Kant writes,

> The restoration [*Die Wiederherstellung*] of the original predisposition to good in us is not therefore the acquisition of a *lost* incentive for the good [*eine verlornen Triebfeder zum Guten*], since we were never able to lose the incentive that consists in the respect for the moral law, and were we ever to lose it, we would also never be able to regain it. The restoration is therefore only

> the recovery [*die Herstellung*] of the *purity* of the law [*der Reinigheit*] as the supreme ground of all maxims.[41]

The return once freed from the problematic of loss brings a different set up into play. Standing opposed to the oscillation between the lost and the found is potentiality and thus force. (And as will be seen there is the possibility of rethinking the ethical beyond the hold of a more generalized problematic of loss.) Recovery here already introduces a sense of production into a concern with the good. Absence is not loss but the failure to actualize; with this failure potentially, precisely because of its anoriginality, still endures. The "original predisposition" remains. This *Anlage* (predisposition) is the basis of the possibility of human morality, thus it is the locus of "pure practical reason" as such. What is recovered therefore, a recovery supplanting loss, is the force of law. That force, law's force, is named here as "the purity of the law"; namely, the law's formal presence (*puram legem*).

———◦———

The next stage in the development of this specific aspect of Kant's project is the identification of the subject position, and the structuring of that position, that is appropriate to a relation between the conditioned and the unconditioned, and where the nature of that relation is expressed in terms of the centrality of the possibility of activity. In this context activity, as has already been noted, is named as striving. To the extent that there has to be a sense of striving and that striving involves the presence of others and not just the self, then the activity demanded by the difference between the conditioned and the unconditioned and which is maintained by the temporality of *at-the-same-timeness*, brings both *being-in-relation* and *being-in-place* into play. Hence, the formulation that "a good that is the *highest good* in the world" could only ever be possible, to use the formulation of *Religion within the Bounds of Mere Reason*, "through our cooperation."[42] The possibility of the worldliness of the world, demands both the world and *being-in-relation* (and, of course, those moments in which relationality, commonality, and place are themselves anoriginally interarticulated.) In regard to the continuity of action, and where that continuity has to be thought in terms of striving, striving is as a result action staging the effective presence of the unconditioned. Striving is linked to the continuity of action that occurs in relation to the unconditioned. In other words, in play here are actions sustaining the force of law. This is a setup that for Kant is encapsulated by the term *duty*. Duty precisely because it is staged in relation to the unconditioned brings a constitutive gap between "maxim" and "deed" in to play. This "between" ("*zwischen*") becomes "a large gap" ("*ein grosser Zwischenraum*"), therefore, a significant and always already present, thus ineliminable, "between space." Hence, it should be understood as a version of *at-the-same-timeness* that maintains, once again, both the activity of duty and the possibility of judgments being made in relation to duty's possible realization.

The centrality of striving allows the relation to the unconditioned and thus to that which has been delimited by the force of law to be renamed as "holiness." Holiness has a specific determination in Kant's writings. As a term it appears in a number of texts. Crucially for these concerns it appear in both the *Critique of Practical Reason* and *Religion within the Bounds of Mere Reason*. It is the context of the second of these texts he argues that,

> The original good is the *holiness of maxims* in the compliance to one's duty, hence merely out of duty, whereby a human being, who incorporates this purity into his maxims, though on this account still not holy as such (for between maxim and deed there still is a wide gap), is nonetheless upon the road of endless progress toward holiness [*dennoch auf dem Wege dazu ist, sich ir im unendlichen Fortschridt zu nähren*].[43]

Holiness as the term is defined in the *Critique of Practical Reason*, is the "complete conformity of the will with the moral law."[44] While this may be an impossible state of affairs if thought in terms of the immediacy of its realization, there needs to be what Kant describes in the passage cited above as a movement toward "holiness." There is an "endless or infinite going forth" ("*ins Unendliche gehend*"). Hence, "holiness," rather than as an end that can be defined in terms of its own necessary actualization, exerts a regulative force precisely because of its presence as unactualized. Moreover, it is possible to think of the "holiness" with(in) human beings as integral to the being of being human's own potentiality. The continuity of the possibilities within and for life, have to be thought as the continual actualization within life, again where the latter is understood as continuity, of finitude's movement toward "holiness"; again the *insistence of finitude*. It is essential here to argue that perfectibility should be understood as perfect-*ibility*. In other words, what the term identifies is a potentiality and thus a capacity for "holiness" (where the latter is defined in terms of striving rather than the necessity of actuality). Unactualizable in its own terms, and of necessity, and therefore has to be understood as given with, and within, the process already identified in terms of "endless progress." Holiness cannot be thought other than in relation to the dominance of the concept of potentiality that remains and endures with its actualization, that has been developed thus far and which creates as much the possibility of judgment as providing a conception of finitude defined in terms of the latter's insistence.

The significant point is therefore that "holiness" is not a position that is external to human being. Rather it is a potentiality with(in) human being. It should be clear therefore that not only is it a term that can be used to describe the relationship between reflection and propriety, what it underscores is the position that what is given by reflection, namely, a sense of inner accord, cannot be thought instrumentally, if the interplay between reflection and propriety is to be maintained. The refusal of instrumentality announces the inscribed presence of the "pure" and of "purity." This is a setting that can be linked to what is identified elsewhere as "the true vocation of reason," which is reason's determinablity. That "vocation" "must be to produce a will that is good, not perhaps *as a means* to other purposes, but *good in itself*, for which reason was absolutely necessary. This will need not, because of this, be the sole and complete good, but it must still be the highest good and the condition of every other, even of all demands for happiness."[45]

In conclusion, there is a confluence of terms: for example, *predisposition holiness, vocation, determinability,* all of which refer to the copresence of a relation between the conditioned and the unconditioned, a relation constituting a necessarily irreparable divide. Held open, activity within it, where that activity can begin to be accounted for in terms of striving, means that the ethical or the moral cannot be separated from life, and thus life as striving. Life as a result becomes insistent. To acknowledge the presence of the *insistence of finitude* is to affirm the necessity of *virtue in being*.

CHAPTER FOUR

JUDGMENT AFTER DERRIDA

Continuing involves, of course, another beginning. If there is a form of continuity, then it is given with the retention of life and thus as life's survival. Its living on, however, is not to be thought in terms that equate life with the demands of nature. The overall contention of this book remains that if there were a philosophical thinking of life, then it has to be located elsewhere. That location has already been given. Life is located, both located and lived out, within the space that has already been held open by the relationship between the unconditioned and the conditioned; a space that brings its own sense of fragility into play. As much as it maintains openness as linked to judgment, it is equally threatened by the possibility of violence. Nonetheless, it is the relation between the unconditioned and the conditioned that allows for finitude to have insistence. Continuing the development of a philosophical anthropology is to continue with finitude. To continue with finitude, is to begin again now with finitude recast as a series of questions. While it is always possible to ask What is finitude?, the question is more aptly posed in terms of what is it to allow for what has already been identified as the *insistence of finitude*? One question is presented with and within the other. Allowing for finitude is to allow for its disclosure. Allowing means therefore maintaining the space in which that disclosure occurs and thus to allow for the space in which finitude obtains. The spacing in which finitude is. The *insistence of finitude* occurs with the unconditioned, with an insistence on it, and thus with its coming to insist. As a consequence it can then be argued, in addition, that the unconditioned also has an insistent presence. In that instance it is a conception of insistence linked to immanence. It is immanent within finitude's disclosure and in so doing it works to allow genuine finitude a place. This is the project with which to continue; to open questioning means to continue with questions.

1.

Is the following an impossible set of questions? Questions asked by Derrida as part of an engagement with processes of forgiving. Derrida's questions intervene within the Arendtian problematic of the pardon by joining activity—pardoning, forgiving, and so on—to the question of the subject. To which it should be added that when the pardon is posed as a question by Derrida, the connection established by Arendt between the pardon and its interruption of time's continuity, and therefore pardon as bound up with the possibility of an experience occasioning interruption, is not present. The non-recognition, by Derrida, of the possibility of continuing as given by the interplay of interruption and renewal is significant. It shows itself, for example, in Derrida's continual use of the word *impossible*, and equally in the recasting of the relationship between the unconditioned and the conditioned in epistemological terms. These are positions that continue to emerge. As point of departure, however, the subject of forgiveness needs to be identified. He writes in *Pardonner*: "Who forgives or who asks whom for forgiveness, at what moment? Who has the right or the power to do this, 'who [to] whom?' And what does the 'who' signify here?"[1] At the outset it should be noted that the question of forgiveness, when posed by Derrida, continues to bring forms of impossibility into play while at the same time refusing to engage with the questions of both "right" and "power" that the formulation demands. (This refusal will return as significant.) As will be argued the problem of "impossibility," and thus the impossibility of forgiveness, needs to be located in relation to a figure, one whose forgiveness would seem problematic. The possibility of an impossible forgiveness and an unpardonable sense of the pardon, when taken together as questions rather than assertions, takes on a more complex quality when they are taken to have pertained, or thought to have pertained to Antigone; or more exactly, to her figured presence. In a way similar to the continual presence of Epicurus as providing a figure in terms of which to continue to rethink finitude in the context of Kant's philosophical project, the figure of Antigone functions in a similar way in relation to the pardon, and, therefore, to a concern with the manner in which both forgiveness and the pardon allows for a staging of the interarticulated presence of the ethical and the ontological, and thus for a further reformulation of what counts as *virtue in being*.

Antigone's is not just any name. What does it mean to begin within Antigone? The name stages a fundamental moment within the philosophical. Continuing, returning, she remains as a source that feeds philosophy. Nourishes it. Philosophy needs her. What is it that philosophy wants of Antigone? Even if her desire were acknowledged, what would it mean for her to be desired? To be wanted by philosophy.[2] At this stage, as an opening, all that can occur are gestures toward an answer. For Antigone what would always have to be maintained, if only as a possibility defining a future to come, is the emergence of a division within the philosophical such that she returns, perhaps despite herself, as a finite being insisting within a transformed conception of finitude. What occurs after the conventions that reduce finitude to the pragmatic is not a further denigration of thought in which philosophy would then return to the banal acriticality of "things" that could only occur with the abandoning both of the ground of thought itself and the positioning of judgment as occasioned by that ground. After finitude, after finitude, when thought other than in relation to its possibility, there is finitude's radical configuration. In other words, there would be a return in which another sense of finitude, the already present recasting of finitude in terms of the latter's insistence, hence, *the insistence of finitude*, played a defining role. There would be a return, in other words, in which finitude would then be thought beyond either its reduction to indifferent particularity or its determination by the concept. An understanding of finitude therefore that continues to occur in the space opened by the anoriginal irreducibility of the conditioned and the unconditioned. A sense of finitude that demands judgment precisely because it allows for it.

The figure of Antigone, who appears within the tragedies of Sophocles and whose place, at least in the play in which her eponymous presence is all, unsettles everything that she encounters. What sense is there in allowing the question of the pardon to be posed in relation to Antigone? In the play *Antigone*, she, the lawbreaker—though in what sense was she, in fact, a lawbreaker and thus ever truly guilty?—did not ask for forgiveness. Antigone's guilt is part of her figured presence. Her guilt is made. That guilt is only even an aftereffect of her having been subjected to the "written law," and this of becoming its subject. Hence, the importance of the question: What would be at stake in establishing a constellation comprised of the two terms, *Antigone* and *forgiveness*? While the question of the pardon, of forgiveness, occurs in a number of Derrida's final works, Antigone as a named presence in the play *Oedipus at Colonus* appears in his writings on cosmopolitanism, however, Antigone as the complicator of law—both civil and family law, laws both written and unwritten—appears, though only with Hegel, perhaps only through Hegel, at her most emphatic in Derrida's *Glas*.[3]

What then of this particular Antigone, her figured presence? The question necessitates paying attention to *Glas*. And yet, prior to that attention being given there needs to be a setting created. In *Pardonner* as part of an attempt to give a precise formulation to way the relationship between the unconditioned and the conditioned is to be understood, at least insofar as that relationship pertains to hospitality and forgiveness, he writes, and this is of course to reprise the formulation of Derrida's with which a beginning was made:

> ... the distinction between unconditionality and conditionality is shifty enough not to let itself be determined as a simple opposition. The unconditioned and the conditional are, certainly, absolutely heterogeneous, and this forever, on either side of a limit, but they are also indissociable. There is in the movement, in the motion of unconditioned forgiveness, an inner exigency of becoming-effective, manifest, determined, and, in determining itself, bending to conditionality [*se plier à la conditionalité*].[4]

There is, in the way the relationship between conditionality and the unconditioned is set up, a recognition on Derrida's part that genuine philosophical thought cannot do without the presence of "the unconditioned," and, moreover, that any sense of the conditional or the conditioned depends on the former's presence. To opt for the latter alone is to reduce thought to no more than either a variant of naturalism or the rule of the merely pragmatic. Thought would have faded, having been rendered otiose by the promulgation of one fallacy after another. There is, however, a genuine philosophical question here. One to which it will be necessary to remain alert, namely, the question that has already been posed: What is meant by the claim of the unconditioned "bending to conditionality" ("*se plier à la condtionalité*")? One aspect that would have to be included in any answer and which concerns how this element of Derrida's thought is to be understood, emerges from the following formulation of "unconditional hospitality" ("*l'hospitalite sans condition*"). Within this particular formulation there is the presence of what Derrida identifies as "pure welcoming" ("*l'accueil pur*"). While the details necessary for a systematic evaluation of this terminology cannot be taken up at this point, it is nonetheless essential to note that the presence of the term *pure* recalls the presence of a similar set of terms in Kant, that is, *reine, pura*.

There are two aspects of Kant's works that are recalled; that is, there is a terminological as well as a conceptual affinity between their projects. Purity in both instances has a specific domain. It is always located beyond the hold of calculation. While there is an affinity, part of the claim to be worked out in this chapter is that the full force of the "pure" when understood as necessarily connected to the development of the already present interarticulation of the ethical and the ontological, summed up in the formulation, *virtue in being*, escapes Derrida. Hence he fails to think the force of the very terms he is using. The rest of Derrida's formulation reads as follows:

> Pure welcoming consists not only in not knowing anything or pretending not to know anything but also to avoid all questions which have to do with the identity of the other, his/her desires, his/her rules, his/her language, his/her aptitude for work and integration. [*L'accueil pur consiste non seulement a ne pas savoir ou a faire comme si on ne savais pas mais a eviter toute question au sujet de l'identite de l'autre, son desir, ses regies, sa langue, ses capacites de travail, d'insertion, d'adaptation.*]⁵

What has to be noted is that in this passage the relationship between the conditioned and the unconditioned is formulated in terms that have a strong epistemological orientation. The formulation of the positions occurs in a language that pertains almost uniquely to either knowledge or belief. It is as though the possibility of maintaining the unconditioned in its relation to the conditioned was itself dependent on what he describes as "not knowing anything." As will be argued this recourse to the epistemological plays a significant role in determining how the presence of the unconditioned in Derrida's work is to be understood. It will be essential to return to this formulation of both the "pure" and the unconditioned, since the limit to Derrida's engagement with the unconditioned can be located in its presentation in quasi-epistemological terms, and then, in the subsequent failure to grasp that what is actually at work in the difference between the unconditioned and the conditioned is a setup whose force resides in the presence of a reconfiguration of the ontological in the terms set by anoriginal irreducibility. In other words, what eludes Derrida's strategy is the force of a setup in which finitude comes to be rethought. Again, what escapes Derrida, thus what he evades, is the possibility of the *othering* of the ontological: that is, a rethinking of the question of being as philosophy's other possibility, in other words, a thinking guided by a relational ontology, thus one in which *being-in-relation* and *being-in-place* play central roles.

And the *Antigone*?[6] The question of the play and thus the creation and the re-creation of the figure of Antigone and its relation to forgiveness are all to be approached here in terms of an engagement with the construction of that figure in Derrida's *Glas*. Hence, the twofold question: What is at work in *Glas*, thus in Derrida's interpretation or reading of the *Antigone*, Sophocles's play? The place of encounter, at the outset, is the character Antigone; the character that appears in Hegel's *Phenomenology of Spirit* and then, perhaps, in light of that appearance, in Sophocles's play. If there were a way of capturing the elements around which this encounter takes place, then it can be located in one of Derrida's fundamental formulations of the relationship between the figure of Antigone and Hegel's system. However, prior to addressing the passage in which this occurs, the question of Antigone has to continue to be posed.

Hegel draws a distinction between Antigone, the sister, the woman, and so forth, and, in a passage quoted by Derrida from the *Aesthetics* what he identifies as a "work of art." Of the later, Hegel writes that it is "the most soothing work of art": Derrida quotes and translates *"la plus apaisante (befriedigendste) oeuvre d'art."*[7] As a beginning it is vital to be clear here about the position Hegel is advancing. Hegel is making a claim about the play by Sophocles, the *Antigone*. He is not making a claim, in this context, about the character Antigone. Why he would claim that the play is the "most soothing" will always be open to conjecture. However, what has to be noted is that here it is not a claim about Antigone the character. Indeed, it is the separation between the play and the figure, not forgetting their moments of imbrication, that will itself come to take on a role of its own.

Derrida also identifies the character Antigone as "a figure." He describes her position within Hegel's interpretation of the brother/sister relation in the *Phenomenology of Spirit*, in the following terms:

> The effect of focusing, in a text, around an impossible place. Fascination by a figure inadmissible to the system. Vertiginous insistence on an unclassable. And what if the inadassimilable, the absolutely indigestible played a fundamental role in the system, abyssal rather, the abyssal playing an almost [*quasi*] transcendental role and letting itself be formed above, as a kind of effluvium, a dream of appeasement [*un reve d'apaisement*]? Isn't there always an element excluded from the system that assures the system's space of possibility? The transcendental has always been, strictly, a transcategorial, what could not be received, formed, terminated in any of the categories in the interior of the system. The system's vomit. And what if the sister, the brother/sister relation represented here the transcendental position, ex-position?[8]

Even for Derrida she is present as a figure. He writes *figure*. Consequently, there is a necessity, or so it would have seemed, to account for her presence as a figure. To ask what the figure figures. Anything else would be to naturalize figuration. Indeed, figures are neither neutral nor natural. She figures in one way, as one modality of figuration, rather than another. She is there. Though she is not just as any figure. Before returning to the question—about whom is Derrida writing? Who or what figures? further elements need to be brought into consideration. Even prior to that however, if only to complicate matters further, language intrudes. It also comes to figure. Hegel's description of the play *Antigone* in Derrida's French as *"la plus apaisante oeuvre d'art"* and then Derrida's description, of the character of Antigone as, *inter alia*, "*un reve d'apaisement*" needs to be noted. Would this dream unsettle? With a shift in the presence of no more than an acute *d'apaisement* would have become *dépaysement?* With this movement, one with its own sense of urgency, the peaceable is sundered by the impossibility of maintaining a singular now. The peaceable, precisely because it involves a form of subduing, once its presence as a complex site takes hold, will have been unsettled. The *now* in which it appears returns, turning back on itself becoming by affirming a specific instance of anoriginal irreducibility. Particularity here is the instant the apparent now within the *now* as plural event. Questions: What then of this acute? What would its introduction, it presence as silent mark to be voiced, have indicated?

Even though it would be almost impossible to try and grasp the detail of Derrida's interpretation of Hegel and the position of the character Antigone within the latter's philosophical project, and then Derrida's response to the same, a sketched summation is possible. The following elements would seem to be central. Sexual difference is thought within and only within the family. The move from the family as a sphere of nature to the domain of civil society means the overcoming of the family and thus the overcoming of sexual difference. In Derrida's terms, writing of Hegel, "the destruction of the family constitutes a step in the realization of *Bürgerlichkeit* [Bourgeoisie civil society] and the properly universal."[9] The retention of the family would both complicate and compromise the presence of what Hegel identifies as "Absolute knowledge," as the latter must involve a necessary form of purity. And yet, sexual difference remains precisely because of the way in which the brother and the sister are related to each other and as significantly Antigone and Kreon stand opposed to each other within a doubling of the law. Of these laws Derrida writes, "Each law is a law of death."[10] As Derrida's analysis continues what emerges with that analysis of what is taken to be an impossibility within, and for, Hegel's argumentation. Sexual difference remains even when there has been the sublation of the family. And therefore, the negation of the setting that was intended to contain the family itself fissures. In fissuring, it causes what should have been defined in terms of the separation, and here this means the separation effected and supposedly maintained by the process of negation, to have come undone. Nothing can relieve the family of its hold, not even the process, it would appear, of relieving it of its hold. Nature intrudes. Civil society both encroaches and will have been encroached on. As the passage noted above makes clear the "figure" of Antigone within Derrida's analysis of Hegel's Antigone, and here the citation underscores that Derrida is indeed constructing a figure, figures as a direct result of that analysis such that she cannot be assimilated to the system and therefore, in that act of exclusion, she becomes the system's "transcendental guarantee." This is the case even if it is a guarantee qualified in advance by the use of the term *almost* (*quasi*). She is there as an outside that secures an inside from which she has been expelled. She remains. However, in remaining, her remaining, thus what remains of her, her remains, become questions, in general terms the question of the remainder, with which various modes of engagement have to be staged.

Derrida's *Glas* begins after all, "What remains, today, for us, here, maintaining now a Hegel?" ("*Quoi du reste, aujourd'hui, pour nous, ici, maintenant d'un Hegel*"?)[11] Of a Hegel though equally of an Antigone. The remainder is always a question and precisely because it is a question, and here Antigone is the remainder, it has to be posed correctly. And yet, to ask what remains of Antigone involves, as a point of departure, not accepting her figured presence—either Derrida's or Hegel's—as natural. Remaining, remaining again, becomes possible, the 'again' is possible, her continuing to remain is possible to the extent that what counts as continuing is linked to the actualization of other potentialities. There is the *now* in which she figures. And thus this remaining, the other remaining, remains to the extent that the actualization of other potentialities has a specific determination, namely an undoing of figures. It should be added here that her construction as a figure is not in doubt. However, that recognition needs to be the beginning of an engagement and not a point of conclusion. Starting with a figure as a remainder means not remaining with the figure. Integral to her construction as a figure and the undoing of that figured presence has to be an opening. Undoing is a reformed deconstruction. The opening, while not determining, sets the conditions in terms of which this other, thus *othered* presence, can be understood. Moreover, at work within this opening are the disequilibria of power whose presence calls upon judgment the ground of which is that which this opening allows. The latter, allowing, needs to be understood as a potentiality the actualization of which is without guarantee. Actualizations and the instances of violence that occur can be judged because of the interconnection between potentiality and both *being-in-place* and *being-in-common*.

Antigone is not just there, remaining. More is involved. Derrida, it could be argued, accepts Hegel's contention that within the confines of the play woman acts in relation to the divine law (and in so acting she becomes woman). And that as a result woman *qua* woman, and Antigone is in this specific way a woman, though perhaps in no other, is, as a result, subject to the demands of the Penates. The Gods of the house dictate and determine their being; which in this in this instance is her being. And yet, of course, this now endures as a possible site of disruption; a possible site as its singularity is produced; a now that is only ever an aftereffect of a *now* harboring other possibilities. Recognizing that any now is an after effect of the *now*, is to recognize that was is at work, inevitably at work, is a setting in which other potentialities remain. This repositions the now, it becomes the *now* and is there as that which holds itself open to processes of transformation: this positioning, a standing, is a condition of its being. Transformation always involves a relation to an outside. Hence transformations cannot be simply self-generated even if their realization endures as an a priori possibility.[12] Created here, in all its complexity, is a setting that remains unnoticed by Derrida. It is as though a concern with processes of figuration are outside his concerns. It is this woman, this specific Antigone, which, in being offered by Hegel, is then taken over by Derrida. The significant point here however is that she is taken over in the terms in which she is given. As though she were fated. This gift and this gift alone is that which then works to undo the hold of the system. In Tina Chanter's succinct formulation of Derrida's position, "she is precisely that which cannot be thought, that which cannot be sublated but she is that upon which nevertheless the system depends."[13] However this limit to thought, Antigone presented as the limit condition, will always have been delimited in advance. This latter point is crucial. Limits can be naturalized. As a result there has been a doubled sense of limitation. Equally, this nature can itself be denatured. A construct can be deconstructed. The *now* can be opened. This is the already noted potentiality inherent in any *now*. Time and being are thought here in terms of the specificity of any instance of the plural event. It is the very condition of the *now* that its opening is a possibility that pertains as an anoriginal condition. Hence, any one now is already present as a plural event (any now is always already the occurrence of the *now*). This is what allows any one specific determination both its presence as a particular and equally that particularity, the particularity of a determination, its contestability.

The next stage in this encounter with what remains is developing a response to this positioning of Antigone by Hegel and then the engagement with that specific Antigone by Derrida. What has to be addressed is the possibility that despite this identification of her as the system's "vomit" Antigone remains. Remaining in a way that resists a complete identification with the figure in Hegel and then with Derrida's naturalization of her figured presence in his acceptance of that figure as Antigone and thus not as a construction to be undone. Moreover, it is an acceptance occurring with and within these terms in order that she can then have attributed to her, by Derrida, a deconstructive reality. The latter is the reality in which she is then the "system's vomit." She is nothing other than "vomit," not even potentially. Antigone is devoid of hope. She could not have figured in any other way. Why, however, should the delimitation imposed by Hegel and then after him by Derrida hold sway? Is there another possibility? Allowing for other possibility gives rise to two questions: Who remains? Who would this (other) Antigone be? These questions do not exist in a vacuum. Not only are there answers, it should not be thought that Antigone herself is unable to answer questions of this nature. Leaving aside both her location within the family and her presence as subject to an "unwritten law" (to evoke, as will be seen, the term that occurs both in the play itself and then also in Aristotle's engagement with it), she is still able to affirm her own identity. This does not occur at the play's end but at her end.

After her project has become impossible, and it should be recalled that Ismene describes her as "in love with the impossible" (90), she says of herself at line 811, that she is dying while still "living" ("ζωσαν"). She is taken to the place that is as much a "tomb" (806) as it is a place reserved for women. She may not be dying because she is a woman; nonetheless she is dying as a woman by dying in a specific place. Understanding the nature of that place occurs a few lines earlier in the play with the evocation of the Daughter of Tantalus. Her resting place, this other daughter, is like Antigone's. For Antigone her resting place is Niobe's. Antigone is Niobe. Or so she says. For Antigone therefore, if self-understanding were to be anything, then her measure and here it will be a self-measure, is set by Niobe and therefore acted out such that she has become the daughter of Tantalus. The language employed by Antigone is precise. For Antigone, there is a "sameness" ("ομοιοτατον") (833), announced by the presence of a shared "fate" ("δαιμων") (832–33). In other words, from Antigone's perspective, they have the same fate. Niobe's fate was to live on while dead. Living mute. Voiceless, speechless, forced to live, to use Arendt's formulation, in a way that is "literally dead to the world."[14] She is "mere life." The object of fate's wrath, fate enacted by Leto leading to the slaughter of Niobe's children by Artemis and Apollo, children killing children, meant that she, Niobe, suffered the death of her family as a result of her actions. Family actions. Antigone suffered as the result of one brother's death, though not directly as a result of the deaths of her brothers. (Though the question is to an extent absurd, could it not be asked: Was the second actually/really a brother?) In both instances what befell Antigone and Niobe pertained to the family. Here—though is it only here?—life had to be lived as defined by fate's ineliminability. Has she become her father's daughter? Is this what Antigone meant by that enigmatic formulation in which "likeness" is defined by the presence of fate? Was Antigone fated? Was she destined to act? Questions that in delimiting fate gesture toward what is other. It is in the *othering* of fate, which is the other of a specific temporal set up, that provides Antigone's other possibility. Fate's *othering* cannot be posited, nor can it be mere revolt, it has to be thought.

Answering the questions pertaining to Antigone's situation and thus her standing cannot occur *in vacuo*. Any answer necessities that "fate" emerge as a philosophical topos.[15] And, moreover, that fate once repositioned as part of such a topos can then be understood as a exercising a determining hold within what has already been identified as a politics of time. The latter is a political setup which when thought philosophically is structured, as has already been suggested, by the presence of the *now* as the site of multiple and inherently conflicting possibilities. The *now* is the locus of a specific concatenation of differing forces and therefore of the presence of founding disequilibria of power. The questions posed above demand answers precisely because they are posed in relation to Antigone's affirmation of her own identity and thus as her own attempt at self-definition. They cannot be avoided as though she was only ever a sister, only a woman. As though her identity as "sister" or "woman" accounts for all that her identity subsumes. Fate is fundamental. The additional point has to be made: Antigone's identity cannot be understood adequately without allowing for fate's registration. Even the chorus, in reminding Antigone that unlike Niobe she is a mortal and not a goddess, still concede comparability on the level of fate. She becomes as a god, insofar as her life, as with the lives of the gods, is subject to fate. Equally, what cannot be forgotten is the extent to which while living a different life, at least on one level, her life becomes her father's precisely because of the claimed effective presence of fate. (The chorus has already described her as: "Unhappy one, child of an unhappy father" [379–80].) Oedipus affirmed fate through revolt. He dismisses the prophetic riddling of Tiresias. As though once Tiresias is absent his words can have no impact. In *Oedipus Tyrannus*, Oedipus is clear: "when you have left you will cause us no more grief."[16] Antigone, on the other hand, responds to fate by yielding to its obligations. Antigone's identification with Niobe is to yield, yielding by constructing a determination of law as ultimately unavoidable. Even if this law were unwritten, the conception of law that pertains within this setting, endures as that which is driven by content, while its form is positioned as fate. The force of law, which here this is the force of the law evoked by Antigone, the law that allows for the comparability between her and Niobe, becomes the force of fate and therefore allows the question of the possibility of another conception of law's force to be thought. Indeed it is the very identification of law with fate that allows the limit to emerge. With that possibility's actualization there would then be importantly different permutations of the force of law. Here, in this precise instance, the force of law is equated with the force of fate. The affirmation of identity through fate, in which to be identified as fated is to have define one's position as a subject positioned by being always already caught within an oscillation between denial (e.g., Oedipus's revolt) and subjection. This oscillation generates a conception of subjectivity as always before the law as fate, before the law of fate, and thus fated before the law. Necessity as fate entails necessity. The latter, which is its enjoined necessity, is there as the result of having been fated.

Fate and law bring a specific form of space into play. It is not just the space that is opened and closed through the law's direct application. Here law's application is immediate in the sense that it works with the assumption of the already determined nature of the particular. Within this setting what passes for judgment is the immediate actualization of the law. (And thus within the terms of the argumentation of the preceding chapters, is not judgment at all.) The unconditioned, and it is only the unconditioned as appearance, is assumed to have been automatically actualized. However, the claim of actualization is of course the undoing of the unconditioned. The unconditioned's impossibility occurs when what is demanded of it is an actual impossibility. (It will be necessary to return to this point.) Actions understood in relation to such a conception of law, that is, where law is positioned in terms of the immediacy of its application, become that which makes the unconditioned impossible. In other words, to the extent that law and action refuse the need for deliberation, then they are nothing other than the already determined acting out of the law. Once again, this is fated necessity as the force of law. It can be argued however that such a conception of law's actuality and thus such a conception of determination is not a decision. Once law's application is immediate what is refused is the space of judgment and potential contestability. And yet, of course, the space of judgment has to be there in relation to the immanent presence of *being-in-place* insofar as judgment and thus decisions cannot be disassociated from the demand that there be a space of contestation: the latter is the locus where contingency encounters contingency and in which the discontinuous continuity of judgment takes place. Once judgment cannot be dissociated from contestability then the limits of fate emerge. Fate refuses contestation. However, once positioned as a judgment, a decision bringing its own *judgeability* into play, then even fate cannot preclude the possibility of a *countermeasure*. While fate's decisions in the end necessitate different forms of violence to secure them, they give rise at the same time to the possibility of the repositioning of fate in terms of another conception of law; namely, a conception of law with a radically reconfigured sense of force. (Law's force would now be the continuity of justice's projected realization.) The result of that reconfiguration would be the suspension of fate. This was a position that Aeschylus understood since in the *Eumenides* the inevitably of fate yielded, that yielding become apparent with the appearance of Athena and then with their disappearance. With Athena justice was relocated. Law's link to fate was suspended and justice was enacted with the inherently contestable decision of citizens. As a result, though more formally, justice would need to be thought as issuing from the anoriginality of *being-in-place* and *being-in-relation*. Justice would always work to secure *virtue in being* on the proviso that judgment maintained a necessary link to contestability a link that announces that othering of fate.

Within the *Critique of the Power Judgment* Kant holds open a domain of judgment that falls beyond the hold of the concept's determination; therefore what occurs is mediacy in the place of immediacy. It is not just that this opening allows for an aesthetic judgment, it is also that allowing for the judgment necessitates maintaining the space of its possibility. Allowing is not just an opening. It registers the hold of potentiality. In section 56 he argues that "If it is granted that we can quarrel about something, then there must be some *hope* [*da muß* Hoffnung *sein*] for us to arrive at agreement about it, so we must be able to count on the judgment's having bases that do not have merely private validity and hence are not merely subjective"[17] (my emphasis). *Hope,* as the term is deployed above, is not futural in any straightforward sense. Hope envisages a possible agreement. However, central to hope is not the agreement but holding to the possibility of agreement. In other words, hope is a condition of the present such that the future is equally a condition of the present. Once emphasis is given to hope rather than the agreement—and thus precluding the possibility that the agreement function as a *telos*—then allowing for the continuity of hope is to defer continually the end. Hope in the context comes to define the present; the *now* rethought here as the locus of "hope," the *now* as plural event.[18]

Contestability needs the open in which contestation can occur; in other words, openness as the place where speech takes place and violence is deferred. Once immediacy occurs and as a consequence *being-in-place* as that which in its particularization provides the locus in which, for example, the judgment of taste seeks approval, then become unnecessary there is a twofold implication. Abandoned in both instances is an understanding, first, of what autonomy will have entailed. Fate forestalls it. And second, what is also displaced is a conception of law in which coercion or compulsion are linked to the necessity of judgment rather than the imposition of that which refused deliberation and demanded that necessity be the outcome of necessity. Within this structure of immediacy what is displaced is law's other path. That other path is attended by a radically different sense of the force of law. On this other path, the possibility of the law, law's possibility, would endure as fundamental such that the grounding of necessity in possibility would mean, first, that necessity yields contingency, and then, second, that contingency would be identified with the nature of judgment itself. Such a conception of contingency would however not have undermined the necessity of law's formal presence. As a result the necessity of law's application would yield contingency as the effect of judgment. Here immediacy returns now as fate since fate stands opposed to the inherent contingency of judgment. Fate, moreover, establishes a tight bind between the force of law and content of law and their incorporation within the structure of immediacy. Within the latter necessity entails necessity and again there is both the impossibility of the unconditioned (and this will especially be the case when the presence of the unconditioned is thought in terms of the temporality of *at-the-same-timeness*) and the space of contestation. In regard to the latter in section 19 of the *Critique of the Power of Judgment*, Kant's argument made in relation to the judgment of taste involves the following important claim concerning the way in which a judgment of taste brings with it a specific set of commitments that pertains equally to the judgment, as they do to place. These judgments do not occur in isolation. The act of judgment both presupposes and demands the place in which the judgment "solicits" assents. Kant's formulation is precise. "Everyone's assent is solicited because there is (*man . . . hat*) a basis for it (i.e. that solicitation) in that which is common to all."[19] Here what is formulated is the necessity of the open as the space of contestation, a space held open by the nature of the judgment itself. This is not the space whose content is fated in advance. Accounting for that spacing, which would form an integral part of a philosophical account of the democratic, necessitates the way judgment depends on an opening staged by the relation between the unconditioned and the conditioned. The further implication is that this relation positions the open as the space in which questions of judgment, once understood as given within the interarticulation of law and life, are lived out (and therefore can themselves be judged). To which it should be added that the structure in which the realization of this complex set of interconnected judgments becomes possible is held in place by the openness created by the anoriginality of relations. Moreover, it is an openness that in conceding the presence of finitude brings, at the same time, criteria of judgment into play. To which it needs to be added, again, that the presence of that in terms of which judgment occurs can only ever have indeterminate relations to the act. Judgment is not the particularization of the universal.

———◆———

Antigone's identification with Niobe, and it is an identification that she makes for herself, an identification that is in part contested by the Chorus, opens up a range of possibilities. Others have noted and drawn on this staged comparison in which Antigone compares herself to Niobe. Writing of the connection Lacan argued: "In effect Antigone declares of herself and since always — I am dead — I want death. When Antigone paints herself as Niobe petrifying, with what is she identifying herself? If not with this inanimated state [inanimé], where Freud teaches us to recognise the form in which the death drive shows itself. This truly is an illustration of the death drive."[20] Lacan is almost literally referring to the passage in *The Ego and the Id*, in which Freud writes that the "task" ("*die Aufgabe*") of the death drive is "to lead organic life back into the inanimate state."[21] Here that would mean both Niobe's petrification and Antigone's entombment. Freud, however, underscores the impossibility of thinking the presence of one drive without the other. "The emergence of life [*Die Entstehung des Lebens*) would thus be the cause of the continuance of life and also at the same time of the striving towards death [*gleichzeitung des Strebens nach dem Tode*]; and life itself would be the conflict [*Kampf*] and compromise between these two strivings [*diesen beiden Strebungen*]."[22] To argue, as Lacan does, that Antigone choses death and that the link to Niobe is based on the attribution to her of the choice of death, seems to miss the point that Antigone herself is making. Dying and living on, living and dying define her stand. In the language of the chorus: "you alone of all the mortals while yet alive descend to Hades" (822). Standing on her own means descending living. What other hope is there?

If there is another question, the continuity of questioning yielding Antigone's other possibility, the process of *othering* Antigone, then its concerns as a question have to move from fate to life and thus to the question of how to understand Antigone and Niobe in relation to life rather than as fated in advance. It may be that what has to be allowed is the possibility of granting to her a sense of life that she may not have granted to others, or even to herself. What then of the claim of a shared *daimon*? This question has to be approached through recognizing the way fate operates. Retaining Antigone's structure of self-understanding for the moment, thus as a beginning, the argument has to be that fate works *via* the relation between sisters and brothers in which both are present in terms of their plurality not their singularity. (And where any singularity would have to be an after effect of this initial plurality.)

Even though Derrida is extremely attentive to what might be described as the fracturing of the sister/sister and then brother/brother relation there still may have been a certain haste in accepting Hegel's Antigone. If there is another way of understanding that set of relations when they are taken more generally then it involves the following considerations: There is neither a sister nor a brother, hence, there was never a brother/sister relation if all the components named here are thought as singularities. And yet, it is not difficult to discern Derrida's point of departure is the acceptance of sibling relations as the relation of putative original singularities. In the *Phenomenology of Spirit*, Hegel writes the following of the sister's relation to the brother: "The loss of a brother is thus irreplaceable to the sister, and her duty towards him is the highest [*und ihre Pflicht gegen ihn die höchste*]."[23] This formulation cannot be taken as mere description. It will always have been more than what occurs within, to use Derrida's formulation, any one "highly determined empirical situation."[24] It should be clear from the start that the state of being "without desire" is produced. Tracing this production is central. The argument has to be, therefore, that Hegel's own claim concerning both brother and sister amounts to the promulgation of an idealized creation which is then naturalized in order that it occur outside the political, with the further implication that this created setting then has to be undone in the move to civil society. What is thereby constructed is as a political gesture that attempts to efface the political by restricting it to "civil society." Recognizing such a setup, a process helping to redefine the work of reflection, is to have recognized the presence of a doubled inscription. Enter Derrida. What becomes untenable, thus, what is there as "inadmissible," is a created figure. Antigone is a figure.[25] Her creation as such, as a figure, marks her in advance. Responding to the presence of the figure and thus what its presence figures, necessitates that attention be paid to the processes of which this figure is itself the aftereffect.[26] If the play the *Antigone*—not the character Antigone—complicates Derrida's system, therefore, it will be for reasons that are entirely different to the ones usually claimed. It will be due to these processes of idealization and naturalization. Both of which are integral to the creation of the figure of Antigone; the figure figuring within the play *Antigone*.

What are the already present relations within which Antigone figures? To equate them with structures of kinship, while this may address part of their truth, fails to address the disequilibrium within them since structures need to be maintained. They demand their own conception of force. As a beginning, it has to be noted that to assume that there is "a" sister, only one sister, and thus to write as Hegel has done of "he sister," where the latter is thought as a singularity, is to have forgotten Ismene. Equally, to assume that there is only one brother—the singular brother—that occurs in Antigone's exclusive focus on the body of Polynikes as though that cadaver alone set the measure, is to have forgotten the body of Eteokles, or, as significantly, to assume that

Kreon's is the only possible engagement with that body; as though, in other words, his body were not allowed to haunt the interplay of conflicting laws and thus to play a role both within the tragedy and then with any subsequent attempt to establish a connection between the concerns of tragedy and a thinking of modernity. Equally, again, forgetting the body of Eteokles is to assume that this particular cadaver is either the locus of singular attention, namely Kreon's, or that it is forgotten. It will not remain. It could only function as a remainder were it to be remembered. Remembering both Ismene and Eteokles, the act occurring in the *now*, undoes, in advance, any claim concerning the possible singularity of either Antigone or Polynikes. Their singularity, in other words, is premised on maintaining a forgetting and thus of attempting to restrict the *now* to a now. What is forgotten is the set of relations that constitute any singularity. (It should be noted here that the majority of contemporary writings on the play would seem to be premised on the twofold forgetting that leads to the failure to think the presence of Antigone and Polynikes as produced and thus remarked entities in which being marked robs them in advance of any form of singularity and where that doubled origin, the original, as anoriginal denoted by the mark's presence, creates the interpretive setting.) Once the construction of the figure plays an integral role in any understanding of what its presence means, meaning as an after effect of its construction and within such a setting presence will have always already been figured in advance, then there will be different set of questions to which to respond. Responding to them needs to form part of the continuity of engagement with the question of finitude.

2.

What occurs with the possibility of acknowledging the forgetting of both Ismene and Eteokles is that a different question comes to be posed. Hence, there is another beginning. The question is the following: What if these other possibilities for the position of sister or brother were remembered?

Remembering here has a complex form of existence, since remembering is not mere chance. Remembering is being caused to remember. This demands that any engagement with Hegel's own reformulation of the brother/sister relation has to occur in a way that does not overlook his own forgetting. Remembering forgetting is significant precisely because what it indicates is that the singularity of the position held by Antigone and the one attributed to Polynikes need to be recognized as produced positions. Their singularity is organized on the basis of having forgotten that founding relation, a relation in which their identities were in fact aftereffects.

In regard to the presence of Antigone, once forgetting is remembered it will then have become impossible to argue, let alone simply to suggest, that her presence can be defined by any form of singularity, since her presence is remarked in advance by her separation from Ismene.[27] Indeed, it must be noted that as the play opens what is announced is the already present status of a relation; an instance of the more general proposition that relationality precedes singularity. Singularity always brings with it the trace of that founding anoriginal relation. (*Being-in-relation* marks human being; being thus has to be thought within a relational ontology.) In sum, both as a general metaphysical claim, and then, specifically, as it pertains to a rethinking of relationality in the *Antigone* at work in the acting out of the presence of an already constructed relation, is *anoriginal relationality*. It is this sense of relationality that, as has already been indicated, produces singularities. And, moreover, were a singularity to be thought as original, as opposed to the plurality that anoriginality brings into play, it would be premised on either forgetting or effacing the anoriginal presence of relationality, and thus the formulation of the being of being human in terms of *being-in-relation*. Recovering relationality as anoriginal therefore means linking finitude and singularity, such that both can be understood as aftereffects. Finitude is, is only what is, in it relation to the unconditioned.

The play—this "soothing" work of art"—begins with Antigone's emphatic statement in which she announces her specific *being-in-relation* with her sister Ismene. The opening line evokes commonality understood as relationality prior to any subsequent sense of singularity. The reverberations of the line continue within the play's unfolding. Audiences remember what they have heard. Theater demands it. The line is clear: "Ω κοινον αυταδελφον" (1). What comes undone therefore as the opening unfolds is this original state of commonality.[28] It is important to nuance this position, however. It is a state commonality that is only there because of a structure of kinship and thus it could be argued that it is not a sense of commonality other than one that is purely formal and consequently whose placeholders are themselves arbitrary. Nonetheless, what is still clear is that relationality precedes singularity; *being-in-relation* in preceding singularity marks it in advance. In the context of the play's opening lines what this means is that the present relation between the sisters, in coming undone, is such that the sister becomes the sisters. While the use of the term κοινον may do no more than emphasize questions of a kindred and familial relation that fails to hold, it is still a relation that comes apart. It comes apart from what it was. Antigone insists, at line 83, that Ismene pursue, "τον σον εξορθου ποτμον" ("your life [or destiny], maintain it as upright"). The latter formulation indicates that their paths have deviated and that not only have they arrived at different positions, they are now pursuing different ways, with different senses of propriety and therefore different senses of what is "right" ("ορθες").

Ismene condemns her sister's decision as "foolish" ("ανους"), but then adds in a hauntingly beautiful line: "τοις φιλοις δ'ὀρθως φιλη." Namely, that Antigone remains, as she says to her: "dear to those to whom you are truly dear." In this context ὀρθως can be read, once again, as underscoring a sense of propriety. The consequences of which is that the split between the sisters has acquired, for each, a different form. A deviation will have been conceded. Their accounts of their coming apart are, however, importantly different. (Evidence, it might be added of the secondary nature of any singularity.) For Antigone Ismene will have remained oblivious to the hold of the "unwritten law." Ismene remains ambivalent before the law because the force of law is mediated for her by the possibility of judgment. As is clear from Ismene's language her view is that "reason" has failed Antigone. Despite this failure she is still loved by those who truly and correctly love her. The key point here, however, is that neither love nor the set of obligations that arise as the result of love, which here is the identification of the ethical with both the place of woman and the family, do not orientate νους. Even though judgment occurs in the opening that holds love within it, love neither forms nor informs that spacing's contunity. There will be that which is other than love.

Ismene's judgment is that there is a fundamental and important distinction at work between love, on the one hand, and "understanding," on the other. This is a distinction which, in virtue of the separation between the emotions (where the latter is a term that continues to stand for the continuity of affect's presence) and the work of reason, allows for their subsequent reconnection. That connection, however, is not necessary. It is not as though family relations are located beyond the possibility of judgment; that is, the possibility that mediacy would stem the hold of immediacy. A stemming that would construct an opening, a place, the place moreover in which finitude holds sway. For Ismene it could be argued that love and reason have to be interarticulated or that the concerns of love have to be subject to reason. (Hence, this might be an intimation of that thinking of finitude in which finitude is defined by the necessity of the universal and thus in relation to the unconditioned.) While for Antigone, on the other hand, there is only one form of obligation. It resides in the "unwritten law" that links Ismene and Antigone in the play's opening lines but which, with the separation of reason and love by the time line 99 is reached, no longer exerts its power. Its force as a locus of commonality has come undone. It was unmade by Antigone. This unmaking recasts finitude. In the process it would have lost its insistence. It becomes a form of subjugation in which fate and unfreedom stem the hold of the decision and thus freedom. Retaining the insistence of finitude is only possible if the opening in which finitude is given within relationality is itself maintained. This position can be reinforced by recalling the point made above concerning the audience. The opening lines are heard and remembered. The undoing of commonality would have been heard. By the time line 99 is reached, the fraying of commonality, the disruption of mediation, and the gradual emergence of conflicting senses of immediacy are all at work. Immediacy occurs because commonality has come undone. This sundering and the different forms it takes, confirms that conflict continues continually marked by its inception and thus its possibility. The conflict is therefore marked in advance.

It is not as though the Antigone remained unnoticed within the history of Greek philosophy. In his *Rhetoric* Aristotle draws an important distinction between "written" and "unwritten laws": "Antigone in Sophocles justifies herself for having buried Polynikes contrary to the law of Kreon [παρα τον του Κρεοντος νομον], but not contrary to the unwritten law [τον αγραφον]."[29] While this examination of the distinction between the written and the unwritten law is of fundamental importance, of greater significance for these current concerns is Aristotle's description of Antigone's actions as "contrary to the law of Kreon" ("παρα τον του Κρεοντος νομον"). In other words, implicit in Aristotle's formulation is the recognition that what is at work are laws that have been simply created. (Therefore, the status of the creator— the author of the law—has to be brought into consideration.) In this context what this means is that they are the laws of a "tyrant."[30] These laws are the ones that Aristotle has already identified as "the laws of Kreon." Within the context of the play his presence as a tyrant is underscored in a number of different ways. When, for example, Haemon says at 745 that Kreon "tramples" on the laws of gods, this is evidence of tyrannical behavior. The counter estimation is of course Hegel's. He argues that: "Kreon is not a tyrant. But rather the championing of something that is also an ethical power."[31] The contention being worked through in this chapter is that Kreon's is not, *stricto sensu*, an ethical position, precisely because judgment brings within it the necessity for what in general terms has to be described as the contestable decision. The latter locates the decision in a setting similar to the finite and the contingent. As a result there would need to be a more complex account of tyranny, one that cannot be reduced to the identification of tyranny with the presence of tyrannical acts. Breaking that reductive identification means that tyranny is better understood within the framework created by Arendt's conception of violence.

In general, it can be argued that tyranny entails that the force of law resides in the relationship between two interrelated forms of necessity. The necessity of law is enacted within the necessity of its actualization. However, in Kreon's case tyranny means that the presence of law is underscored by the simultaneity of the presence of force and violence set within a disequilibrium of power. Hence, the identification of force and violence opens up the possibility of a different formulation of the force of law. Kreon invents a law that positions Antigone as outside the law. And yet in *Oedipus at Colonnus*, Oedipus pleads that he not be thought of as *anomos*. "Do not look upon me as outside the law." ("μη μ'ικετευω προσιδητ ανομον.") Given his own blindness his evocation of "being seen" or "looked at" ("προσεῖδον") is particularly significant. Oedipus recognizes that being outside the law is a produced position. The ubiquity of *nomos* entails that there is a sense in which subjects are always already before the law. Hence, it matters how the force of law is both understood and enacted. In other words, being positioned outside the law is not an original position and that it is always generated by the effacing of relationality (and the latter's claim to another possibility for the law). In *Oedipus at Colonus* relationality occurs in terms of the necessity and ubiquity of the stranger/host relation. A positioned affirmed at the play's beginning when Oedipus addresses himself to Antigone in the following terms: "Lead me, then daughter, so that we may tread where piety dictates, speaking and listening to others, and may not be at war with necessity. [και μη χρεια πολεμωμεν.]"[32] While what is meant here by "necessity" is open to different forms of interpretation, the argument is that once it is linked to "treading with piety" in the first instance and then "speaking and listening to others" in the second, what the passage signals is the necessity to engage with the presence of *nomos*. However, it has to be to a form of engagements that takes the dissymmetrical relation of stranger/host as the point of orientation in the first instance and *nomos* as an anoriginal condition of human sociality in the second.

In the *Antigone*, Antigone positions herself, locating herself before a law, the law to which she subjects herself where the law in question endures as "unwritten." Hence, as Aristotle wrote, her actions are "not contrary to the unwritten law [τον αγραφον]." And yet, when viewed more broadly, this "unwritten law" is not just another possibility for law, it is law as fate.[33] While Kreon demands that the response to a law devised by a tyrant and enacted tyrannically is immediate, the immediacy in question is not ground in fate as the "unwritten" but in the interplay of violence and creation. While these conceptions of law differ radically, one in relation to each other, they both coalesce around the presence of that conception of immediacy that closes the space of judgment. What matters therefore is as much the nature of the difference between the way the force of law operates with Antigone and Kreon as well as with the difference between them.

At work are two different modalities of immediacy that preclude the possibility of deliberation, the necessity of the mutable and thus the inevitability of contingency. Effaced, in Kreon's case with literal violence, is the very structure of judgment itself.[34] At work here, in other words, is a different, importantly different, sense in which necessity entails necessity. For Antigone it is a conception of law and finitude positioned by the necessary hold of fate. Fate is a form of necessity that would be countered by presence of the necessity of contingency. Fate precludes the thought of contestability and the space of contestation. This accounts for why actual places are so central to the play. Actual contingency, fate's *countermeasure*, is inextricably bound up with the necessity of contestability and the retention of the space of contestation. Hence, as examples, there is the keen sense of the relation between place and *nomos* that occurs in the opening of *Oedipus at Colonus*, there is the location of the body of Polynikes outside the city wall, then there is the doubled presence of the tomb. Living on in the place of death, she is to be buried as the bride. Developing this counter, a position inherently more difficult than thinking fate's negation, is to continue to respond to questions concerning how this other space of possibility would itself take form.[35]

3.

Note Derrida's concession of the relation that *Glas*, perhaps *Glas*'s protagonist, has to the character Antigone.

> Like Hegel we have been fascinated by Antigone, [*Comme Hegel nous avons été fascinés par Antigone.*] by the unbelievable relation. By this powerful liaison without desire [*sans desire*], this immense impossible desire which could not live, capable only of reversing, paralysing or exceeding a system and a history, of interrupting the life of the concept, of cutting the breath from it or rather, that which amounts to the same of supporting it from the outside or beneath a crypt.[36]

While on one level the opening of this account of fascination cannot be faulted. After all who would exclude themselves from the proposition, "we have been fascinated by Antigone." However, it needs to be added that fascination is the inability not to look: Orpheus turned, Eurydice vanished. Here, with Antigone/*Antigone* there is more than just fascination. The crypt to which Derrida refers is the "tomb." She is only ever outside because she is positioned as such by the system that has created her to be entombed. There will be a place of death. In it she lives on, to deploy the language of the play, as "the bride of Acheron" (816).[37] She is only "without desire" because Hegel has created her thus. Within both the *Phenomenology of Spirit* and *Glas* she becomes her figure. There would have to be another way therefore, another way for Antigone that resists the specular oscillation between the tomb and its outside; a space that falls beyond the tomb and its other. If there is another possibility for Antigone then it will demand rethinking her place as a finite being, and thus her possibilities as a being in place. There would need to be a thinking that allowed for *being-in-place*.

If there is a response to Derrida's engagement with the figure of Antigone, it is to be located in the way that he understands the figure's presence and how it comes to figure. As a point of departure it could be suggested that what Derrida does not take up is the possibility that the construction of the figure—and construction here has to be thought in terms of needing to maintain the anoriginal relationality, for example, Antigone and Ismene—marks the figure in advance precisely because the production of a singularity will always have been marked in advance. Hegel's forgetting of the figure figuring in the construction of Antigone as figure—that is, Ismene and then the joined and separated Polynikes and Etecoles—means, within the recognition of that forgetting, that she is simply unable to function as a singularity other than as a produced singularity and thus not singular at all. As such it would be impossible for her ever to function as a limit condition. She is produced by the system as its limit. She does not limit the system. She has been tamed in advance. What would cause the system to be limited therefore is the recognition of the process of her construction. The object or site of engagement is not the figure taken as an end in itself (precisely because it could never be such an end) but what produces it. Inherent in that production is the attribution to fate of a capacity both to produce figures and then subject them to the law of fate (fate as law). What is produced is a limit. This means that it is only by her complexity having been subdued that she could then be assimilated to the position of the figure that cannot be assimilated. What is "vomited," to return to Derrida's formulation, is her figured presence. That limitation would give rise to the question of what other possibility would there be for Antigone? This question opens up the possibility of there being differences within figuration. Responding necessitates taking up the already present demand of what would it mean to forgive Antigone and, in forgiving her, allow her to figure beyond the hold of fate and guilt. Could she have another fate? Could she figure in a different way? Finally, is there a form of living on without the continuity of guilt, divesting her of that continuity such that the economy of guilt will not have had an always already determining presence in advance? The force of this question, both its force and the only possibility of an answer, lies in having recognized that guilt cannot be disassociated from the subject position demanded by the presence of a twofold positing. First, there is the positing of guilt as an ineliminable quality of human being. Second, and relatedly, there is the positing of fate's inevitability. The *othering* of Antigone resides in the possibility of an ethics that is not determined by the interplay of impossibility and guilt. As a beginning this demands the reflective awareness of the positing of fate, of its having been posited. A setup which once recognized, as a consequence of that recognition, will have already undone fate's hold.

There is a defining element in the extraordinary passage in which Hegel identifies Antigone as indebted from the start. What defines her, Hegel claims, is that she knows herself to be guilty. To which it should be added that this is, of course, uniquely Hegel's supposition, moreover it would be guilt that determined the demand for forgiveness. The interplay of guilt and fate indicates that a specific logic is at work. Within it forgiveness and guilt would have an original interarticulation. Hegel wrote:

> It can be that the right which lay in reserve is not on hand in its distinctive shape for the acting *consciousness* but is only on hand *in itself*, that is, in the inner guilt of the decision and the action. However, ethical consciousness is more complete and its guilt purer if it both *knows* the law *beforehand* and the power [*die Macht*] against which it takes an opposing stance, and it takes them to be violence [*Gewalt*] and wrong [*Unrecht*], to be an ethical contingency, and then, like Antigone, knowingly commits the crime. The accomplished deed turns the point of view of ethical consciousness topsy-turvy. What the *accomplishment* itself articulates is that the *ethical* must be *actual*, for the *actuality* of the purpose is the purpose of acting. Acting directly articulates the *unity* of *actuality* and *substance*. It says that

actuality is not accidental to essence, but rather that, in league with essence, there is nothing which is granted that is not a true right. In terms of this actuality and in terms of its deed, ethical consciousness must recognize its opposite as its own. It must acknowledge its guilt: [*Das sittliche Bewußtsein muß sein Entgegengesetztes um dieser Wirklichkeit willen, und um seines Tuns willen, als die seinige, es muß seine Schuld anerkennen;*]

> Because we suffer, we
> acknowledge that we have erred.
> [*weil wir leiden, anerkennen wir,
> daß wir gefehlt.*]³⁸

Antigone suffers. And yet, *contra* Hegel, she neither acknowledges guilt nor links guilt to suffering.³⁹ At no point has she erred. It is in response to this passage, therefore, that it has to be argued that, returning to Derrida's terminology, "vomit," to have been vomited, to be vomit, and thus to be maintained at, and as, the limit depends on an acceptance and eventual normalization of the nexus between fate, guilt, and suffering. Suffering and erring working to delimit who Antigone is and thus to produce her figured presence. There is a set of questions that announce possible *countermeasures*: What if that nexus weren't accepted? What if the figure of Antigone were not defined by fate, guilt, and suffering? Giving rise to the further question: What if she weren't thought to be originally guilty? And thus what if she weren't held within a sense of an original disposition in which fate and guilt collided? Might it even be asked: What if she were forgiven? Clarification is necessary. She would not need to be forgiven her "crime," since she is produced as guilty. Rather, she would be forgiven her fate. The difficulty of these questions means that in order to answer them there needs to another configuration of forgiveness, one that brings with it the possibility of another figure of Antigone.

In the *Philosophy of Right* in his engagement with the way "extenuating circumstances" may have an impact of legal decisions, Hegel argues the following in regard to the possibility of pardoning of criminals: "The sphere where those circumstances [*Umstände*] as mitigating circumstances come into consideration in relation to the penalty [*Strafe*] is other than that of rights, it is the sphere of the pardon [*Sphäre der Gnade*]."[40] It is not just that what is involved here is the move beyond the "sphere" of rights, more significantly pardoning necessitates the introduction of another distinct realm and thus another domain of sovereignty. The sovereign for Hegel is "outside of right." Hegel is explicit. The formulation clear: "The right to pardon criminals [*Begnadigungsrecht*] arises from the sovereignty of the monarch, since it alone actualizes the power of spirit to make undone what has been done and to negate [*vernichten*] the crime by its being forgiven and forgotten [*Vergeben und Vergessen*]."[41]

Neither the crime nor the punishment is lived out. There is a form of absolution that attempts to separate the crime from life. The crime is both "forgiven" and "forgotten." This is the result of its having been nullified. It is as though, *qua* crime, the act had not taken place. The scars of the crime would have healed. The extraordinary line from the *Phenomenology of Spirit* would have been recalled: "The wounds of the spirit heal, with no scars remaining." ("*Die Wunden des Geistes heilen, ohne daß Narben bleiben*").[42] Or so the argument would run.

While it is always difficult to generalize from such a setting it is nonetheless clear that what is stake here is the problem of a relationship between the registration of guilt and the possibility of forgiveness in the first instance, and then the separation of the monarch's decision from the sphere of right, in the second. In other words, the monarch's decision is immediate, and as a consequence positioned beyond the hold of contestation. The decision is singular. It attempts to rid itself of the possibility of any appeal since appeal would necessitate, almost as a minimal condition, the evocation of rights. While differing determinations of forgiveness pervade Hegel's writings, appearing in one form in *The Spirit of Christianity and Its Fate* and another in the *Phenomenology of Spirit*, what matters in the case of Antigone (her figured presence) is that her guilt is defined in relation to law (hence, the affinity with the treatment of the pardon in the *Philosophy of Right*).⁴³ Indeed, it is possible to go further and suggest that any understanding of Antigone's positions as a Hegelian figure necessitates drawing a connection between law and fate as providing the way ahead. As a result what is left to one side is the discussion of forgiveness as it appears in the *Phenomenology of Spirit*. Moreover, if within Hegel's writings Antigone remains fated, guilty, and suffering, then she is not alone. And this despite clear differences.

Throughout *The Spirit of Christianity and Its Fate*, the Jews are defined in relation to fate. The two passages cited below present this position with great clarity. Within them what is important is the possibility (or rather in this instance what would amount to the impossibility) of Jews having another figure. This is, of course, another important instance of the naturalization of the process of figuration.⁴⁴

> The subsequent circumstances of the Jewish people up to the mean, abject, wretched circumstances in which they still are today, have all of them been simply consequences and elaborations of their original fate. By this fate an infinite power which they set over against themselves and could never conquer they have been maltreated and will be continually maltreated until they appease by the spirit of beauty and so annul it by reconciliation.⁴⁵

In the same text Hegel separates the concerns of the Jews from those of Greek tragedy. Nonetheless, what insists in both instances is the work of fate. He writes that the,

> great tragedy of the Jewish people is no Greek tragedy; it can rouse neither terror nor pity, for both of these arise only out of the fate which follows from the inevitable slip of a beautiful character; it can arouse horror alone. The fate of the Jewish people is the fate of Macbeth who stepped out of nature itself, clung to alien Beings, and so in their service had to trample and slay everything holy in human nature, had at last to be

forsaken by his gods (since these were objects and he their slave) and be dashed to pieces on his faith itself.[46]

The Jews were fated. They were, for Hegel, fated to live according to the fate that ruined them. Hegel could not construct the future for Jews beyond either self-ruination in which they are "dashed to pieces," or, in an act of self-completion, they overcame their fate through an act of self-overcoming. Judaism is overcome in the process. Paul's work becomes here the work of fate.[47] In both instances what emerges is the possibility of a *countermeasure*. The central question is therefore the possibility of living one within and on account of fate's subversion. What is constructed can be understood as their "fate." Moreover, what is constructed by fate is the subject position of the Jew. Fate, present here as a mode of historical time and a determination of identity, is integral to that mode of subjectivization that creates and maintains the figure of the Jew. Once the hold of fate is identified, identified as fate, then what has to emerge is the question of what is involved in the overcoming of fated existence. The question that attends the possibility of a *countermeasure*, attending by staging it, is the following: Is there an interruption of fate? For Hegel the interruption of fate was the arrival of Jesus. However that arrival is equally the completion of Judaism. (Again Paul is on hand.) Could there be, therefore, another thinking of the *othering* of fate. What matters in regards to both Hegel's Jews as well as Hegel's Antigone/*Antigone* is the possibility that both, the Jew and Antigone, could survive their fate. That the Jews might survive as Jews. And that Antigone live on. Antigone's living on, her survival, demands a form of speculation. What would then have to have figured is another form of survival. This speculation is not mere conjecture; it is bound to a form of the possible. In the fragmentary remains of Aeschylus's *Niobe*, Niobe spoke.[48] If that were possible, could there be a remainder in which Antigone survived? Could there be a possible fragment of survival?

Moving on from the hold of fate, perhaps allowing for the suspension of fate, what Antigone's figured presence would then demand is that forgiveness be understood as a possibility both in relation to the law and, therefore, also in relation to whomsoever it is that is empowered to forgive. In regard to the latter the questions of forgiveness, signaled by Derrida—that is, Who forgives? By what right?—must endure. The question that returns is clear: What does it mean to pardon? Pardoning may be one thing when what is involved are human relations and thus where the setting in question is not determined automatically by legal concerns. However, pardoning takes on a different quality when the law defines guilt. While it can be argued that Kreon's law is not the conception of law envisaged by Hegel's engagement with "right," nonetheless, what is important about the conception of law in both instances is that sovereignty is located in the possibility that the law be set aside. That there be the suspension of the law where law is defined in terms of relationship between necessity and necessity. Interrupting the already determined relation between necessity and necessity amounts to a genuine critique of law, namely, one occurring in the name of law.

Despite the presence of important differences, Hegel on the pardon repeats the conception of law that Kreon enacts in the precise sense that in both instances pardoning, were it to be possible, would depend on a similar sense of sovereignty.[49] Tyranny and Hegel's monarch are both situated outside the "sphere of right." Even though both may seek to invoke a conception of right as that which grounds law. Equally, of course, Antigone could not pardon. However, and this is the significant point, she is not guilty in any original sense because guilt is constructed by the identification of the force of law with the force of fate. She in constructed both as guilty and as "vomit." Moreover, the weave between the two is ineluctable. What has to occur, therefore, is what was identified earlier as a deconstruction of that construction. The response to this setup in which guilt and vomit figure as figures would have to be positioned in relation to Derrida on the pardon. It is only that placing that would allow for the overlap of Antigone and *the insistence of finitude*. There will be a return that continues to be there in terms of fate's *othering*. A turn that still awaits.

4.

In *Pardonner* Derrida writes: "There is only forgiveness, if there is such a thing, of the un-forgivable. Thus forgiveness, if it is possible, if there is such a thing, is not possible, it does not exist as possible, it only exists by exempting itself from the law of the possible, by impossibilizing itself, so to speak, and in the infinite endurance of the im-possible as impossible."[50] What has to be argued is that Derrida's formulation, while in part accurate, also contains systematic failures. As a beginning, accuracy and failure are both held in place by the term *impossibility*. "Impossibility" marks for Derrida the consequence of the relation between the unconditioned and the conditioned. It is as though the necessary presence of the unconditioned is not simply challenged but would be checked irreparably and thus rendered impossible by the exigencies that accompany the presence of the conditioned and thus conditioned acts. What will have to emerge is that neither the nature of finitude nor how finitude comes to acquire the quality that it has have been understood. Forgiveness, the pardon, as conditioned acts, and thus as moments in which finitude's insistence obtains, already depend on the nonactualizability of the unconditioned. What this means, of course, is that "impossibility" has an importantly different register. This is the very condition of singularity and thus the possibility of the decision, decisions enjoining responsibility. Hence, the presence of the setting in which necessity entails contingency. It is not as though absolute forgiveness is impossible. The point is that the unconditioned cannot be thought in terms of either its own possibility or impossibility. The immanent presence of the unconditioned, recalling Kant's formulation, "immanent for practical purposes," demands another thinking, first, of what presence means in such a context and therefore, second, of how singularity is both to be understood and judged.

While the structure is correct insofar as the hold of the unconditioned does generate a sense of impossibility, what it makes possible is an ethics without the nexus of fate and guilt.⁵¹ Guilt would cede its place to the conception of responsibility that arises with the recognition of finitude as descriptive of life to which the already present status of *being-in-relation* and *being-in-place* provide the ground of judgment. However, this for Derrida is an impossibility. Even though he writes, tentatively and inconclusively of the possibility of the pardon, what remains is a description of a guilt "beyond all expiation."⁵² And here the point is that guilt, rather than having been produced, takes on an original form. Derrida accepts the fate of guilt by accepting guilt as fate. It is the setting provided by the accepted originality of guilt and fate that needs to be connected to the affirmed retention of guilt that occurs in the following:

> I have just said "experience" of forgiveness or the gift, but the word "experience" may already seem abusive or precipitous here, where forgiveness and gift have perhaps this in common, that they never present themselves as such to what is commonly called an experience, a presentation to consciousness or to existence, precisely because of the aporias that we must take into account; and for example—to limit myself to this for the time being—the aporia that renders me incapable of giving enough, or of being hospitable enough, of being present enough to the present that I give, and to the welcome that I offer, such that I think, I am even certain of this, I always have to be forgiven, to ask forgiveness for not giving, for never giving enough, for never offering or welcoming enough. One is always guilty, one must always be forgiven the gift. And the aporia becomes more extreme when one becomes conscious of the fact that if one must ask forgiveness for not giving, for never giving enough, one may also feel guilty and thus have to ask forgiveness on the contrary, for giving, forgiveness for what one gives, which can become a poison, a weapon, an affirmation of sovereignty, or even omnipotence or an appeal for recognition.⁵³

What this passage signals—and its detail resists complete exploration—is a sustained misunderstanding of the relationship between the unconditioned and the conditioned. Note that Derrida writes of "the aporia that renders me incapable of giving enough [*assez*], or of being hospitable enough [*assez*]." What is the status of this "enough" ("*assez*")? And then how is the ensuing *aporia* to be understood? Two aspects of what is involved need to be stated in advance. First, since nothing has been lost, there is nothing to mourn. Invoking mourning is to do no more than resist the demands of finitude's insistence. Second, this incapacity is not a locus of guilt. It is the locus of responsibility. A space in which activity, here the continual actualization of that which is only ever "enough," can be recast, to recall Kant's formulation, as "striving." This setting yields a subject who is never guilty if guilt has what might be described as an "always already" quality. Maintaining such a quality is nothing other than guilt's location within the nexus of fate, guilt, and suffering. In lieu of guilt, there is only ever responsibility. The place of the guilty subject cedes it place to the anoriginally relational subject positioned continually by *being-in-place*. As a result, this "enough" is simply not an "enough," thus never just an enough, as if the latter signaled, what may be presented again as "merely enough," and thus is simply a continuity of failure. The "enough" is the mark of finitude, the mark of finitude's insistence, *the insistence of finitude* within placed relationality. There can only ever be this enough, the "enough" is not just good enough. On the contrary, it is the mark of the ethical act. All there is, is this "enough." There isn't an *aporia*. It is the moment, the determined "now"— and it will only ever be "a moment" this "now"—the moment within/of *at-the-same-timeness* in which the unconditioned is there "bending to conditionality" ("*se plier à la conditionalité*").

And again this "enough"' remains. It endures, though now as a question. What if this "enough," as suggested above, continued to mark out the only possibility for the ethical precisely because the enough, now a generalized condition and not just a mere citation, was not the locus of guilt and a conception of impossibility marked by differing problematic of loss. What if this 'enough' were simply the conditioned? And thus the insistent presence of an *aporia* could then be redefined in terms of an anoriginal spacing held in place by the temporality of *at-the-same-timeness*? This would have been the *othering* of the aporetic. While it is taken out of context, the line that has to be retained, if only to allow it to be acknowledged as a key formulation within the conception of the ethical within Derrida's philosophical project, is the following: '*One is always guilty*" (emphasis added). It cannot be reinforced enough that the only force that this claim can have, leaving aside directly theological notions of "original sin," is that the process of being a subject is defied by fate. To which the rider of the impossibility of that fate's suspension then needs to be added. In sum, the argument is not that Derrida cannot think beyond the hold of guilt. It is, rather, that guilt only holds because of its interarticulated presence with fate. Finitude is not a locus of guilt. It is the name of the conditionality to which the unconditioned continues to bend.

If there is a way of bringing this overall project to a close— closing again by providing beginnings—then it can be located in Derrida's return to the law and the law's involvement. Both occur for these purposes in his engagement with the unconditioned. He writes of: "The Law [*La Loi*] of unconditional hospitality," and then goes on to add in relation to it that in its application it is "offered *a priori* to all others [à tout autre] to all who arrive [à tout arrivant] regardless, and the conditional laws of a right to hospitality without which the Law of hospitality would risk remaining a pious desire, irresponsible, without form and without effect, indeed of perverting itself in each instance."[54]

In other words, for Derrida, there is a necessity built into the unconditioned. Indeed, it is the unconditioned that provides that necessity. There is a move from that which is "*a priori*," a formulation that accords with the elements of anoriginality, to conditioned actions. Those actions, for Derrida occurs such that any form of "comportment is not dictated, programmed or normalized by anything which serve as a rule of mechanical application."⁵⁵ While this becomes a formulation of finitude, moreover, it is a conception of finitude as that which is disclosed by the infinite, that is, the unconditioned—and moreover there is the absence of obligation that accords with the link established between contingency and the *insistence of finitude*, there is fundamental absence in this formulation. Further, it is an absence that has a sustained ubiquity in Derrida's engagements with this topic.

What is lost is a ground of judgment. How could any claim be made in relation to actions undertaken, or more significantly not undertaken in regard to pragmatic instances pertaining to hospitability (though the argument then extends to include, responsibility, forgiveness, etc.) without the ground of judgment being given within, and as, the unconditioned. Once this is the case, then there is the enjoined project, again not undertaken, to think the unconditioned. The unconditioned can acquire content without there being any undoing of its unconditioned nature. The unconditioned is not undone by the possibility of application. There is a conception of the relation between the unconditioned and the conditioned that is not just that of "mechanical application." Moreover, it necessitates retaining what was referred to earlier as the unconditionality of the unconditioned. This is what makes striving possible. In addition, it is precisely this state of affairs for which Kant was allowing in his use of the term *immanent*. The error that is made is to think that because of the absence of a determinate or causal relation between the unconditioned and the conditioned it is then possible to go on and argue that any conception of the latter is already an undoing of the unconditioned nature of the unconditioned. Hence Derrida's use of formulations presenting complex sets of connections defined in terms of the possibility of the impossible.⁵⁶ At risk here is not the possibility of the unconditioned, since the unconditioned is by definition unpresentable (which simply means that in order for it to remain effective it cannot be actualized). It is rather that without having provided the unconditioned with content while still allowing for its unconditionality to be retained, this is after all what was at work in the use of the formulations *being-in-relation* and *being-in-place*, what is then lost is the possibility of judgment itself. This is the point that has it be pursued.

Note the two following formulations of the "law," and the way that for Derrida the relationship between the law and the unconditioned is presented given the ineliminability of laws (the latter always in the plural). In sum, the former is always present as a form of singularity, while second is always in the plural.

> 'La loi' [The Law] as the unconditioned is above the laws. It is therefore illegal, transgressive, outside the law [*hors la loi*], as an anomic law nomos a-nomos, law above the laws and law outside the law . . . [(*comme une loi anomique*), *nomos a-nomos, loi au-dessus des lois et loi hors la loi* . . .][57]

> This unconditional law of hospitality, if one can think that, will be therefore a law without imperative, without order and without obligation. In sum, a law without law. [*ce serait donc une loi sans impératif, sans ordre et sans devoir. Une loi sans loi, en somme*].[58]

The same problem is repeated in both passages. The problem can be summed up in terms of a type of positioning. The *above* and the *without* and the *outside*, all of which are Derrida's terms, are deployed to provide positions that ruin in advance the possibility of any form of productive relationality between the unconditioned and the conditioned, and when taken together they recast the unconditioned in epistemological terms such that it appears as the unknowable. And yet, the unconditioned need not have that quality. Moreover, the significant point is that it cannot have that quality if judgment is going to be possible. What this means is that while the unconditioned is *apart* from the conditioned such a positioning is contemporaneous with its also being, and at the same time, *a part* of the conditioned. This is the conception of the relationship between the conditioned and the unconditioned that was developed earlier in terms of both anoriginal spacing and the temporality of *at-the-same-timeness*. As has already been argued, this is positioning in which content was understood in terms of *being-in-place* and *being-in-relation*. It can be suggested further that such a conception of relationality is what Derrida had already suggested in the claim that the unconditioned was there "bending to conditionality" ("*se plier à la conditionalité*"). Contrary then to the formulations Derrida provides in both instances concerning the use of the "outside," the argument has to be that there is no outside the law. As has been suggested, this is Oedipus's recognition, equally it is the error made by the "man from the country" in Kafka's parable *Before the Law*.[59] The only "out-law" is the one who is produced as such. Hence, it is not an impossible position. It is, rather, possible only because it is produced as such. The produced out-law is marked by the law that produces that position. As a result the "out-side" is only ever inside. Antigone is outside Kreon's law; produced as such. Oedipus knew that he was only ever before the law. Taken as a claim made within the development of a philosophical anthropology, the impossibility of any outside is given by the anoriginality of *being-in-place* and *being-in-relation*. Further, when Derrida suggests that to be "above the law" is to be "outside the law" ("*hors la loi*") then this is to conflate two different senses of law. Law as the conditioned is either the statute and the pragmatic act made in relation to it. It may even be the case that in such a setting the law begins to incorporate the meaning of both convention and norm. However, law as the unconditioned, is neither the presence of an abstraction nor of law's absence. Law, as the unconditioned, would be the locus in which there would be an interconnection between justice, *being-in-place* and *being-in-relation*. Law as the unconditioned therefore has as its corollary the anoriginality of *virtue in being*. This is not law as an outside. It is rather the possibility of giving content to the law as the unconditioned. Derrida is wrong to suggest that it is "outside the law," other than as a produced position that causes the "outside" to founder in advance.. The correct formulating is to argue that it is apart from laws, where *laws* as a plural term marks the plurality of pragmatic instances of law (be they statutes, decisions made in relation to them, norms, or conventions). There is a relation that would undo the claim that the singularity contradicts the presence of laws in the plural. What emerges is the contrary. Namely, the possibility and the need to think their interarticulated presence.

If there is a way of bringing this overall project to a close—closing again by providing beginnings—then it will occur by noting what is implicit in evocation of Derrida's formulation of that which occurs "without obligation." Its presence needs to be linked to the position that emerged at the beginning of the chapter. There it was suggested that while, in the case of Arendt's formulations in which the pardon and the promise could be understood as allowing for both interruptions and beginnings, Derrida's approach to the pardon, defined by its relation to impossibility as the ground of the pardon's possibility, could not account for what it would mean to continue in the wake of having pardoned. In the passage in which it is used the formulation "without obligation" is intended to identify the presence of a "law without a law." And yet that it is not the case. What it identifies is an element of thought that is both far more important, if inherently fragile. What is identified is contingency and thus finitude. It would be to fail to understand the concerns of the ethical if they are thought to produce obligations without that account incorporating the difference between pathology and the conception of movement—for example, striving—that defines duty. It is a difference that can itself be explained in terms how of both the difference and the relation between the unconditioned and the conditioned is structured and continues, and then the way *being-in-relation* and *being-in-place* figure within that relation. Taken together they identify not just law's ineliminability, but how a reconfiguration of law's force occurs once what is taken as central is the continual possibility of the actualization of *virtue in being*.

NOTES

INTRODUCTION

1. Jacques Derrida, "La Différance," in *Marges de la philosophie* (Paris: Les editions de minuit, 1972).
2. The engagement with relationality throughout this book is part of an ongoing project whose concern is the development of a relational ontology. Part of the more general argument is that relationality is an already present force within the history of philosophy. However, relationality is effaced in the name of a singularity that is taken to preexist relationality. It is this position that has to be countered. I have developed a more sustained account of this project in my *Towards a Relational Ontology: Philosophy's Other Possibility* (Albany: SUNY Press, 2015). For the statement that forms a precursor to the argument presented here, see my, "The Place of the Ethical," *Irish Philosophical Journal* 5, (1988), 31–45. This book could be understood therefore as the next step in the development of what has been called the anoriginality of relationality.
3. G. W. F. Hegel, *Phenomenology of Spirit*, trans. A. V. Miller, (Oxford: Oxford University Press, 1998), 111.
4. Mary Wollstonecraft, *Vindication of the Rights of Women* (London: T. S. Unwin), 1891), 258.

5. The term *Vita activa* is central to the writings of Hannah Arendt. This book could be situated in the same domain of concerns, namely, the development of a philosophical account of life, that takes life as a complex set of activities as that which defines life. For a discussion of the term in relation, specifically, to her writings as a whole see James T. Knauer, "Rethinking Arendt's 'Vita Activa': Towards a Democratic Theory of Praxis," *PRAXIS International* 2 (1985), 185–194; Eric Wainwright, "The Vita Activa of Hannah Arendt," *Politikon* 16, no. 2 (1989), 22–38; and Jean Yarbrough and Peter Stern, "Vita Activa and Vita Contemplative: Reflections on Hannah Arendt's Political Though in the Life of Mind," *Review of Politics* 43, no. 3 (1981), 323–54.
6. There is an additional point here, namely, that the presence of "capacity," when the term is understood more generally, still does not entail the necessity of its actualization.
7. The insistence on the importance of potentiality as a concept that plays a decisive role within the history of philosophy as has been argued, in general, by Giorgio Agamben and in relation to the work of Walter Benjamin, by Samuel Weber. In regard to the former, see, among others works, the papers collected in *Potentialities*, trans. Daniel Heller-Roazen (Stanford: Stanford University Press, 1999). In regard to the latter, see his *Benjamin's –abilities* (Cambridge, MA: Harvard University Press, 2010). The position advanced here, and throughout other writings, has argued equally for the centrality of potentiality. The nature of the augmentation and how potentiality has been understood involve important differences. Nonetheless there is an affinity of concern.
8. This formulation of the relationship between law and life echoes the debate between Rosenzweig and Buber known as the *Die Bauleute*. This text is available in English translation in Franz Rosenzweig, *On Jewish Learning* (New York: Schocken Books, 1955). For other attempts to interpret this relationship, see Maurice Friedman, "Dialogue, Speech, Nature and Creation. Franz Rosenzweig's Critique of Buber's *I and Thou*," *Modern Judaism* 13 (1993), 109–118;

Richard A. Cohen, *Elevations: The Height of the Good in Rosenzweig and Levinas* (Chicago: University of Chicago Press, 1994), 28–39. Cohen's is a detailed and scholarly account of the exchange.

9. The central relationship that determines the argumentation of this book is between the "unconditioned" and the "conditioned." Other forms taken by that relationship include the "infinite" and the "finite."

CHAPTER 1.
TOWARD THE UNCONDITIONED

1. The formulation *disequilibrium of power* is central to the argumentation of this book and to other work done in attempting to develop a relational ontology. There cannot be any naïveté in regards to terms such as *relationality* and *difference*. A disequilibrium of power may be at work in sustaining difference. Equally power may sustain a sense of relationality that furthers inequality: the latter is both a relation and a relation involving difference. Arendt's conception of power and its opposition to violence becomes one way of understanding how a *disequilibrium of power* necessitates violence for its continuity and how a another conception of power is central to the construction (or recovery) of a counter to its naturalized continuity.
2. *Nietzsche Werke*, Kritische Gesamtausgabe, vol. I3 (Berlin: Walter de Gruyter. 1973), 177. There are many treatments of the "free spirit" throughout Nietzsche's writings. See, for example. *Nietzsche Werke*, Kritische Gesamtausgabe, vol. I3 (Berlin: Walter de Gruyter,1973), 55–56; *Nietzsche Werke*, Kritische Gesamtausgabe, vol. I2 (Berlin: Walter de Gruyter, 1968), 417.
3. *Nietzsche Werke*, Kritische Gesamtausgabe, vol. I3 (Berlin: Walter de Gruyter, 1973), 291.
4. For an opening development of this approach see my: "Having to Exist," *Angelaki*, no 2, 51–57.
5. The formulation "politics of time" is taken from Peter Osborne's seminal work, *The Politics of Time* (London:

Verso, 1989). While I have developed the term such that it has a different inflection, it is clear that Osborne is right to see that what is at work within the political—and it could be added, when the political is thought philosophically—is a conflict occurring within and defining the present between different forms of historical time. I have developed how the term is understood in my work most recently in my *Working with Walter Benjamin: Recovering a Political Philosophy* (Edinburgh: Edinburgh University Press, 2013).

6. Garve's *Philosophische Anmerkungen und Abhandlungen zu Cicero's Büchern von den Pflichten* was published in 1788, the same year as the publication of the first edition of the *Critique of Practical Reason*. For a detailed investigation of Kant's relation to both eighteenth-century translations of Cicero and Seneca, see José M. Torralba, "Stoic *katórthôma*, perfect duty and Kant's notion of acting *aus Pflicht*. The relevance of the *oikeiôsis* doctrine for the notions of moral good and inner attitude (Gesinnung) in Kantian ethics." In A. Vigo (ed.), *Oikeiôsis and the Natural Basis of Morality: From Ancient Stoicism to Modern Philosophy* (Hildesheim–Zürich–New York: Olms, 2012), 295–346.

7. Cyril Bailey, *Epicurus, the Extant Remains* (Oxford: Oxford University Press, 1926). This particular line is to be found in the *Letter to Menoeceus*.

8. Seneca, Letter XXI. See Seneca, *Epistles* 1–65, transl. Richard M. Gummere. (Cambridge, MA.: Loeb Classical Library, 1917).

9. Lorenzo Valla, *On Pleasure: De voluptate*, trans. A. Kent Hieatt and Maristella Lorch (New York: Abaris Books, 1977), 267.

10. The allusion here is intended to see a the possibility of a relation between moral action as presented throughout Kant's writings, and the notion of the genius developed in the *Critique of the Power of Judgment*. In regard to the latter, see: Immanuel Kant, *Critique of the Power of Judgment*, trans. Eric Matthews (Cambridge: Cambridge University Press, 2001), §46.

11. The use of the term *always the same* is intended to highlight the presence of differing ways of thinking about

difference. The *always the same* points to a conception of difference as variety. In other words, this is a conception of difference that involves quantity. The force of the claim here is that difference has to involve forms of irreducibility, and thus it is a conception of difference, understood as an ontological terms, that takes quality as its central element. Anoriginal difference allows for the possibility of judgment and therefore criticality.

12. The term *plural event* was first introduced along with the term *anorginal* in *The Plural Event*, (London: Routledge, 1993). All my subsequent work has involved attempts to develop both what these terms mean and then the extension they might have.
13. Tranquillity is to be understood here as a translation of Epicurus's conception of αταραξια. While it will be taken up toward the end of this paper, it is important to note that in Seneca's presentation of Epicurus he translates it as *"inertia."* See Seneca, *De Constantia*, XV. 4 (in Seneca, *Moral Essays, Volume I*, trans. John W. Basore [Cambridge: Harvard University Press, 1927]).
14. For a general discussion of the role of time in Nietzsche, see: Robin Small, *Time and Becoming in Nietzsche's Thought* (Continuum: London, 2010).
15. Both Derrida and Walter Benjamin have taken up the question of the possibility of suspending the death penalty and how such a possibility should be understood philosophically. I have discussed their different approaches in my *Working with Walter Benjamin: Recovering a Political Philosophy* (Edinburgh: Edinburgh University Press, 2013). 115–17.
16. For a detailed study of this section in *Daybreak*, see Morgan Rempel, *Daybreak* 72, "Nietzsche, Epicurus, and the After Death." *Journal of Nietzsche Studies* 43, no. 2 (2012). And for a survey of Nietzsche's relation to Epicurus, see both Marcin Milkowski, "Idyllic Heroism: Nietzsche's View of Epicurus," *Journal of Nietzsche Studies* 15 (Spring 1998), 70–79; and Richard Bett, "Nietzsche, the Greeks, and Happiness" (with Special Reference to Aristotle and Epicurus), *Philosophical Topics* 33, no. 3 (Fall 2005). For Nietzsche's relation to both Epicurus and the history of Greek skepticism, in

general, see Jessica N. Berry, *Nietzsche and the Ancient Skeptical Tradition* (Oxford: Oxford University Press, 2011).
17. For a critical engagement with the viability of arguments pertaining to *ataraxia* as it emerges in Epicurus's own writings see: James Warren, *Facing Death, Epicurus and His Critics* (Oxford: Clarendon Press, 2004), 153–59.
18. For a general discussion of the role of Epicurus within modern thought—that is, post-Renaissance—see Catherine Wilson, *Epicureanism and the Origins of Modernity* (Oxford: Oxford University Press, 2008).
19. There is an extensive literature on this topic: see, in particular, Anthony Curtis Adler, "Sensual Idealism: The Spirit of Epicurus and the Politics of Finitude in Kant and Hölderlin," in *Dynamic Reading: Studies in the Reception of Epicureanism*, ed. Brook Holmes and W. H. Shearin (Oxford: Oxford University Press, 2012), 199–238.
20. A detailed investigation of the relationship between Epicurus and Lucretius is staged in David Sedley, *Lucretius and the Transformation of Greek Wisdom* Cambridge: Cambridge University Press), 1998.
21. Immanuel Kant, *Critique of the Power of Judgment*, trans. Eric Matthews (Cambridge: Cambridge University Press, 2001), §53, 207.
22. The version of the text hat has been consulted here is Cyril Bailey, *Epicurus, the Extant Remains* (Oxford: Oxford University Press), 1926.
23. Immanuel Kant, *Practical Philosophy*, trans. Mary J. Gregor (Cambridge: Cambridge University Press, 1999), 261.
24. The connection between Maimonides and Alexander of Aphrodisias was established by Shlomo Pines. The latter's research is summed up in his introduction to his translation of *The Guide* (Chicago: University of Chicago Press, 1963). Herbert A. Davidson also suggest that Maimonides had not read Epicurus. See his *Moses Maimonides. The Man and His Works* (Oxford: Oxford University Press, 2005), 111.
25. Moses Maimonides, *The Guide for the Perplexed*, trans. M. Friedlander (London: Routledge & Kegan Paul, 1971), 173.
26. On the question of Epicurus's atheism, see: D. Obbink, "The Atheisim of Epicurus," *GRBS* 30 (1989), 187–223.

27. In Diogenes of Oenoanada, Fragment 29, there is the same formulation of "the blessed and immortal being" ("το μακαπιω και αφθαρτον"). Fragment 29 lower. This needs to be compared to Epicurus's actual text, *Diogenes of Oinoanda: The Epicurean Inscriptions*, ed. and trans. Martin Ferguson Smith (Naples: Bibliopolis, 1992). In Ambrosius Traversarius's 1535 translation, *Diogenis Laertii Clarissimi historici de uita*, The same position is formulated as '*deu esse animal immortale acbeatu,*' 664. The significance of underscoring the presence not simply of the words of Epicurus in the continuity of inscription and translation is that the differing presentations of his position allow God the constancy that the original position had always maintained. Ambrosius Traversarius's translation that involves the notion of God as an *animal immortale* is a position that continues to maintain the centrality of God. While definitions may be contestable, God endures. Hence, the actual issue cannot be atheism per se. Rather, it resides both in the conception of God and then in the relation between God and the activity of human life. It is in terms of this relationship that possible forms of affinity with Kant emerge.
28. Evidence for this position can also be found in Plutarch. See his *Non posse suaviter vivi secundum Epicurum*, 1011, B 21. Plutarch is quoting either Philodemus or Epicurus, though he is assuming that he is quoting the latter: "Now we should I grant you remove superstition [την δεισδαιμονιαν] from our belief in Gods like rheum from the eye." For a more general discussion of Epicurus's relation to the "gods" and the question of theism and possible atheism, and which is situated in current debates on the topic see David Konstan, "Epicurus on the Gods," in *Epicurus and the Epicurean Tradition*, ed. Jeffery Fish and Kirk R. Sanders (Cambridge: Cambridge University Press, 2011), 53–71.
29. Hermann Cohen. *Religion der Vernunft aus den Quellen des Judentums* (Leipzig: Gustav Fock, 1919).
30. See in addition A. A Long, *From Epicurus to Epictetus: Studies in Hellenistic and Roman Philosophy* (Oxford: Oxford University Press, 2006), 188–89. For a specific investigation

of Epicurus's positive engagement with the question of "community," and therefore with a sense of the common, see Pierre-Marie Morel, "Les communautés humaines," in *Lire Épicure et les épicuriens*, ed. Alain Gigandet and Pierre-Marie Morel (Paris: PUF, 2007).

31. Gassendi, Pierre. *De vita, et moribus Epicuri*, Liber Quartus Caput IV (Apud Gulielmum Barbier, 1647).
32. The key text here is Arthur Warda, *Immanuel Kants Bücher* (Berlin: Verlag von Martin Breslauer,1922). In regard to direct knowledge of Epicurus, Hegel also notes in the *Vorlesungen über der Geshiichte der Philosophie* that knowledge of Epicurus, even at the time he was writing his lectures, was based on Diogenes Laertius. See his *Vorlesungen über der Gescjichte der Philosophie* II, 300. Allen Wood argues that Kant's "knowledge of classical Greek philosophy was mostly at second hand (mainly through Cicero's Latin popularizations and via J. J. Brucker's *Historia critica philosophica* (1742–44)." See his Kant's "History of Ethics" in *Studies in the History of Ethics*.
33. Cicero, *De Finibus*, Book 1, 63 (Cicero, *On Ends*, trans. H. Rackham [Harvard University Press, Cambridge, 1914]).
34. Raphael Woolf, "What Kind of Hedonist Was Epicurus?" *Phronesis* 49, no. 4 (2004), 303–22.
35. Immanuel Kant, *Practical Philosophy*, trans. Mary J. Gregor (Cambridge: Cambridge University Press, 1999), 233. Equally within the complex history of Jewish philosophy, while Epicurus was taken to be an atheist, it was still possible to write of him that "he was not so deficient in discernment and philosophy as to deny of conclusive and convincing arguments." A position advanced by Uriel da Costa in his *Exame Das tradicoes Phariseas conseridas com á lei escrita*, 1623–24.
36. Seneca *Letter 90*, in Seneca, Epistles 66–92, trans. Richard M. Gummere, 1920.
37. See in this regard my "Raving Sybils, Signifying Gods: Noise and Sense in Heraclitus: Fragments 92 and 93," *Culture, Theory and Society* 46, no. 1 (April. 2005).
38. "Religion within the Bounds of Mere Reason," in Immanuel Kant, *Religion and Rational Theology*, trans Allen W.

Wood and George di Giovanni (Cambridge: Cambridge University Press, 2001).
39. See my, "A Missed Encounter: Plato's Socrates and Geach's Euthyphro," *Grazer Philosophische Studien* 29,145–70.
40. Immanuel Kant, *Critique of Pure Reason*, translated Allen W. Wood (Cambridge: Cambridge University Press, 1999), 702.
41. Immanuel Kant, *Critique of Pure Reason*, trans. Allen W. Wood (Cambridge: Cambridge University Press, 1999), 703.
42. Immanuel Kant, *Critique of Pure Reason*, trans. Allen W. Wood (Cambridge: Cambridge University Press, 1999), 500.
43. See in this regard 4. Proposition VII of the *Ethics*. Of equal importance is 4. XXI. "Nemo potest cupere beatum esse, bene agree, & bene vivere, qui simul non cupiat esse, ageree, & vivere, hos ext, actu existere." While it cannot be undertaken here, it is clear that the development of a philosophical anthropology that holds to the centrality both of judgment and inscribes the latter's possibility in the effective presence of the distinction between the "unconditioned" and the "conditioned" has to take a stand on the nature of ontology that involves a radical distancing of Spinoza and the legacy of his thought (primarily Nietzsche and Deleuze).
44. Kant *Dissertation* §9. In Immanuel Kant, *Werke*, Band 111 ed. Wihelm Weischedel (Darmstadt: WBG, 2001), 38.
45. Rodolphe Gasché is right to argue that pure means "separation and isolation." However, what needs to be added in addition is that the "pure" is located outside calculation. See Gasché *The Idea of Form: Rethinking Kant's Aesthetics* (Stanford, CA: Stanford University Press, 2003), 19.
46. For a more detailed study of section 9 of the dissertation in relation to Epicurus and the role of Epicurus in Kant's philosophy, see Klaus Reich, "Kant and Greek Ethics (1)," *Mind* 48, no. 191 (July 1939), 338–54.
47. The argument concerning abstraction and the limitations of abstraction will be developed in greater detail in chapter 2.

48. Immanuel Kant, *Practical Philosophy*, trans. Mary J. Gregor (Cambridge: Cambridge University Press, 1999), 90–91.
49. This is not to argue that there have not been attempts to see a profound rapprochement between Kant and Spinoza. See, for example, Beth Lord, *Kant and Spinozism: Transcendental Idealism and Immanence from Jacobi to Deleuze* (London: Palgrave, 2011).
50. Boris Nikolsky, "Epicurus on Pleasure," *Phronesis* 46, no. 4 (November 2001), 440–65.
51. I have tried to address this question in the context of both Sophocles and Hölderlin in my *"Leben und Glück:* Modernity and Tragedy in Walter Benjamin, Hölderlin and Sophocles," in *Tragedy and the Idea of Modernity*, ed. Joshua Billings and Miriam Leonard (Oxford: Oxford University Press, 2014).
52. Immanuel Kant, *Notes and Fragments*, trans. Curtis Bowman and Fredrick Rauscher (Cambridge: Cambridge University Press, Cambridge, 2010). Fragment 6837, 1776–78, *Pr* IX.
53. The force of the formulation—the worldliness of the world—is that it introduces a space of abstraction. Hence how is worldliness to be understood? This question will allow for the identification of a relationship between being and value that may have not been enacted in and by the world. Hence worldliness becomes a place of potentiality. Equally, as has been suggested, it is "worldliness" that allows for a distinction between life and "mere life" to be sustained.
54. Hannah Arendt, *The Human Condition* (Chicago: University of Chicago Press, 1998), 176.
55. Cyril Bailey, *Epicurus, the Extant Remains* (Oxford: Oxford University Press, 1926), 91.
56. It should not be thought that the reception of Kant and Epicurus has not involved attempts to reconcile their projects. See in this regard, Jules Vuillemin, "Trois philosophes intuitionnistes: Epicure, Descartes et Kant," *Dialectica* 35, no's. 1–2 (1981).
57. Immanuel Kant, *Practical Philosophy*, trans. Mary J. Gregor (Cambridge: Cambridge University Press, 1999), 230.

58. Bailey suggests that μελετᾶν could also be understood as "meditate upon." See Bailey, *Ioan Scapulae Lexicon Graeco-latinum*, 1663, 321. Provides a Latin translation as *"meditatio."*
59. See, in this regard, the important argument by Gisela Striker concerning both Stoics and the Epicureans. She claims that:

> They rightly started from the assumption that there is a significant distinction to be made between the human good and what people might imagine that to be, so that even believing that one has got all that one might wish for will not be sufficient for a good life. Hence they saw their task as determining what should count as a real good, and eventually to show that a happy life required virtue.

Gisela Striker, "Ataraxia: Happiness as Tranquility," *The Monist* 73, no. 1, Hellenistic Ethics (January 1990), 97–110; here 109.
60. Cyril Bailey, *Epicurus, the Extant Remains* (Oxford: Oxford University Press), 1926, 87.
61. I have tried to explore this tension in Kant's writings in a number of places. See my, "Towards an Affective Structure of Subjectivity: Notes on Kant's An Answer to the Question: What Is the Enlightenment?" *Parallax*, 18, no. 4 (2012), 26–41.
62. Kant, *Religion within the Bounds of Mere Reason*, 282.
63. G. W. F. Hegel, *Vorlesungen über die Geschicte der Philosophie*, II (Frankfurt am Main: Suhrkamp Verlag, 1982), 297.
64. Immanuel Kant, *Critique of Pure Reason*, trans. Allen W. Wood (Cambridge: Cambridge University Press, 1999), B372.

CHAPTER 2.
ARENDT AND THE TIME OF THE PARDON

1. Jacques Derrida, *Pardonner* (Paris: Editions Galilée, 2010). There are other arguments and other versions of this form

of forgiveness. See Eve Garrard and David McNaughton, "In Defense of Unconditional Forgiveness," *Proceedings of the Aristotelian Society, New Series* 103 (2003), 39–60.
2. In the end the process of "bending" and the sense and directionality of the movement that it entails will need to be brought into a productive affinity with the following methodological claim made by Derrida in both *Glas* (Paris: Editions de Galilée, 1974). "Si l'érection est habité par la contrbande, par ce qui la produit en la coupant, si donc elle est d'avance, déjà, l'anthérection, il peut, il doit y avoir une castration de la castration, une anthérection de l'anthérection, et ainsi à l'infini" (149).
3. I have taken up the question of "holiness" in a different but related context in my "Recovering Holiness and the Place of Others: Notes on *Vayikra* 19:34," *Parallax* 19, no. 4 (2013), 36–48.
4. Hannah Arendt, *The Human Condition* (Chicago: University of Chicago Press, 1998), 176.
5. The concept of "mere life" does not have a single point of origination. However, it is clearly at work in writings of both Walter Benjamin and Hannah Arendt. It reappears in regard to the figure of the *homo sacer* in the work of Giorgio Agamben. In regard to the latter, see his *Homo Sacer: Sovereign Power and Bare Life* (Stanford, CA: Stanford University Press, 1998). In regards to the way this term continues to figure with contemporary political philosophy, see: Jessica Whyte, *Catastrophe and Redemption: The Political Thought of Giorgio Agamben* (Albany: SUNY Press, 2014).
6. Hannah Arendt, Letter to Jaspers 1951. *Correspondence: Hannah Arendt, Karl Jaspers, 1926–1969* (New York: Mariner Books, 1993). The significant element of the overall letter are as follows:

> What radical evil is I don't know, but it seems to me that it somehow has to do with the following phenomenon: *making* [*zu machen*] human beings as human beings superfluous. . . . This happens as soon as all unpredictability—which, in human

beings, is the equivalent of spontaneity [*die Spontaneität*]—is eliminated. And all this in turn arises from—or, better, goes along with—the delusion of the omnipotence (not simply the lust for power) of an individual man. If an individual man qua man were omnipotent, then there is in fact no reason why men in the plural should exist at all—just as in monotheism it is only God's omnipotence that makes him ONE [*zu EINEM macht*]. (Letter 109, page 222/166) (italics added for emphasis; "unpredictability" in the original in English)

7. Hannah Arendt, *The Origins of Totalitarianism* (New York: Harcourt, Brace, Jovanovich, 1973, 459).
8. For a possible link between this potentiality and what Hans Jonas has described as "our potentiality for the Good," see *Mortality and Morality* (Evanston, IL: Northwestern University Press, 1996), 105. *A Search for the Good after Auschwitz*, 105.
9. Hannah Arendt, *The Human Condition* (Chicago: University of Chicago Press, 1998), 176.
10. There is an extensive literature on Kant's relation to Hume. Indeed it could be argued that the divisions within the history of philosophy—Europeans contra analytic—depends on how this encounter is understood. Kant's project is not to deny the reality of the empirical world but rather to account both for how it can be known and how life should be lived within it.
11. David Hume, *A Treatise of Human Nature* (Oxford: Oxford University Press, 2000), 19.
12. Kant. *On the common saying: That may be correct in theory, but it is of no use in practice*. In Immanuel Kant, *Practical Philosophy* trans. Mary J. Gregor (Cambridge: Cambridge University Press, 1999), 144. For a detailed discussion both of this text as well as the prevision on an exemplary account of Kant's ethical writings set in the context of his metaphysics, see Kristi E. Sweet, *Kant on Practical Life: From Duty to History* (Cambridge. Cambridge University Press, 2013.

13. Immanuel Kant. *Practical Philosophy*, trans. Mary J. Gregor (Cambridge: Cambridge University Press, 1999), 144.
14. A strong summary position of Kant's relation to both Epicurus and the Stoics can be identified in the following fragment:

    Fragment 6619. 1769–70? (1764–68?) *Pr* IX.

    Epicurus takes the subjective ground of execution, which moves us to action, for the objective ground of **adjudication**. Zeno reverses this. That Epicurus reduces it all to bodily stimuli appears to be more an opinion, used to explain the decisions of human beings, than a prescription. The **greatest spiritual** joys find the ground of their own approbation in the intellectual concept, to be sure, but their *elateres* in the sensible. (424)

15. Aristotle, *Politics* 1261. 19. (Aristotle, *Politics*, trans. H. Rackham [Cambridge, MA: Harvard University Press, 1932]).
16. There is an important philological project that could be undertaken here concerning the dictionaries that Kant might have used or which were used at the time. For example, in Corn. Schrevelli, *Lexicon manuale græco-latinum et latino-græcum*. Holland.1670, ευδαιμον is translated as *beatus* and ευδαιμονια as *felicitas*. The connection of these terms to the contextual understanding of *Glückseligkeit* would be important to establish.
17. Kant Fragments 6619, 1769–70? (1764–68?), *Pr* IX. In Immanuel Kant, *Notes and Fragments*, trans. Curtis Bowman and Fredrick Rauscher (Cambridge: Cambridge University Press, 2010).
18. In a letter that Moses Mendelssohn sent to Kant on December 25, 1770, he suggested in response to Kant's interpretation of Epicurus that for the latter, "the feeling of pleasure is not only a criterion of goodness [*criterium boni*] but is itself the highest good [*summum bonum*]," 123.

From which it must be concluded that Mendelssohn had failed to grasp the point of Kant's argument.
19. Immanuel Kant, *Critique of the Power of Judgment*, trans. Eric Matthews (Cambridge: Cambridge University Press, 2001), §9.
20. Immanuel Kant, *Notes and Fragments*, trans. Curtis Bowman and Fredrick Rauscher (Cambridge: Cambridge University Press, 2010), 240.
21. Immanuel Kant, *Critique of Pure Reason*, trans. Allen W. Wood (Cambridge: Cambridge University Press, 1999), B365.
22. Plato, *Phadeo*, 99b.
23. Immanuel Kant, *Practical Philosophy*, trans. Mary J. Gregor (Cambridge: Cambridge University Press, 1999), 24.
24. Derrida, *Glas* (Paris: Editions de Galilée, 1974), 91.
25. See to this end Rebecca Comay, *Mourning Sickness: Hegel and the French Revolution* (Stanford, CA: Stanford University Press, 2011), 34–35.
26. *The Contest of the Faculties*, §6, in Immanuel Kant *Practical Philosophy*, trans. Mary J. Gregor (Cambridge: Cambridge University Press, 1999).
27. Probably the most important contemporary contribution to the undoing and thus rethinking of the opposition between the sensible and the indelible can be located in the writings of John Sallis. While it emerges in a number of places it is deployed with telling force in his discussion of painting. See, for example, his *Transfigurements: On the True Sense of Art* (Chicago: University of Chicago Press, 2011).
28. Immanuel Kant, *Critique of Pure Reason*, trans. Allen W. Wood (Cambridge: Cambridge University Press, 1999), B365.
29. For a development of the issues involved in Arendt's conception of forgiveness, see among others, Bernadette Meyler, "Does Forgiveness Have a Place? Hegel, Arendt, and Revolution," *Theory and Event* 6, no. 11 (2002); Roger Berkowitz, "'The Angry Jew Has Gotten His Revenge': Hannah Arendt on Revenge and Reconciliation,"

Philosophical Topics 39, no. 2 (Fall 2011), 1–20; Sigrid Weigel, "Secularization and Sacralization, Normalization and Rupture: Kristeva and Arendt on Forgiveness," *PMLA* 117, no. 2 (March 2002), 320–323; Edith Wyschogrod, "Repentance and Forgiveness: The Undoing of Time," *International Journal for Philosophy of Religion* 60, no. 1/3; "Self and Other: Essays in Continental Philosophy of Religion," *International Journal for Philosophy of Religion* (December 2006), 157–168.

30. Hannah Arendt, *The Human Condition* (Chicago: University of Chicago Press), 237.
31. Hannah Arendt, *The Human Condition* (Chicago: University of Chicago Press), 246.
32. The argument is too elaborate to sustain here. Nonetheless the conjecture would be that Arendt links modernity to a conception of freedom that has to be thought in terms of an experience of creative destruction, namely, a thinking of destruction and creation that cannot be assimilated to the prevailing order of power. This conception of both freedom and agency yields a conception of authentic subjectivity that breaks free of the continuity—a continuity to be discovered—of *"being-towards-death."* For a detailed and brilliant examination of Arendt's thinking of the revolutionary, see: Paul A. Kottman, "Novus Ordo Saeclorum: Hannah Arendt on Revolutionary Spirit," in *Political Theology and Early Modernity*, ed. Graham Hammill and Julia Reinhard Lupton (Chicago: University of Chicago Press, 2012), 143–58. See, in addition, the discussion of Arendt in Anne O'Byrne, *Natality and Finitude* (Bloomington: Indiana University Press, 2010.)
33. Hannah Arendt, *The Human Condition* (Chicago: University of Chicago Press), 199.
34. "Wherever people gather together, it is potentially there, but only potentially, not necessarily and not forever," Hannah Arendt' *The Human Condition* (Chicago: University of Chicago Press), 199.
35. Hannah Arendt, *The Human Condition* (Chicago: University of Chicago Press), 204.

36. Hannah Arendt, *On Violence* (New York: Harcourt Brace Jovanovich, 1970), 52.
37. Hannah Arendt, *On Violence* (New York: Harcourt Brace Jovanovich, 1970), 51.
38. Hannah Arendt, *The Human Condition* (Chicago: University of Chicago Press), 200.
39. Hannah Arendt, *The Human Condition* (Chicago: University of Chicago Press), 202.
40. Kant, "An Answer to the Question: What Is Enlightenment?," in Immanuel Kant: Practical Philosophy, trans. Mary J. Gregor (Cambridge: Cambridge University Press, 1999).
41. Hannah Arendt, *The Human Condition* (Chicago: University of Chicago Press), 193.
42. Aristotle *Metaphysics* 1048b25. A detailed study of this aspect of Aristotle's work will appear chapter 2. Following the path opened up by the problem of potentiality taken as a project in its own right necessitate a study of Heidegger's own engagement with this aspect of Aristotle. Heidegger profoundly affects Agamben's interpretation of Aristotle, which has recently acquired considerable importance in its own right. See Martine Heidegger, *Aristotle's Metaphysics Θ 1–3, On the Essence and Actuality of Force*, trans. Walter Brogan and Peter Warnek (Bloomington: Indiana University Press, 1995). For an extended treatment of Agamben's interpretation of Aristotle and then his own thinking of potentiality, see William Watkin, *Agamben and Indifference* (London: Rowman and Littlefield, 2014).
43. For Aristotle, as Arendt notes, while the "polis" "comes into existence for the sake of life, it exists for the good life. [γινομένη μέν του ζήν ένεκεν ούσα δε εύ ζήν.]" (Aristotle *Politics* 1252b29).
44. See Aristotle *Metaphysics* 1046b 29ff.
45. Hannah Arendt, *The Human Condition* (Chicago: University of Chicago Press), 176.
46. Hannah Arendt, *The Human Condition* (Chicago: University of Chicago Press), 179.

47. Hannah Arendt, *On Violence* (New York: Harcourt Brace Jovanovich, 1970), 175.
48. It can be argued that there is a considerable amount of contemporary French philosophy that has exerted an influence here. Works by Jean-Luc Nancy and Marc Crépon have been particularly important. See *La communauté désoeuvrée* (Paris: Christian Bourgois, 1990), and *Vivre avec* (Paris: Herman, 2008). The difference here is that commonality has been understood in terms of a relational ontology that incorporates both value and equally an account of the potentiality for justice. Hence the philosophical basis of an argument for *virtue in being* has a different orientation.
49. Kant, "An Answer to the Question: What Is Enlightenment?," in *Immanuel Kant: Practical Philosophy*, trans. Mary J. Gregor (Cambridge: Cambridge University Press, 1999). "A revolution may well bring about a falling off of personal despotism and of avaricious or tyrannical oppression, but never a true reform in one's way of thinking; instead new prejudices will serve just as well as old ones to harness the great unthinking masses," (18). What this passage opens up is the need to give much more thought to what Kant means by the revolution.
50. Hannah Arendt *The Human Condition* (Chicago: University of Chicago Press, 208).
51. Immanuel Kant, *Practical Philosophy*, trans. Mary J. Gregor (Cambridge: Cambridge University Press, 1999).
52. Immanuel Kant, *Practical Philosophy*, trans. Mary J. Gregor (Cambridge: Cambridge University Press), 1999, 241.
53. Immanuel Kant, *Practical Philosophy*, trans. Mary J. Gregor (Cambridge: Cambridge University Press,1999), 286.

CHAPTER 3.
KANT, EVIL, AND THE UNCONDITIONED

1. Immanuel Kant, *Practical Philosophy*, trans. Mary J. Gregor (Cambridge: Cambridge University Press, 1999), 232.
2. Immanuel Kant, *Lectures on Logic*, trans. Peter Heath (Cambridge: Cambridge University Press, 2001).

> The liberal arts have an inner worth, without serving for gain[.] E.g., the art of the carpenter, of the builder, are arts for earning one's bread[;] other arts have a worth in themselves. E.g., poetry, oratory. These have an immediate pleasantness in themselves and need no *auctoramentum*; these are liberal arts, because they have an inner worth by themselves. If liberal arts are used as arts for earning one's bread, then their inner worth, i.e., their dignity, is degraded. One gives them the worth of a means, although they have an unconditioned worth. (419–20)

3. Immanuel Kant, *Practical Philosophy*, trans. Mary J. Gregor (Cambridge: Cambridge University Press, 1999), 329.
4. Immanuel Kant, *Critique of Pure Reason*, trans. Allen W. Wood (Cambridge: Cambridge University Press, 1999), B418. "Now one can think of this unconditioned either as subsisting merely in the whole series, in which thus every member without exception is conditioned, and only their whole is absolutely unconditioned, or else the absolutely unconditioned is only a part of the series, to which the remaining members of the series are subordinated but that itself stands under no other condition" (465).
5. Immanuel Kant, *Practical Philosophy*, trans. Mary J. Gregor (Cambridge: Cambridge University Press, 1999), 341.
6. A similar critique of the equation of the political with pragmatic can be identified in *The Contest of the Faculties*, in Immanuel Kant, *Religion and Rational Theology*, trans. Allen W. Wood and George di Giovanni (Cambridge: Cambridge University Press, 2001), 143.
7. In Immanuel Kant, *Practical Philosophy*, trans. Mary J. Gregor (Cambridge Cambridge University Press, 1999), 341.
8. Kant, *Critique of Practical Reason*, in Immanuel Kant, *Practical Philosophy*, trans. Mary J. Gregor (Cambridge: Cambridge University Press, Cambridge, 1999).
9. Immanuel Kant, *Lectures on Logic*, trans. J. Michael Young, 2004), 201.

10. Immanuel Kant, *Critique of the Power of Judgment*, trans. Eric Matthews (Cambridge: Cambridge University Press, 2001).
11. *Religion within the Bounds of Mere Reason*, in Immanuel Kant, *Religion and Rational Theology* trans. by Allen W. Wood and George di Giovanni (Cambridge: Cambridge University Press, 2001), 94.
12. Giorgio Agamben, *Potentialities*, trans. Daniel Heller-Roazen (Stanford, CA: Stanford University Press, 1999), 182.
13. The term *actative* underscores a thinking of the anoriginality of action. The locative pertains to place, and thinking the necessity of location. The actative pertains to the necessity of action. A capacity for action as an intrinsic presence.
14. Immanuel Kant, *Critique of the Power of Judgment*, trans. Eric Matthews (Cambridge: Cambridge University Press, 2001).
15. Immanuel Kant, *Critique of the Power of Judgment*, trans. Eric Matthews (Cambridge: Cambridge University Press, 2001), 208.
16. There is a similar formulation in Schiller's *Über Anmut und Würde*. In his treatment of "dignity" he will note that animals "*must* [*muß*] strive to avoid pain," however humans are able do so. In other words, they can chose pain if they wish. Striving has an important division within it. However, prior to that position Schiller notes that human beings can try and bring their two natures—sensible and intelligible—into a type of harmony. "But this beauty of character, the ripest fruit of humanity, is a mere idea that they can never vigilantly strive [*streben*] to live up to, yet, despite all efforts can never fully attain [*nie ganz erreichen kann*]." Here, as with Kant, "striving" depends on the necessarily unactualizable nature of the idea. Friedrich Schiller, *Werke in Drei Banden*, Band II (München: Carl Hanser Verlag), 1966), 410–11.
17. For an important discussion of Derrida's relation to Kant see: Marguerite La Caze, "At the Intersection: Kant,

Derrida, and the Relation between Ethics and Politics," *Political Theory* 35, no. 6 (December 2007), 781–805.
18. On evil as a philosophical topos and evil in Kant see: Henry Allison, *Kant's Theory of Freedom* (Cambridge: Cambridge University Press, 1990); Peter Dews, *The Idea of Evil* (Oxford: Blackwell, 2008); Alan D. Schrift (ed.) *Modernity and the Problem of Evil* (Bloomington: Indiana University Press, 2005); Patrick R. Frierson, "Character and Evil in Kant's Moral Anthropology," *Journal of the History of Philosophy* 44, no. 4 (October 2006), 623–34; Richard J. Bernstein, "Reflections on Radical Evil: Arendt and Kant," *Soundings: An Interdisciplinary Journal* 85, no. 1/2 (Spring/Summer 2002), 17–30.
19. *Religion within the Bounds of Mere Reason*, in Immanuel Kant, *Religion and Rational Theology*, trans. Allen W. Wood and George di Giovanni (Cambridge: Cambridge University Press, 2001), 69.
20. While it cannot be pursued here, it would be useful to look in more details at the threefold division with which Leibniz locates his concern with "evil" ("mal"). See his *Essais de Théodicée*, in G. W. Leibniz, *Die philosophischen Schriften*, Band 6, 115.
21. *Religion within the Bounds of Mere Reason*, in Immanuel Kant, *Religion and Rational Theology* trans. Allen W. Wood. George di Giovanni (Cambridge: Cambridge University Press, 2001), 76.
22. *Religion within the Bounds of Mere Reason*, in Immanuel Kant, *Religion and Rational Theology*, trans. Allen W. Wood and George di Giovanni (Cambridge: Cambridge University Press, 2001), 75.
23. These determined conditions become the sites in which an already presented disequilibria of power is played out.
24. G. W. F. Hegel, *Phenomenology of Spirit* (Oxford: Oxford University Press, 1976), 254.
25. *Religion within the Bounds of Mere Reason*, in Immanuel Kant, *Religion and Rational Theology*, trans. Allen W. Wood and George di Giovanni (Cambridge: Cambridge University Press, 2001), 74.

26. *Lectures on the Philosophical Doctrine of Religion*, in Immanuel Kant, *Religion and Rational Theology*, trans. Allen W. Wood and George di Giovanni (Cambridge: Cambridge University Press, 2001), 411.
27. Immanuel Kant, *Critique of Pure Reason*, trans. Allen W. Wood (Cambridge: Cambridge University Press, 1999), A111.
28. Immanuel Kant, *Critique of the Power of Judgment*, trans. Eric Matthews (Cambridge: Cambridge University Press, 2001), 145.
29. What is opened here is the possibility of another writing of nature. It would be the denaturing of nature in terms of another nature that would save nature from its identification with the mechanistic.
30. *Religion within the Bounds of Mere Reason*, in Immanuel Kant, *Religion and Rational Theology*, trans. Allen W. Wood and George di Giovanni (Cambridge: Cambridge University Press, 2001), 76.
31. *Religion within the Bounds of Mere Reason*, in Immanuel Kant, *Religion and Rational Theology*, trans. Allen W. Wood and George di Giovanni (Cambridge: Cambridge University Press, 2001), 76.
32. *Critique of Practical Reason*, in Immanuel Kant, *Practical Philosophy*, trans. Mary J. Gregor (Cambridge: Cambridge University Press, 1999), 210.
33. Immanuel Kant, *Lectures on Metaphysics*, trans. Karl Ameriks and Steve Naragon (Cambridge: Cambridge University Press, 2001, *Metaphysik L.* 64–65.
34. Kant, *Practical Philosophy*, trans. Mary J. Gregor (Cambridge: Cambridge University Press, 1999), 50.
35. *Critique of the Power of Judgment*, §1
36. This is the position I have tried to argue that is integral to the philosophical project of Walter Benjamin. See my *Working with Walter Benjamin* (Edinburgh: Edinburgh University Press, 2013).
37. *Religion within the Bounds of Mere Reason*, in Immanuel Kant, *Religion and Rational Theology*, trans. Allen W. Wood and George di Giovanni (Cambridge: Cambridge University Press, 2001), 82.

38. *Religion within the Bounds of Mere Reason* in Immanuel Kant, *Religion and Rational Theology*, trans. Allen W. Wood and George di Giovanni (Cambridge: Cambridge University Press, 2001), 87.
39. *Religion within the Bounds of Mere Reason* in Immanuel Kant, *Religion and Rational Theology*, trans. Allen W. Wood and George di Giovanni (Cambridge: Cambridge University Press, 2001), 79.
40. Immanuel Kant, *Critique of the Power of Judgment*, trans. Eric Matthews (Cambridge: Cambridge University Press, 2001).
41. *Religion within the Bounds of Mere Reason*, in Immanuel Kant, *Religion and Rational Theology* trans. Allen W. Wood and George di Giovanni (Cambridge: Cambridge University Press, 2001), 91.
42. *Religion within the Bounds of Mere Reason* in Immanuel Kant, *Religion and Rational Theology*, trans. Allen W. Wood and George di Giovanni (Cambridge: Cambridge University Press, 2001), 282.
43. *Religion within the Bounds of Mere Reason* in Immanuel Kant, *Religion and Rational Theology*, trans. Allen W. Wood and George di Giovanni (Cambridge: Cambridge University Press, 2001), 91.
44. Immanuel Kant, *Critique of the Power of Judgment*, trans. Eric Matthews (Cambridge: Cambridge University Press, 2001), 238.
45. *Groundwork of the Metaphysic of Morals*, in Immanuel Kant, *Practical Philosophy*, trans. Mary J. Gregor (Cambridge: Cambridge University Press, 1999). 52.

CHAPTER 4. JUDGMENT AFTER DERRIDA

1. Jacques Derrida *Pardonner* (Paris: Editions Galilée, 2010), 15. In addition, the evocation of right within this passage means that the question of the ground of right then has to be posed. The answer, in the end, has to be the immanent presence of the unconditioned.
2. See in relation this question the essay by Stathis

Gourgouris, "Philosophy's Need for Antigone," in his *Does Literature Think?* (Stanford, CA: Stanford University Press, 2003). This paper is one of the most significant to be written on the Antigone. Even if the argument involves different considerations, there is an affinity between his critique of Derrida on singularity and the argument developed here.
3. Jacques Derrida, *Glas* (Paris: Editions de Galilée, 1974).
4. Jacques Derrida, *Pardonner* (Paris: Editions Galilée, 2010, 62).
5. Jacques Derrida, 7.
6. The definitive study of the history of the interpretations and rewritings of the Antigone remains George Steiner, *Antigones* (Oxford: Oxford University Press, 1984).
7. Jacques Derrida, *Glas* (Paris: Editions de Galilée, 1974), 170.
8. Jacques Derrida, *Glas* (Paris: Editions de Galilée, 1974), 171–83
9. Jacques Derrida, *Glas* (Paris: Editions de Galilée, 1974), 211.
10. Jacques Derrida, *Glas* (Paris: Editions de Galilée, 1974).
11. Jacques Derrida, *Glas* (Paris: Editions de Galilée, 1974, 211).
12. In the *Critique of Pure Reason* Kant uses the term *epigenesis* to account for the origin of the "categories" (B167). He then goes on to add that they are that which makes experience possible. In other words, the unconditioned and a priori cannot be accounted for within the terms created to account for what they makes possible. Kant's use of the term *epigenetic* here is to account for the self-caused occurrence that generates and sustains relationality. The latter occurs with the conditioned (where the latter names the experienced).
13. Tina Chanter, *Whose Antigone? The Tragic Marginalization of Slavery* (Albany: SUNY Press, 24).
14. Hannah Arendt, *The Human Condition* (Chicago: University of Chicago Press).
15. The approach to the presence of fate as a philosophical *topos* that has to be taken up follows from the work

of Walter Benjamin. In particular, it follows both from an interpretation of the way "fate" is analyzed in his "Fate and Character," and then with the way the relationship between fate and "mythic violence" is established in his "Toward a Critique of Violence." I have discussed this connection in considerable detail in my: *Working with Walter Benjamin* (Edinburgh: Edinburgh University Press, 2013).
16. Sophocles, *Oedipus Tyrannus*, 446. In Sophocles Volume I, *Ajax. Electra. Oedipus Tyrannus*, trans. Hugh Lloyd Jones (Cambridge: Harvard University Press, 1994).
17. Immanuel Kant, *Critique of the Power of Judgment*, trans. Eric Matthews (Cambridge: Cambridge University Press, 2001), §56.
18. For an extended treatment of this conception of hope see my *Present Hope: Philosophy, Architecture, Judaism* (London: Routledge, 1997).
19. See in this regard my "On Tolerance: Working through Kant," *Contretemps* 2 (2002).
20. Jacques Lacan, *L'éthique de la psychanalyse* (Paris: Éditions de Seuil, 1986), 327.
21. S. Freud, *The Ego and the Id*, vol. XIX, Standard Edition, trans. James Strachey (London: Hogarth Press, 1990), 40.
22. S. Freud, *The Ego and the Id*, vol. XIX, Standard Edition, trans. James Strachey (London: Hogarth Press, 1990), 40–41. What could also be pursued, albeit in another context, is the nature of the relationship between what Freud names in this passage with the term *gleichzeitung* and what has also emerged in terms of the temporality of *at-the-same-timeness*.
23. G. W. F. Hegel, *Phenomenology of Spirit* (Oxford: Oxford University Press, 1976), §456.
24. Jacques Derrida, *Glas* (Paris: Editions de Galilée, 1974), 186.
25. I have tried to develop this particular conception of the figure in a number of recent writings. See, in regard to the figure of the Jew and the figure of the animal, my *Of Jews and Animals* (Edinburgh: Edinburgh University Press), 2010.

26. It is not as though Derrida is unaware of the creation of figures. He shows how the figure of Jew is constructed. See *Glas* (Paris: Editions de Galilée, 1974), 65.
27. Derrida's text *Retrait de la métaphore* (in *Psyche: Inventions de l'autre* [Paris: Éditions Galilée, 1998]) provides a way of beginning to understand this claim. What can never be excised is an original and constituting "trait." There will always be the mark of a founding impurity. The difficulty is that Derrida is unable to account for the presence of this mark of anoriginal relationality because there is the failure to recognize that this mark is constitutive of the marked object being an object. Hence, it has to be thought as the mark of an already present and operative relational ontology. The further point is that the presence of this "trait" would be damaging to any insistence on the original singularity of Antigone.
28. See in this regard Nicole Loraux, "La main d'Antigone," *Mètis*1, no. 2 (1986), 165–96.
29. Aristotle *Rhetoric* 1375a–75b: Aristotle, *Art of Rhetoric*, trans. J. H. Freese (Cambridge, MA: Harvard University Press, 1926).

> Let us first then speak of the laws, and state what use should be made of them when exhorting or dissuading, accusing or defending. For it is evident that, if the written law is counter to our case, we must have recourse to the general law and equity, as more in accordance with justice; and we must argue that, when the dicast takes an oath to decide to the best of his judgment, he means that he will not abide rigorously by the written laws; that equity [επιεικες] is ever constant [αει μενει] and never changes, even as the general law, which is based on nature, whereas the written laws often vary (this is why Antigone in Sophocles justifies herself for having buried Polynikes contrary to the law of Kreon [παρα τον του Κρεοντος νομον], but not contrary to the unwritten law [τον αγραφον].

30. There is a range of philosophical as well as historical work on Kreon as a tyrant. See, for example, Peter J. Ahrensdorf, "The Limits of Political Rationalism: Enlightenment and Religion in *Oedipus the Tyrant*," *Journal of Politics* 66, no. 3 (2004), 773–99; James F. McGlew, *Tyranny and Political Culture in Ancient Greece* (Ithaca, NY: Cornell University Press, 1993); David A. Teegarden, "Tyrant-Killing Legislation and the Political Foundation of Ancient Greek Democracy," *Cardozo Law Review* 34, no. 3 (February 2013), 965–82.
31. G. W. F. Hegel. *Lectures on the Philosophy of Religion*, vol. 11 (Oxford: Oxford University Press, 2007), 66.
32. *Oedipus at Colonus* in Sophocles, vol. II, *Antigone. The Women of Trachis. Philoctetes. Oedipus at Colonus* trans. Hugh Lloyd Jones (Cambridge, MA: Harvard University Press, 1994).
33. The complex relationship between law, fate, and tragedy in the Antigone is a continual site of investigation. See, for example, Martin Cropp, "Antigone's Dinal Speech (Sophocles *Antigone* 891–928)," *Greece and Rome* 44, no. 2 (1997), 137–60; Costas Douzinas, "Law and the Postmodern Mind: Law's Birth and Antigone's Death: On Ontological and Psychoanalytic Ethics," *Cardozo Law Review* 16 (1995), 1325; Alfred R. Ferguson, "Politics and Man's Fate in Sophocles' 'Antigone,'" *Classical Journal* 70, no. 2 (1974, 1975), V41–49; Mark S. Howenstein, "The Tragedy of Law and the Law of Tragedy in Sophocles' *Antigone*," *Legal Studies Forum* 193 (1999); Stephen Palmer, "Martyrdom and Conflict: The Fate of Antigone in Tragic Drama," *Mortality* (2014), 1–18.
34. While it cannot be pursued here there is an important connection between this aspect of judgement and Aristotle's engagement with the distinction between constancy and mutability. See Aristotle, *Nicomachean Ethics*, Book VII.
35. This would be the one in which, following the lead of Judith Butler, Antigone would have become, "the occasion for a new field of the human, achieved through political catachresis, the one that happens when the less than

human speaks as a human, when gender is displaced, and kinship founders on its own founding laws." Judith Butler, *Antigone's Claim: Kinship between Life and Death* (New York: Columbia University Press, 2000), 82.
36. Jacques Derrida, *Glas* (Paris: Editions de Galilée, 1974), 187.
37. The presence of Antigone as a "bride"—living and dying, as a bride—and equally the effect of Kreon's actions in denying his son a bride are fundamental elements within the play. See to this end, Rush Rehm, *Marriage to Death: The Conflation of Wedding and Funeral Ritual in Greek Tragedy* (Princeton, NJ: Princeton University Press, 1994), 9–71.
38. Hegel, *Phenomenology of Spirit* (Oxford: Oxford University Press, 1976), §470, 284. A great deal more needs to be said about the relation between deed and acts. It is in terms of the immediacy of their relation that Antigone refuses to allow Ismene to take on part of the responsibility for the burial of Polynikes. Ismene demanded a space of judgment; a space that the immediacy of the relation between deed and act closes down.
39. The question of guilt will continue to return. In part this is inspired by the analyses of guilt in the work of Walter Benjamin. See my discussion of this *topos* in my *Working with Walter Benjamin: Recovering a Political Philosophy* (Edinburgh: Edinburgh University Press, 2013). For a more general analysis of the question of guilt in Greek tragedy see: N. J. Sewell-Rutter, *Guilt by Descent: Moral Inheritance and Decision Making in Greek Tragedy* (Oxford: Oxford University Press, 2007).
40. G. W. F. Hegel, *Philosophy of Right*, trans. T. M. Knox (Oxford: Oxford University, 1967), 89.
41. G. W. F. Hegel, *Philosophy of Right*, trans. T. M. Knox (Oxford: Oxford University, 1967), 186.
42. Hegel, *Phenomenology of Spirit* (Oxford: Oxford University Press, 1976).
43. There is a range of important papers on the topic of forgiveness in Hegel's early writings. Two of the most important are Theodore George, "Forgiveness, Freedom, and Finitude in Hegel's Spirit of Christianity," *International*

Philosophical Quarterly 51, no. 1 (2011), 39–53; María del Rosario Acosta López, "Hegel and Derrida on Forgiveness: The Impossible at the Core of the Political," *Derrida Today* 5, no. 1 (2012), 55–68. In this instance, however, a distinction is being drawn between forgiveness or pardoning when what is stake is a claim made in relation to the law. Hence, while Hegel's arguments in his early writings concerning "forgiveness" are important and while those texts provide an interesting and important contribution to an understanding of the relationship between fate and guilt, they are not defined in relation to the "law." It is for this reason that emphasis has been given to the possibility of the "pardon" as it is present in the *Philosophy of Right*.

44. For an earlier and fundamentally important discussion of the construction of the figure, see Élisabeth de Fontenay, *Les Figures juives de Marx: Marx dans l'idéologie allemande* (Paris: Editions Galilée, 1973).
45. G. W. F. Hegel, "The Spirit of Christianity and Its Fate," in *Hegel's Early Theological Writings*, trans. T. M. Knox (Philadelphia: University of Pennsylvania Press, 1971), 199.
46. G. W. F. Hegel, "The Spirit of Christianity and Its Fate," in *Hegel's Early Theological Writings*, trans. T. M. Knox (Philadelphia: University of Pennsylvania Press, 1971), 204.
47. See in this regard the extensive contemporary literature on Paul. While some is no more than Christian apologetics disguised as radical thought (Badiou), there are important engagements with the presence of the Pauline thinking of interruption. Fundamental here is Giorgio Agamben, *The Time That Remains: A Commentary on the Letter to the Romans* (Stanford, CA: Stanford University Press, 2005).
48. Aeschylus *Niobe*, in Aeschylus, III, *Fragments* trans. Alan H. Sommerstein (Cambridge, MA: Harvard University Press, 2009).
49. See the point made by Derrida in relation to Hegel on the "pardon." While the context is more general, see in this regard *Glas* (Paris: Editions de Galilée, 1974), 247.
50. Jacques Derrida, *Pardonner* (Paris: Editions Galilée, 2010), 68.
51. The details of this position is outlined by Derrida thus:

> . . . there is in forgiveness, in the very meaning of forgiveness a force, a desire, an impetus, a movement, an appeal (call it what you will) that demands that forgiveness be granted, if it can be, even to someone who does not ask for it, who does not repent or confess or improve or redeem himself, beyond, consequently, an entire identificatory, spiritual, whether sublime or not, economy, beyond all expiation even. But I will leave this suggestion in a virtual state.

52. Jacques Derrida, *Pardonner* (Paris: Editions Galilée, 2010), 28.
53. Jacques Derrida, *Pardonner* (Paris: Editions Galilée, 2010), 10–11.
54. Jacques Derrida, *Cosmopolites de tous pays encore un effort!* (Paris: Editions Galilée, 1997), 7.
55. Jacques Derrida, "Responsabilité et hospitalité," in *De l'hospitalité: Autor de Jacques Derrida*, ed. Mohammed Seffahi (Genouilleux, France: Éditions la passé du vent, 2001), 133.
56. Jacques Derrida, *L'autre cap*. (Paris: Les éditions de minuit, 1991), 43.
57. Jacques Derrida, *De l'hospitalité*. (Paris: Calmann-Lévy, 1997), 73.
58. Jacques Derrida, *De l'hospitalité*. (Paris: Calmann-Lévy, 1997), 77.
59. Within Kafka's text *"Before the Law"* (*"Vor dem Gesetz"*), which in its final form is contained in the novel *The Trial* (*Der Process*), the "man from the county" asks for access to the law. The mistake within the question is the failure to have recognized that he is anoriginally—thus always already—before the law. There isn't a position "before the law," if such a position were thought to be prior to the law.

BIBLIOGRAPHY

Adler, Anthony Curtis. "Sensual Idealism: The Spirit of Epicurus and the Politics of Finitude in Kant and Hölderlin." In Brook Holmes and W. H. Shearin (editors), *Dynamic Reading: Studies in the Reception of Epicureanism*. Oxford: Oxford University Press, 2012, 199–238.

Aeschylus. III, *Fragments*. Translated by Alan H. Sommerstein. Cambridge: Harvard University Press, 2009.

Agamben, Giorgio. *Potentialities*. Translated by Daniel Heller-Roazen. Stanford: Stanford University Press, 1999.

———. *Homo Sacer: Sovereign Power and Bare Life*. Stanford: Stanford University Press, 1998.

———. *The Time That Remains: A Commentary on the Letter to the Romans*. Stanford: Stanford University Press, 2005.

Ahrensdorf, Peter J. "The Limits of Political Rationalism: Enlightenment and Religion in *Oedipus the Tyrant*." *Journal of Politics* 66, no. 3 (2004), 773–799.

Allison, Henry. *Kant's Theory of Freedom*. Cambridge: Cambridge University Press.

Arendt, Hannah. *The Human Condition*. Chicago: University of Chicago Press, 1998.

———. *On Violence*. New York: Harcourt Brace Jovanovich, 1970.

———. *The Origins of Totalitarianism*. New York: Harcourt, Brace, Jovanovich, 1973.

Arendt, Hannah, and Karl Jaspers. *Correspondence 1926–1969*. New York: Mariner Books, 1993.
Aristotle. *Politics*. Translated by H. Rackham. Cambridge: Harvard University Press, 1932.
———. *Art of Rhetoric*. Translated by J. H. Freese. Cambridge: Harvard University Press, 1926.
Bailey, Cyril. *Epicurus, the Extant Remains*. Oxford: Oxford University Press, 1926.
Benjamin, Andrew. The Place of the Ethical. *Irish Philosophical Journal* 5 (1988), 31–45.
———. *Present Hope: Philosophy, Architecture, Judaism*. London: Routledge, 1997.
———. *Of Jews and Animals*. Edinburgh: Edinburgh University Press, 2010.
———. *Working with Walter Benjamin: Recovering a Political Philosophy*. Edinburgh: Edinburgh University Press, 2013.
———. *Towards a Relational Ontology: Philosophy's Other Possibility*. SUNY Press, 2015
———. *Leben und Glück*. Modernity and Tragedy in Walter Benjamin, Hölderlin and Sophocles. In *Tragedy and the Idea of Modernity*. Edited by Joshua Billings and Miriam Leonard. Oxford: Oxford University Press, 2015.
Berkowitz, Roger. "The Angry Jew Has Gotten His Revenge": Hannah Arendt on Revenge and Reconciliation. *Philosophical Topics* 39, no. 2 (Fall 2011), 1–20.
Bernstein, Richard J. Reflections on Radical Evil: Arendt and Kant. *Soundings: An Interdisciplinary Journal* 85, no. 1/2 (Spring/Summer 2002), 17–30.
Berry, Jessica N. *Nietzsche and the Ancient Skeptical Tradition*. Oxford: Oxford University Press, 2010.
Bett, Richard. Nietzsche, the Greeks, and Happiness (with special reference to Aristotle and Epicurus). *Philosophical Topics* 33, no. 3 (Fall 2005).
Butler, Judith. *Antigone's Claim: Kinship between Life and Death*. New York: Columbia University Press, 2000.
Chanter, Tina. *Whose Antigone? The Tragic Marginalization of Slavery*. Albany: SUNY Press, 2011.
Cohen, Hermann. *Religion der Vernunft aus den Quellen des Judentums*. Leipzig: Gustav Fock, 1919.

Cohen, Richard A. *Elevations: The Height of the Good in Rosenzweig and Levinas*. Chicago: University of Chicago Press, 1994.
Comay, Rebecca. *Mourning Sickness: Hegel and the French Revolution*. Stanford: Stanford University Press, 2011.
Crépon, Marc. *Vivre avec*. Paris: Herman, 2008.
Cropp, Martin. Antigone's Dinal Speech (Sophocles *Antigone* 891–928). *Greece and Rome* 44, no. 2 (1997), 137–60.
Derrida, Jacques. La Différance in *Marges de la philosophie*. Paris: Les editions de minuit, 1972.
———. *Glas*. Paris: Editions de Galilée, 1974.
———. *L'autre cap*. Paris: Les éditions de minuit, 1991.
———. *De l'hospitalité*. Paris: Calmann-Lévy, 1997.
———. *Cosmopolites de tous pays encore un effort!* Editions Galilée. Paris 1997.
———. *Retrait de la métaphore*. In *Psyche. Inventions de l'autre*. Paris: Éditions Galilée, 1998.
———. *Donner La Mort*. Paris: Editions de Galilée, 1999.
———. *Pardonner*. Paris: Editions Galilée, 2010.
———. Responsabilité et hospitalité. In *De l'hospitalité. Autor de Jacques Derrida*. Edited by Mohammed Seffahi. Genouilleux: Éditions la passé du vent, 2001.
Dews, Peter. *The Idea of Evil*. Oxford: Blackwell, 2008.
Diogenes of Oenoanda. *The Epicurean Inscriptions*. Edited and translated by Martin Ferguson Smith. Naples: Bibliopolis, 1992.
Douzinas, Costas. Law and the Postmodern Mind: Law's Birth and Antigone's Death. On Ontological and Psychoanalytic Ethics. *Cardozo Law Review* 16 (1995), 1325.
Ferguson, Alfred R. Politics and Man's Fate in Sophocles' "Antigone," *Classical Journal* 70, no. 2 (1974), 41–49.
Fontenay, Élisabeth de. *Les Figures juives de Marx: Marx dans l'idéologie allemande* (Paris: Editions Galilée, 1973.
Freud, S. *The Ego and the Id*, vol. XIX. The Standard Edition. Translated by James Strachey. London: Hogarth Press.
Friedman, Maurice. Dialogue, Speech, Nature and Creation: Franz Rosenzweig's Critique of Buber's *I and Thou*. *Modern Judaism* 13 (1993), 109–18.
Frierson, Patrick R. Character and Evil in Kant's Moral

Anthropology. *Journal of the History of Philosophy* 44, no. 4 (October 2006), 623–34.

Davidson, Herbert A. *Moses Maimonides: The Man and His Works*. Oxford: Oxford University Press, 2005.

Garrard, Eve, and David McNaughton. In Defense of Unconditional Forgiveness. *Proceedings of the Aristotelian Society, New Series* 103 (2003), 39–60.

Gasché, Rodolph. *The Idea of Form: Rethinking Kant's Aesthetics*. Stanford: Stanford University Press, 2003.

Gassendi, Pierre. *De vita, et moribus Epicuri*. Liber Quartus Caput IV. Apud Guillelmum Barbier, 1647.

George, Theodore. Forgiveness, Freedom, and Finitude in Hegel's Spirit of Christianity. *International Philosophical Quarterly* 51, no. 1 (2011), 39–53.

Gourgouris, Stathis. Philosophy's Need for Antigone. In *Does Literature Think?* Stanford: Stanford University Press, 2003.

Heidegger, Martin. *Aristotle's Metaphysics Θ 1–3. On the Essence and Actuality of Force*. Translated by Walter Brogan and Peter Warnek. Bloomington: Indiana University Press, 1995.

Hegel, G. W. F. The Spirit of Christianity and Its Fate. In *Hegel's Early Theological Writings*. Translated by T. M. Knox. Philadelphia: University of Pennsylvania Press, 1971.

———. *Vorlesungen über der Geschicte der Philosophie*, II. Frankfurt am Main: Suhrkamp. Verlag, 1982.

———. *Phenomenology of Spirit*. Oxford: Oxford University Press, 1976

———. *Philosophy of Right*. Translated by T. M. Knox. Oxford: Oxford University, 1967.

———. *Lectures on the Philosophy of Religion*, vol. 11 Oxford: Oxford University Press, 2007, 66.

Howenstein, Mark S. The Tragedy of Law and the Law of Tragedy in Sophocles' *Antigone. Legal Studies Forum* 193 (1999).

Hume, David. *A Treatise of Human Nature*. Oxford: Oxford University Press.

Jonas, Hans. *Mortality and Morality: A Search for the Good after Auschwitz*. Evanston: Northwestern University Press, 1996.

Kant, Immanuel. *Lectures on Logic*. Translated by Peter Heath. Cambridge: Cambridge University Press, 2001.
———. *Religion and Rational Theology*. Translated by Allen W. Wood and George di Giovanni. Cambridge: Cambridge University Press, 2001.
———. *Werke*, Band 111. Edited by Wihelm Weischedel. Darmstadt: WBG, 2001.
———. *Critique of the Power of Judgment*. Translated by Eric Matthews. Cambridge: Cambridge University Press, 2001.
———. *Critique of Pure Reason*. Translated by Allen W. Wood. Cambridge: Cambridge University Press, 1999.
———. *Practical Philosophy*. Translated by Mary J. Gregor. Cambridge: Cambridge University Press, 1999.
———. *Notes and Fragments*. Translated by Curtis Bowman and Fredrick Rauscher. Cambridge: Cambridge University Press, 2010.
Knauer, James T. Rethinking Arendt's "Vita Activa": Towards a Democratic Theory of Praxis. *PRAXIS International* 2 (1985), 185–94.
Konstan, David. Epicurus on the Gods. In *Epicurus and the Epicurean Tradition*. Edited by Jeffrey Fish and Kirk R. Sanders. Cambridge: Cambridge University Press, 2011, 53–71.
Kottman, Paul A. Novus Ordo Saeclorum: Hannah Arendt on Revolutionary Spirit. In *Political Theology and Early Modernity*. Edited by Graham Hammill and Julia Reinhard Lupton. Chicago: University of Chicago Press, 2012, 143–58.
Lacan, Jacques. *L'éthique de la psychanalyse*. Paris: Éditions de Seuil, 1986.
La Caze, Marguerite. At the Intersection: Kant, Derrida, and the Relation between Ethics and Politics. *Political Theory* 35, no. 6 (December 2007), 781–805.
Leibniz, G. W. *Essais de Théodicée*. In *Die philosophischen Schriften*. Hildesheim: Georg Olms Verlagsbuchhandlung, 1960.
Long, A. A *From Epicurus to Epictetus: Studies in Hellenistic and Roman Philosophy*. Oxford: Oxford University Press, 2006.
López, María del Rosario Acosta. Hegel and Derrida on Forgiveness: The Impossible at the Core of the Political. *Derrida Today* 5, no. 1 (2012), 55–68.

Lord, Beth. *Kant and Spinozism: Transcendental Idealism and Immanence from Jacobi to Deleuze*. London: Palgrave, 2011.

Loraux, Nicole. La main d'Antigone. *Mètis* 1, no. 2 (1986), 165–96.

Maimonides, Moses. The Guide for the Perplexed. Translated by M. Friedlander. London: Routledge & Kegan Paul, 1971.

McGlew, James F. *Tyranny and Political Culture in Ancient Greece*. Ithaca: Cornell University Press, 1993.

Meyler, Bernadette. Does Forgiveness Have a Place? Hegel, Arendt, and Revolution. *Theory and Event* 6, no. 11 (2002).

Milkowski, Marcin. Idyllic Heroism: Nietzsche's View of Epicurus. *Journal of Nietzsche Studies* 15 (Spring 1998), 70–79.

Morel, Pierre-Marie. Les communautés humaines. In *Lire Épicure et les épicuriens*. Edited by Alain Gigandet and Pierre-Marie Morel. Paris: PUF, 2007.

Nancy, Jean-Luc. *La communauté désoeuvrée*. Paris: Christian Bourgois, 1990.

Nietzsche. Werke. *Kritische Gesamtausgabe*, VI2. Berlin: Walter de Gruyter, 1968.

———. Werke. *Kritische Gesamtausgabe*, VI3. Berlin: Walter de Gruyter, 1973.

Nikolsky, Boris. Epicurus on Pleasure. *Phronesis* 46, no. 4 (November 2001), 440–465

Obbink, D. The Atheisim of Epicurus. *GRBS* 30 (1989), 187–223.

O'Byrne, Anne. *Natality and Finitude*. Bloomington: Indiana University Press, 2010.

Osborne, Peter. *The Politics of Time*. Verso, 1989.

Palmer, Stephen. Martyrdom and Conflict: The Fate of Antigone in Tragic Drama. *Mortality* (2014), 1–18.

Rehm, Rush. *Marriage to Death: The Conflation of Wedding and Funeral Ritual in Greek Tragedy*. Princeton: Princeton University Press, 1994.

Reich, Klaus. Kant and Greek Ethics (1). *Mind* 48, no. 191 (July 1939), 338–54.

Rempel, Morgan. *Daybreak* 72: Nietzsche, Epicurus, and the After Death. *Journal of Nietzsche Studies* 43, no. 2 (2012).

Rosenzweig, Franz. *On Jewish Learning*. New York: Schocken Books, 1955.

Sallis, John. *Transfigurements: On the True Sense of Art*. Chicago: University of Chicago Press, 2011.
Sewell-Rutter, N. J. *Guilt by Descent: Moral Inheritance and Decision Making in Greek Tragedy*. Oxford: Oxford University Press, 2007.
Schrevelli, Corn. *Lexicon manuale græco-latinum et latino-græcum*. Holland, 1670
Schrift, Alan D. (ed.). *Modernity and the Problem of Evil*. Bloomington: Indiana University Press, 2005.
Sedley, David. *Lucretius and the Transformation of Greek Wisdom*. Cambridge: Cambridge University Press, 1998.
Seneca. *Epistles* 1–65. Translated by Richard M. Gummere. Cambridge, MA: Harvard University Press, 1917.
———. *Epistles* 66–92. Translated by Richard M. Gummere, 1920.
———. *Moral Essays*, vol. Translated by John W. Basore. Cambridge: Harvard University Press, 1927.
Schiller, Friedrich. *Über Anmut und Würde*. In *Werke in Drei Banden*, Band II. München: Carl Hanser Verlag, 1966, 410–11.
Small, Robin. *Time and Becoming in Nietzsche's Thought*. London: Continuum, 2010.
Sophocles, Volume I. *Ajax. Electra. Oedipus Tyrannus*. Translated by Hugh Lloyd Jones. Cambridge: Harvard University Press, 1994.
———. Volume II. *Antigone. The Women of Trachis. Philoctetes. Oedipus at Colonus*. Translated by Hugh Lloyd Jones. Cambridge: Harvard University Press, 1994.
Striker, Gisela. Ataraxia: Happiness as Tranquility. *The Monist* 73, no. 1, *Hellenistic Ethics* (January 1990), 97–110.
Sweet, Kristi E. *Kant on Practical Life. From Duty to History*. Cambridge: Cambridge University Press, 2013.
Teegarden, David A. Tyrant-Killing Legislation and the Political Foundation of Ancient Greek Democracy. *Cardozo Law Review* 34, no. 3 (February 2013), 965–82.
Torralba, José M. Stoic Katórthôma, Perfect Duty and Kant's Notion of Acting aus Pflicht: The Relevance of the Oikeiôsis Doctrine for the Notions of Moral Good and Inner Attitude (Gesinnung) in Kantian Ethics. In *Oikeiôsis and the*

Natural Basis of Morality: From Ancient Stoicism to Modern Philosophy. Edited by A. Vigo. Olms, Hildesheim–Zürich–New York, 2012, 295–346.

Traversarius, Ambrosius. *Diogenis Laertii Clarissimi historici de uita.* 1535.

Valla, Lorenzo. *Valla On Pleasure: De voluptate.* Translated by A. Kent Hieatt and Maristella Lorch. New York: Abaris Books, 1977.

Vuillemin, Jules. Trois philosophes intuitionnistes: Epicure, Descartes et Kant. *Dialectica* 35, no. 1–2 (1981).

Wainwright, Eric. The Vita Activa of Hannah Arendt. *Politikon* 16, no. 2 (1989), 22–38.

Warda, Arthur. *Immanuel Kants Bücher.* Berlin: Verlag von Martin Breslauer, 1922.

Warren, James. *Facing Death, Epicurus and His Critics.* Oxford: Clarendon Press, 2004.

Watkin, William. *Agamben and Indifference.* London: Rowman and Littlefield, 2014.

Weber, Samuel. *Benjamin's -abilities.* Cambridge: Harvard University Press, 2010.

Weigel, Sigrid. Secularization and Sacralization, Normalization and Rupture: Kristeva and Arendt on Forgiveness. *PMLA* 117, no. 2 (March 2002), 320–23.

Whyte, Jessica. *Catastrophe and Redemption: The Political Thought of Giorgio Agamben.* Albany: SUNY Press, 2014.

Wilson, Catherine. *Epicureanism and the Origins of Modernity.* Oxford: Oxford University Press, 2008.

Wollstonecraft, Mary. *Vindication of the Rights of Women.* London: T. S. Unwin, 1891.

Woolf, Raphael. What Kind of Hedonist Was Epicurus? *Phronesis* 49, no. 4 (2004), 303–22.

Wyschogrod, Edith. Repentance and Forgiveness: The Undoing of Time. *International Journal for Philosophy of Religion* 60, no. 1/3, Self and Other: Essays in Continental Philosophy of Religion (December 2006), 157–68.

Yarbrough, Jean, and Peter Stern. Vita Activa and Vita Contemplative: Reflections on Hannah Arendt's Political Thought in the Life of Mind. *Review of Politics* 43, no. 3 (1981), 323–54.

INDEX

actative, 101, 103, 110, 112, 118–119, 188
Aeschylus, 140, 159, 197
aftereffect, 3–4, 13, 27, 55, 80, 91, 105, 118, 119, 128, 135, 145, 147
Agamben, Giorgio, 170, 180, 185, 188, 197
Ahrensdorf, Peter J., 194
Alexander of Aphrodisiensis, 30, 174
Allinson, Henry, 189
anoriginal, 2–9, 19–21, 25, 27, 51, 53–55, 57–58, 62, 71, 74–76, 78, 81, 84–85, 88, 90–93, 95–96, 99, 103–105, 107, 109–110, 112, 120–121, 128, 131, 133, 136, 140, 143, 146–47, 152, 154, 163–164, 166–167, 169, 173, 194, 198
Antigone, 127–128, 131–139, 143–160, 167, 191–192, 194–196
a part/apart, 2, 4, 15, 21, 37, 43, 49, 55, 59, 63, 68–71, 78, 90, 99, 110, 112, 148, 166–167
Arendt, Hannah, 5, 9–10, 28, 40–41, 51, 53–57, 59, 61, 63, 65, 67, 69, 71, 73–85, 94, 107–109, 117, 126, 137, 151, 168, 170–171, 178–181, 183–186, 189, 192
Aristotle, 5, 10, 42, 60–63, 77–79, 81–82, 99–100, 107, 115, 137, 150, 173, 182, 185, 194–195
at-the-same-timeness, 2, 7, 57, 68–69, 71–72, 78, 81, 95–96, 104, 107, 109–113, 118, 120–121, 142, 163–164, 167, 193

Bailey, Cyril, 172, 178–179
being-in-common, 7, 46, 56–57, 88, 135
being-in-place, 7–8, 13, 40, 55–57, 61–62, 72, 77, 80–81, 85, 88, 90–92, 101, 115, 119–120, 131, 135, 140–141, 154, 162–163, 166–168
being-in-relation, 3, 8, 13, 38, 40, 46, 54–57, 81–82, 85, 91–92, 101, 115, 119–120, 131, 140, 147–148, 161, 166–168
being-toward-death, 74, 184
Benjamin, Walter, 76, 108, 170–173, 178, 180, 190, 192–193, 196

INDEX

Bernstein, Richard J., 189
Berry, Jessica, 174
biological life, 17,
Breslauer, Martin, 176
Brucker, Johann J., 32, 176
Butler, Judith, 195

Chanter, Tina, 136, 192
Cicero, 23, 32–35, 42, 172, 176
Cohen, Hermann, 175
Cohen, Richard, 171
Comay, Rebecca, 183
Countermeasure, 9, 56, 59, 81–82, 140, 156, 159
Crépon, Marc, 186
Cropp, Martin, 195

Deleuze, Gilles, 177–178
del Rosario Acosta López, María, 196
denaturing, 22, 190
Derridá, Jacques, 2–3, 5–6, 28, 52, 57, 87, 99, 102, 112, 125–137, 139, 144–145, 153–154, 156, 160–169, 173, 179–180, 183, 188–189, 191–194, 196–198
Dews, Peter, 189
Diogenes Laërtius, 32, 176
Diogenes of Oenoanda, 31, 175
Douzinas, Martin, 195

Epicurus, 5, 15, 23–24, 26–36, 38–46, 49–50, 60, 62–63, 115, 127, 173–179, 182
eudaimonia, 29, 38, 41–42, 44–45, 50, 62, 77–79, 81–82, 85

Ferguson, Alfred R., 195
Fichte, Johann Gottlieb, 106,
finitute, 5, 13, 27, 31, 37, 44, 52, 57, 64, 84, 88, 93–84, 102–105, 112, 118–119, 122–123, 125–128, 131, 143, 146–147, 149, 152, 160–165, 168, 174, 184, 196
de Fontenay, Élisabeth, 197
"free play of the faculties," 64–66

Freud, Sigmund, 143, 193
Friedman, Maurice, 170
Frierson, Patrick R., 189

Garve, Christian, 172
Gasché, Rodolphe, 177
Garrard, Eve, 180
Gassendi, Pierre, 32, 176
George, Theodore, 196
Glückseligkeit, 15, 29, 37–39, 42–45, 47, 49, 60, 62–64, 67, 115–116
Gourgouris, Stathis, 191

Hegel, G. W. F., 3, 5, 13, 46, 50, 107, 128, 131–136, 144–145, 147, 150, 153–160, 169, 176, 179, 183, 189, 193, 195–197
Heidegger, Martin, 73, 185
Hobbes, Thomas, 60
Hölderlin, Friedrich, 178
Howenstein, Mark S., 195
Hume, David, 58–59, 64, 181

immanence, 68, 73–74, 84, 95, 126, 165, 178
insistence of finitude, 64, 84, 112, 119, 122–123, 125–126, 128, 149, 160, 161, 163, 165
Ismene, 137, 145–149, 154, 196

Jesus Christ, 159
Jonas, Hans, 181

Kafka, Franz, 167, 198
Kant, Immanuel, 2, 5–7, 11–12, 15, 23, 25, 27–30, 32–40, 43–46, 48–49, 53, 57–60, 62–64, 66–70, 75, 77–79, 81–84, 87–107, 111–122, 127, 130, 141–142, 161, 163, 165, 172, 174–179, 181–183, 185–193
Knauer, James T., 170
Konstan, David, 175
Kottman, Paul, 184
Kreon, 133, 146, 150–152, 160, 167, 194, 196

INDEX

Lacan, Jacques, 143–144, 193
Leibniz, Gottfried Wilhelm, 189
Le Caze, Marguerite, 188,
Locke, John, 91
Long, Anthony A., 175
Loraux, Nicole, 194
Lord, Beth, 178
Lucretius, 26, 28, 174

Maimonides, Moses, 30, 174
McGlew, James F., 195
McNaughton, David, 180
Mendelssohn, Moses, 182–183
mere life, 40–41, 49 53–54, 80, 101, 108–109, 114, 137, 178, 180
Meyler, Bernadette, 183
Morel, Pierre-Marie, 176

Nancy, Jean-Luc, 186
naturalism, 14, 28, 51, 54, 58–59, 62, 64, 93, 102, 129
nature, 20–21, 54, 60–62, 72, 97, 102, 111, 125, 133–134, 136, 188, 190, 194
Nietzsche, Friedrich, 18, 26–27, 38, 171, 173–174, 177
Nikolsky, Boris, 178
Niobe, 137–139, 143–144, 159, 197
now, 8–10, 21, 25–27, 98–99, 103, 113, 117–119, 133–136, 138, 141, 146, 163

O'Byrne, Anne, 184
Oedipus, 138–139, 151, 167
Orpheus, 153
Osborne, Peter, 171
othering, 8–9, 14, 22, 59, 131, 138, 140, 144, 155, 159–160, 164

Palmer, Stephen, 195
Paul, Saint, 159, 197
Philodemus, 175
philosophical anthropology, 1, 6–7, 42, 52, 55, 87–88, 100, 119, 125, 167

phronesis, 41–43, 47, 50
Pines, Shlomo, 174
Plato, 35, 47, 67–68, 70, 177, 183
Plutarch, 34, 175

Rehm, Rush, 196
Reich, Klaus, 177
relationality, 3–4, 7–8, 13, 18, 20, 45, 47, 54, 55, 57, 64, 67, 73, 75, 81, 109, 121, 147–149, 151, 154, 163, 166–167, 169, 171, 192, 194

Sallis, John, 183
Schiller, Friedrich, 188
Schrift, Alan D., 189
Sedley, David, 174
Seneca, 23, 32–33, 172–173, 176
Sewell-Rutter, N. J., 196
Sophocles, 42, 128, 131, 150, 178, 193–195
Spinoza, Baruch, 38, 178
Steiner, George, 192
Stoicism, 60, 179, 182
Striker, Gisela, 179
Striving, 12, 49, 82–84, 101–104, 119–123, 143–144, 163, 165, 168, 188
Sweet, Kristi E., 181

Tantalus, 137
Teegarden, David A., 195
the pardon, 6, 53, 72–73, 79, 84–85, 126–128, 157–158, 160–162, 168, 197
the promise, 72–73, 79, 81, 84, 168
Torralba, José, 172

Valla, Lorenzo, 23–24, 172
virtue in being, 1, 4–5, 18–19, 23, 40, 50–51, 56, 85, 90, 96, 104, 115, 123, 127, 130, 140, 167–168, 186
vocation (Bestimmung), 103–104, 106, 123
Vuillemin, Jules, 178

Wainright, Eric, 170

Warda, Arthur, 176
Warren, James, 174
Watkin, William, 185
Weber, Samuel, 170
Weigel, Sigrid, 184
Whyte, Jessica, 180
Wollstonecraft, Mary, 3, 13, 169

Wood, Allen, 176
Woolf, Raphael, 176
worldliness of the world, 20, 39–40, 47, 53–54, 80–81, 93, 101, 108, 120, 178
Wyschograd, Edith, 184

www.ingramcontent.com/pod-product-compliance
Lightning Source LLC
LaVergne TN
LVHW041205030526
837769LV00030B/328